Charles Dickens, 1940-1975

an analytical subject index
to periodical criticism of
the novels and Christmas books

JOHN J. FENSTERMAKER

G.K.HALL &CO.

70 LINCOLN STREET, BOSTON, MASS.

Copyright © 1979 by John J. Fenstermaker

Library of Congress Cataloging in Publication Data
Fenstermaker, John J
  Charles Dickens, 1940-1975, an analytical subject index to
periodical criticism of the novels and Christmas books.

  1. Dickens, Charles, 1812-1870 — Dictionaries, indexes, etc.
2. Dickens, Charles, 1812-1870 — Criticism and
interpretation — History.   3. Periodicals — Indexes.
I. Title.
PR4580.F4   823'.8   78-21696
ISBN 0-8161-8064-4

This publication is printed on permanent/durable acid-free paper
MANUFACTURED IN THE UNITED STATES OF AMERICA

Contents

Contents

Preface

A commonplace among Dickens critics today is that the most significant and fruitful phenomenon of English literary scholarship and
criticism of the past half-century--the elevation of Charles Dickens
to the rank of major artist--grew from seeds planted during an especially fertile few years around 1940. The period between 1935 and
1941 saw publication of a number of books and essays concerning Dickens, the more important of which contributed to a radical alteration
of conventional ways of viewing the man and his work: e.g., the re-
vealing accounts of Dickens's private life in Thomas Wright's Life of
Charles Dickens (1935) and his Autobiography (1936), and in Gladys
Storey's Dickens and Daughter (1939); T. A. Jackson's Marxist analysis, Charles Dickens: The Progress of a Radical (1937); the Nonesuch
Edition of the letters (1938); and the major statements by George
Orwell, "Charles Dickens" in the collection Inside the Whale (1940),
by Edmund Wilson, "Dickens: The Two Scrooges" in The Wound and the
Bow (1941), and by Humphry House, The Dickens World (1941). Although
each depended on biographical detail, each viewed Dickens from a
slightly different angle, and collectively they described or provided
the material which soon allowed others to describe a Dickens markedly
different from the comic and sentimental writer with a social histo-
rian's eye who had become so much a part of popular lore.

During the three-and-one-half decades since 1940, Wilson's essay
has come to be regarded as the work which stands as "the watershed
between the new view of Dickens and the old," to use the words of Ada
Nisbet, who claims that Wilson's essay "has served as a catalyst to
so much criticism of Dickens that it is now customary to refer to individual critics as pre- or post-Wilsonian." As every student of
Dickens knows, the period since 1940 has witnessed an ever-increasing
flood of articles and books that have created for us a portrait of
Dickens, dark with shadows, emphasizing his complex nature as an artist and as a man. The present volume is an index that attempts to
make readily accessible a major portion of this scholarly activity.
It provides a topical key to the journal articles appearing in English during the major phase of this reassessment, 1940-1975, select-
ing for indexing those articles devoted to substantive considerations
of Dickens as novelist, specifically those focusing upon one or more
of his novels or Christmas books.

vii

The size of this output in the journals is impressive. The sheer quantity and, no less, the over-all quality of the material make indispensable a comprehensive topical analysis of its content. At present, a researcher must spend valuable time compiling a working bibliography and then, because so many titles give no precise description of their content, he or she must work through the books and articles themselves until all the material on the desired subject is identified. This Index will provide a partial solution—a subject key to the articles that deal with Dickens as novelist, the major portion, that is, of the critical material on Dickens appearing in the journals. This volume functions in the manner of an index to a single book: it refers the reader to the precise page or pages where the desired subject can be found. In this case, however, the "book" indexed is the 1100 articles of the more than 2000 items, excluding reviews, that were read and analyzed for this compilation. The guiding criterion for including an article has been the question, "Does the discussion bear directly on the interpretation or critical evaluation of one or more of the novels or Christmas books, on Dickens's reputation as a novelist, or on his influence as a novelist on other writers?" If an article contains substantive consideration of any of these issues, the pertinent pages of that discussion are indexed, even when the major portion of the item in question is devoted to matters unrelated to Dickens's career as a novelist and hence beyond the scope of this Index.

The Index proper is divided into twenty-two sections, one devoted to each Dickens novel and Christmas book, and two general sections, one entitled "NOVELS" preceding the sections on the novels and one entitled "CHRISTMAS BOOKS" before the individual Christmas books. The "NOVELS" section indexes those articles dealing with the major characteristics of the novels as a group—influences, character types, aspects of language and style, Dickens's religious and social attitudes and his theories of fiction, and general surveys of critical commentary on his works. Following this section are those devoted to the individual novels, listed in order of the dates of their original publication; following the sections on the novels are the much shorter sections devoted to the Christmas books, listed in the order of their publication.

Each article is represented in the Index by as many topical entries as there are definable and reasonably significant topics in that item. A broad discussion, for example, may be cited in several different sections: Dorothy Van Ghent's "The Dickens World: A View from Todgers's" [SR, 58 (1950), 419-38] has seventeen topical entries under five novels and in the "NOVELS" section; even an article of modest length and limited to a single novel such as Trevor Blount's eight pages on Chancery in Bleak House [DiS, 1 (1965), 112-20] often provides a number of topic entries, in this case nine.

A bibliography of all items appearing in a section follows each section for ease of reference. Thus, the Van Ghent article appears in six different bibliographies, in the "NOVELS" section and in the ones for each of the five novels considered in it; Blount's article, on the other hand, appears only in the bibliography for <u>Bleak House</u>, that being the only work discussed by him.

The breakdown of major subject headings is the same in each section of the Index; seventeen or fewer major headings, with appropriate subheadings, are arranged alphabetically as follows:

CHARACTERIZATION

CHARACTERS

COMPOSITION

CRITICAL ASSESSMENT

EXPLANATORY NOTES, HISTORICAL BACKGROUND, and SOURCES

ILLUSTRATIONS

INFLUENCES

LANGUAGE and STYLE

LITERARY PARALLELS

PLOT

POINT OF VIEW

PUBLICATION

SETTING

STRUCTURE/UNITY

TECHNIQUES, VARIOUS

TEXT

THEMES

Certain of the major headings include cross-references to other major categories dealing with similar subjects, such as with "INFLUENCES" and "LITERARY PARALLELS," and with "COMPOSITION," "PUBLICATION," and "TEXT." However, because of the relative brevity of each section in the Index and because of the futility of trying to effect a comprehensive system, no cross-referencing occurs among minor or sub-categories. Persons using the Index are encouraged to survey the entire section under the particular novel or Christmas book they are investigating and to supplement such searches, when necessary, with a similar survey of the "NOVELS" or "CHRISTMAS BOOKS" sections. By quickly scanning the entire <u>Bleak House</u> section, for example, a person interested in spontaneous combustion will soon isolate material on that subject indexed under "CRITICAL ASSESSMENT/ Contemporary reaction," under "EXPLANATORY NOTES, HISTORICAL BACKGROUND, and SOURCES," under "INFLUENCES," under "LITERARY PARALLELS," and under "TECHNIQUES, VARIOUS."

Spontaneous combustion in <u>Bleak House</u>, however, may constitute an atypical example in that few subjects as specific as spontaneous combustion find critics approaching them from as many as five different points of view. For a broader subject and, hence, a more typical "quest," one might take the topic "imagery" in a novel such as <u>Hard Times</u>. The researcher would, of course, turn to the <u>Hard Times</u> section of the Index and then locate the sub-category "Imagery" under "LANGUAGE and STYLE" to find citations to the specific pages considering imagery in all the articles published on <u>Hard Times</u> between 1940 and 1975. As with the instance of spontaneous combustion, for the sake of thoroughness the user would want to check the other categories in the <u>Hard Times</u> section that might include or be related to the subject of imagery (for example, the category "Symbolism," since so many of Dickens's images can be and often are discussed also as symbols). If the investigator then wishes to find articles focusing on imagery in the other novels or Christmas books, he or she would locate that information in this same way under the pertinent section for each work; the "NOVELS" and "CHRISTMAS BOOKS" sections, of course, are also available.

While the reader will find the Index largely self-explanatory, a brief description of some categories may be helpful:

CHARACTERIZATION: Normally, the first major category in each section of the Index is "CHARACTERIZATION." In the sections dealing with individual novels and Christmas books, most discussion of characterization is pinned directly to consideration of a specific character and is, therefore, indexed under that person's name in the second category, "CHARACTERS." Nevertheless, the "General" sub-category under "CHARACTERIZATION" for each novel and Christmas book is very important, especially for minor characters who have received little critical attention in their own right. If the Index indicates little or no discussion of such a character, the material under "CHARACTERIZATION/General" should be considered. Much discussion cited there involves characters grouped by critics in order to make general observations about Dickens's techniques of characterization, but, in that no specific character is the focus of these discussions, what is said about a minor character may be overlooked unless these entries are checked.

CRITICAL ASSESSMENT: The general content of this category is clear in most of its minor headings: e.g., "Contemporary reaction" (i.e., consideration of the reaction of Dickens's contemporaries), "Criticism, survey of" (surveys of commentary on Dickens usually limited to a single work or to a year or period of years). The first minor category, "General," however, is more involved than these others. Under "CRITICAL ASSESSMENT/General" are grouped whole discussions or brief parts of longer ones which cover a range of topics, usually in little detail, for the purpose of asserting a "general" assessment of some broad facet of Dickens's achievement. A second use of "CRITICAL ASSESSMENT/General" is to parallel and supplement "CRITICAL ASSESS-

MENT/Contemporary reaction." Under "Contemporary reaction," there
are instances in which specific critics are singled out, as in "Contemporary reaction (Forster)." In the "General" category, this pattern is repeated in cases where the criticism of a specific commentator who was not one of Dickens's contemporaries is cited, as in
"CRITICAL ASSESSMENT/General (Chesterton)," and in the instance of
criticism on Dickens from a particular country, as in "CRITICAL AS-
SESSMENT/General (in Russia)."

THEMES: Needing comment in this category is not what does appear but
what seems not to. From one standpoint, virtually all critical discussion of Dickens's work would deal directly or indirectly with
theme, in that at base most critical commentary addresses what the
writer meant. But the emphasis of the criticism indexed in this volume has not centered upon what Dickens meant so much as in how he
conveyed his meaning--matters of technique. Few critics have offered
extensive commentary about Selfishness in <u>Martin Chuzzlewit</u> or Pride
in <u>Dombey and Son</u>. Rather the tendency has been to assume that much
about theme is well known, virtually a given in most cases, and that
what needs analysis is Dickens's method, his artistry. The most
casual glance through the Index will demonstrate this fact; mention
of it here is merely to forestall surprise that so little comment on
theme <u>per se</u> has developed over these years, even of novels which
come immediately to mind as strident social commentaries. The material which does occur under the rubric "THEMES," of course, repre-
sents discussion specifically focused on that identified theme.

These, then, are the major categories in the Index. Within each,
the most important minor category is "General," which always precedes
the alphabetical list of all other minor categories. In addition to
directing the user to discussions which frequently are only brief
summaries, entries in this category also refer to extensive treat-
ments of the subject; the primary function of this category is to
guarantee that the complete discussion of the subject is cited, not
just that which is broken down under specific headings elsewhere.
This pattern for comprehensiveness is followed throughout the Index,
and the particular importance of this minor category cannot be over-
estimated, especially under very broad major headings such as "CHAR-
ACTERIZATION," "TECHNIQUES, VARIOUS," and "THEMES."

Finally, a word about the form of entry: all material in the
Index is entered in a two-part structure. A sample entry will help
explain this basic pattern:

CHARACTERIZATION

    Heroes: Coolidge, <u>North Dakota Quarterly</u>, 30 (Jan. 1962), 9;
       Hardy, <u>VS</u>, 5 (1961), 49-67; Milner, <u>Philologica</u>, 9 (1957),
       61-67; Wilson, <u>REL</u>, 2 (July 1961), 10-18; (Byronic): Har-
       vey, <u>NCF</u>, 24 (1969), 305-16.

The material preceding a colon is "topical"; the material following a colon and preceding a semicolon or a period is "critical." Normally a topical breakdown does not exceed three levels of specificity: major heading--"CHARACTERIZATION"; minor category--"Heroes"; and a sub-category within the minor one--"(Byronic)." Within each level, entries appear alphabetically. Citations of the "critical" material include only the author's surname, journal, volume, date, and pagination; these citations are arranged alphabetically by author. When two or more items are cited for a given author under the same category, they are listed in the order of publication.

The fact that this compilation was computer-assisted accounts for a few arbitrary features of form and organization which would have been avoided had it been edited wholly by hand. The only one which may cause a user any perceptible difficulty is that involving two or more authors with the same surname. The form of entry does not allow for distinguishing in these cases according to given names; however, this and all other possible difficulties arising from the abridged form may be quickly resolved in the bibliography which follows each section and cites full documentation for every item appearing in that section.

This Index, then, provides a subject key to journal articles considering the achievement of Dickens as novelist. In addition to these scholarly and critical investigations and assessments, however, there is another body of evaluative commentary in the periodicals which has influenced in very important ways critical opinion of Dickens over the thirty-five years covered in this volume--i.e., the reviews of Dickensian scholarship. Hence, this Index includes two supplements: Appendix I, a selection of books considering Dickens as novelist published 1940-1975 and selected important reviews of these works; Appendix II, a list of editions of the novels and Christmas books published 1940-1975 and their reviews in the journals. An Author Index is also provided for the user's convenience. Listed there are each occurrence of a critic's work in the Index proper, the first citation of that work in one of the bibliographies, and each citation in Appendix I and Appendix II.

In closing it may be both helpful to the user of this Index and appropriate as a way of paying homage to the giant of a man--Charles Dickens--to note some of those aspects of his life and career which lie outside the purview of this volume. Unless it bears directly on interpretation of the novels or Christmas books, commentary on Dickens is generally excluded if it falls into the following categories: all material dealing with exhibitions, and with locations of manuscripts and first editions; all material dealing with Dickens's journalism, his philanthropic and humanitarian activities, his acting and play-writing, his public readings, his letters, his other books, and his short fiction. Even so, this volume offers access to a reasonably full record of the modern view of Charles Dickens. With the information provided here, a person pursuing research on Dickens should have a key not only to what has been thought and said on his or her subject over these three-and-one-half decades but also to the major voices during this exciting period of critical reassessment.

Acknowledgments

Many people have contributed to the completion of this volume, and I would like to mention several: Richard D. Altick, who originally conceived the idea of an index to Dickens criticism and who offered advice and direction through the production of an earlier version of this compilation; C. Eugene Tanzy, who suggested important modifications of format in the final stages and who helped work out how best to explain this tool to potential users; Thomas G. Whitney, who must remain forever frustrated that weak understanding of computer science prohibits my fully comprehending the extent of his accomplishment in creating programs to sort and print, according to MLA style, the thousands of pieces of information I have given him; Mary Fuller Hayes, who assisted in identifying and verifying the reviews in the Appendixes; the Florida State University Foundation and the English Department, each of which provided a small grant to help defray travel and computer costs.

Periodical Abbreviations

AI	American Imago
AM	Atlantic Monthly
AN&Q	American Notes and Queries (New Haven, Conn.)
AS	American Speech
ASch	American Scholar
AUMLA	Journal of the Australasian Universities Language and Literature Association
AWR	The Anglo-Welsh Review (Pembroke Dock, Wales)
BJRL	Bulletin of the John Rylands Library
BNYPL	Bulletin of the New York Public Library
BuR	Bucknell Review
CE	College English
CentR	The Centennial Review (Mich. State U.)
CL	Comparative Literature
CLS	Comparative Literature Studies
CQ	The Cambridge Quarterly
CritQ	Critical Quarterly
Di	Dickensian
DiS	Dickens Studies
DR	Dalhousie Review
DSA	Dickens Studies Annual
DSN	Dickens Studies Newsletter
DUL	Durham University Library
EA	Etudes Anglaises
E&S	Essays and Studies by Members of the English Association
EIC	Essays in Criticism (Oxford)
EJ	English Journal
ELH	Journal of English Literary History
ELN	English Language Notes (U. of Colo.)
EM	English Miscellany
ES	English Studies
ESA	English Studies in Africa (Johannesburg)
FitzN	Fitzgerald Newsletter
FMLS	Forum for Modern Language Studies (U. of St. Andrews, Scotland)
FurmS	Furman Studies
GaR	Georgia Review
HLB	Harvard Library Bulletin
HLQ	Huntington Library Quarterly

HSL	Hartford Studies in Literature
HudR	Hudson Review
JAmS	Journal of American Studies
JEGP	Journal of English and Germanic Philology
JFI	Journal of the Folklore Institute (Ind. U.)
JHI	Journal of the History of Ideas
JNT	Journal of Narrative Technique
KR	Kenyon Review
L&P	Literature and Psychology (U. of Hartford)
Lang&S	Language and Style
LWU	Literatur in Wissenschaft und Unterricht (Kiel)
MD	Modern Drama
MFS	Modern Fiction Studies
MinnR	Minnesota Review
MLN	Modern Language Notes
MLQ	Modern Language Quarterly
MLR	Modern Language Review
MP	Modern Philology
MQR	Michigan Quarterly Review
MSE	Massachusetts Studies in English
MSpr	Moderna Sprak
MTJ	Mark Twain Journal
N&Q	Notes and Queries
NCF	Nineteenth-Century Fiction
NHQ	New Hungarian Quarterly
NSN	New Statesman and Nation
NYTBR	New York Times Book Review
OGS	Oxford German Studies
PBSA	Papers of the Bibliographical Society of America
PLL	Papers on Language and Literature
PMASAL	Papers of the Michigan Association of Science, Arts, and Letters
PMLA	Publications of the Mod. Lang. Assn. of America
PQ	Philological Quarterly (Iowa City)
PR	Partisan Review
PsyR	Psychoanalytic Review
PULC	Princeton University Library Chronicle
QQ	Queen's Quarterly
REL	Review of English Literature
RES	Review of English Studies
RLV	Revue des Langues Vivantes (Bruxelles)
RMS	Renaissance and Modern Studies
RS	Research Studies (Wash. State U.)
RUS	Rice University Studies
SAQ	South Atlantic Quarterly
SatR	Saturday Review
SB	Studies in Bibliography: Papers of the Bibliographical Society of the University of Virginia
SEER	Slavonic and East European Review
SEL	Studies in English Literature 1500-1900
SNNTS	Studies in the Novel (North Texas State U.)

SoR	Southern Review (Louisiana State U.)
SoRA	Southern Review (Australia)
SP	Studies in Philology
SR	Sewanee Review
SSF	Studies in Short Fiction (Newberry Coll., N.C.)
SWR	Southwest Review
TC	Twentieth Century
TSL	Tennessee Studies in Literature
TSLL	Texas Studies in Literature and Language
UTQ	University of Toronto Quarterly
VN	Victorian Newsletter
VQR	Virginia Quarterly Review
VS	Victorian Studies (Ind. U.)
WHR	Western Humanities Review
YES	Yearbook of English Studies
YR	Yale Review
YULG	Yale University Library Gazette

Novels

Novels

CHARACTERIZATION

General: Allen, Listener, 43 (1950), 302; Axton, UTQ, 37 (1967),
32-34; Coolidge, Mississippi Quarterly, 15 (Spring 1962),
68-73; Cox, E&S, N.S. 11 (1958), 92-99; Dunn, DiS, 1 (1965),
37-38; Goodheart, Di, 54 (1958), 35-37; Hamilton, Nineteenth
Century, 142 (1947), 40-49; Jump, BJRL, 54 (1972), 391-97;
Morse, PR, 16 (1949), 277-80, 281-82, 288-89.

Caricature: Hall, UTQ, 39 (1970), 242-56.

Children: Fiedler, New Leader, 41 (14 Apr. 1958), 22-23; Lucas,
YR, 29 (1940), 727-28; Manheim, SNNTS, 1 (1969), 189-95.

Child-wives: Stedman, Di, 59 (1963), 112-18.

Chimney-sweeps: Phillips, Di, 59 (1963), 39-42.

Comic: Coolidge, VN, 18 (Fall 1960), 9-11; Cox, E&S, N.S. 11
(1958), 87-92; Cross, WHR, 17 (1963), 143-49; Ganz, DSA, 1
(1970), 25-40; Pritchett, Listener, 51 (1954), 971-73.

Devil, use of: Lane, DR, 51 (1971), 326-27.

Disguise, use of: Kelly, MLQ, 30 (1969), 396-97.

Dissenters: Adrian, NCF, 10 (1955), 190-93; Blount, MLQ, 25
(1964), 295-307.

Doctors: Easton, Di, 41 (1944/45), 152-56.

Dogs: Gibson, Di, 53 (1957), 145-51.

Doubling: Hardy, VS, 5 (1961), 52-67; Kelly, MLQ, 30 (1969),
398-400.

Dramatic: Churchill, Scrutiny, 10 (1942), 363-67.

Dreams, use of: Kelly, MLQ, 30 (1969), 388-92.

Dualism: Wilson, New Republic, 102 (4 Mar. 1940), 297-98.

Fools and madmen: Manheim, DSA, 2 (1972), 73-97.

Forms of address (status indicators): Page, Di, 67 (1971),
16-19.

3

Novels

Heroes: Coolidge, <u>North Dakota Quarterly</u>, 30 (Jan. 1962), 9;
    Hardy, <u>VS</u>, 5 (1961), 49-67; Milner, <u>Philologica</u>, 9 (1957),
    61-67; Wilson, <u>REL</u>, 2 (July 1961), 10-18; (Byronic): Harvey,
    <u>NCF</u>, 24 (1969), 305-16.

Heroines: Lucas, <u>YR</u>, 29 (1940), 708-17; Wilson, <u>REL</u>, 2 (July
    1961), 10-18.

Illusions, use of: Colburn, <u>Di</u>, 54 (1958), 110-18; Kelly, <u>MLQ</u>,
    30 (1969), 393-95.

Imagery: Smith, <u>RMS</u>, 3 (1959), 134-42; (animal): McMaster, <u>UTQ</u>,
    31 (1962), 354-61.

Inner life: Kelly, <u>MLQ</u>, 30 (1969), 386-401.

Introduction and reintroduction of characters: Coolidge, <u>SAQ</u>, 61
    (1962), 405-10.

Jews: Johnson, <u>Commentary</u>, 9 (1950), 47-50; Lane, <u>PMLA</u>, 73
    (1958), 94-100; Stone, <u>VS</u>, 2 (1959), 228-31, 233-35, 240-42,
    243-53; 3 (1960), 459-60.

Language: Stoll, <u>RES</u>, 18 (1942), 264-66; (dialect): Brook,
    <u>BJRL</u>, 47 (1964), 32-48; (speech): Quirk, <u>REL</u>, 2 (July 1961),
    20-22, 25-26.

Ministers: Dunstan, <u>Di</u>, 56 (1960), 105-13.

Minor characters: Garley, <u>Di</u>, 39 (1942/43), 147-48, 203-204; 40
    (1943/44), 45-46, 64, 159-60.

Music and musicians: Ruff, <u>Di</u>, 68 (1972), 35-42.

Names: Bromhill, <u>Di</u>, 41 (1944/45), 92-93; Harder, <u>Names</u>, 7
    (Mar. 1959), 35-42.

Natural vs. artificial: McMaster, <u>SNNTS</u>, 1 (1969), 134-45.

Oral context: Watt, <u>DSA</u>, 3 (1974), 177-79.

Passions, use of: Hardy, <u>NCF</u>, 24 (1970), 451-66.

Preparing or eating food: Hill, <u>Di</u>, 37 (1940/41), 145-51,
    191-99; 38 (1941/42), 23-31, 95-101, 167-71, 197-205;
    39 (1942/43), 5-15; Ward, <u>Personalist</u>, 45 (1964), 401-403.

Soldiers: Williams, <u>Di</u>, 41 (1944/45), 48-50.

Storytellers: Hardy, <u>Di</u>, 69 (1973), 71-78.

Through confinement: Reed, <u>DSA</u>, 1 (1970), 41-54.

Transposition into objects: Van Ghent, <u>SR</u>, 58 (1950), 420-23.

Types: Wenger, <u>PMLA</u>, 62 (1947), 213-32.

Villains: Coolidge, North Dakota Quarterly, 30 (Jan. 1962), 9-10; Kreutz, NCF, 22 (1968), 331-48; Shuckburgh, Di, 46 (1949/50), 18-23; Stoll, RES, 18 (1942), 265-68.

Widows: Brumleigh, Di, 38 (1941/42), 103-12.

Women: Lucas, YR, 29 (1940), 706-28; Manheim, TSLL, 7 (1965), 181-200; Manning, Di, 71 (1975), 67-74; Pope, DSN, 5 (1974), 4-7; Wenger, PMLA, 62 (1947), 224-25; Woollen, Di, 36 (1939/40), 178-80.

COMPOSITION (See also PUBLICATION and TEXT)

General: Butt, Listener, 47 (1952), 341-42; Jump, BJRL, 54 (1972), 386-97; (around characters): Coolidge, North Dakota Quarterly, 31 (Jan. 1963), 8-10.

Manuscripts and working notes: Butt, YULG, 36 (1962), 149-57.

Memoranda notes: Butt, Di, 45 (1948/49), 129-38.

CRITICAL ASSESSMENT

General: Allen, Listener, 43 (1950), 302-303; Burns, CE, 18 (1956), 145, 148-49; Donoghue, NCF, 24 (1970), 383-84; Gold, EJ, 58 (1969), 205-11; Holloway, Listener, 73 (1965), 287-89; House, Listener, 37 (1947), 147-48; Levin, ASch, 39 (1970), 670-76; Marcus, NYTBR, 7 June 1970, pp. 1, 46-49, 51; Miller, Listener, 83 (1970), 704-705; Pearson, Universities and Left Review, 1 (Spring 1957), 52-56; Priestley, Di, 40 (1943/44), 61-63; Pritchett, Listener, 51 (1954), 970-73; Rodriques, Literary Criterion, 7 (1966), 41-45; Tomlin, EA, 23 (1970), 113-24; Tomlinson, Critical Review, 15 (1972), 64-65; Ward, Listener, 69 (1963), 870-71, 874; Wilson, New Republic, 102 (4 Mar. 1940), 297-98, 339-42; The Month, 189 (May 1950), 349-60; Susquehanna University Studies, 6 (Apr.-June 1959), 422-57; CritQ, 2 (1960), 101-108; Listener, 83 (1970), 701-703; (Chesterton): Blount, DSN, 6 (1975), 15-16; Bray-brooke, Di, 41 (1944/45), 77-80; Churchill, DSN, 5 (1974), 34-38; Fielding, DSN, 6 (1975), 14-15; Monod, Di, 66 (1970), 111-13; DSA, 3 (1974), 219-28; (Dickens in DNB): J., N&Q, 184 (1943), 92-93; (E. A. Robinson): Cary, AN&Q, 2 (1963), 35-36; (Gissing): Monod, DSA, 3 (1974), 219-21; (in Germany): Gibson, Di, 43 (1946/47), 71-74; (in Holland): Verkoren, Di, 55 (1959), 46; (in Russia): Anikst, TLS, 4 June 1970, p. 617; Gifford, FMLS, 4 (1968), 48-52; Gilenson, Di, 57 (1961), 56-58; Senelick, DiS, 1 (1965), 129-44; (Orwell): Warncke, SAQ, 69 (1970), 373-81; (Shaw): Monod, Di, 66 (1970), 104-106; Shaw, Di, 69 (1973), 44-45.

Novels

Areas of Dickens studies needing additional research: Axton and
Patten, DSN, 2 (1971), 106-11.

Biographies: Hill, Di, 47 (1950/51), 11-15, 72-79.

Contemporary reaction: Collins, Di, 70 (1974), 5-19; Miller, Di,
43 (1946/47), 200-202; (Acton): Bennett, ELN, 7 (1970),
282-85; Schoeck, Di, 52 (1955/56), 77-80; (American): Mason,
Di, 36 (1939/40), 163-68; (Carlyle): Thomas, DSN, 6 (1975),
5-7; (Chartist reviewers): Peyrouton, Di, 60 (1964), 84-88,
152-61; (Fonblanque): Brice, DSN, 3 (1972), 69; (Forster):
ibid., 69-70; Di, 70 (1974), 185-90; Fielding, Di, 70 (1974),
165-69; (French): Flibbert, CL, 23 (1971), 18-31; (Hunt):
Brice, DSN, 3 (1972), 70-76; (James): Fielding, Di, 66
(1970), 94-97; (Lang, Andrew): Green, Di, 41 (1944/45),
10-14; (Lewes): Haight, PMLA, 71 (1956), 175-77, 179; (Longfellow): Wagenknecht, Di, 52 (1955/56), 12-15; (Ludwig):
Thomas, Hermathena, 111 (1971), 36-41; (Morley): Brice, DSN,
3 (1972), 76-78; (Poe): Grubb, NCF, 5 (1950), 15-18, 119-20,
215-19; (Thackeray): Mauskopf, NCF, 21 (1966), 21-33;
(Twain): Gardner, PMLA, 84 (1969), 93-101; (1870-1900):
Fielding, Di, 66 (1970), 85-100.

Criticism, survey of: Churchill, TLS, 23 July 1970, p. 814;
21 Aug. 1970, p. 927; Johnson, VN, 7 (Apr. 1955), 4-9; SatR,
10 Feb. 1962, pp. 31, 69; Nisbet, NCF, 24 (1970), 379-82;
Slater, TLS, 7 Aug. 1970, p. 878; Snow, TLS, 9 July 1970,
p. 737; Zabel, Nation, 169 (Sept. 1949), 279-81; (in Russia):
Anikst, TLS, 4 June 1970, p. 617; Senelick, DiS, 1 (1965),
129-44; (Jackson to Johnson): Boege, NCF, 8 (1953), 171-87;
(modern American vs. modern British): Giddings, DSN, 6
(1975), 47-55; (1900-1920): Monod, Di, 66 (1970), 101-20;
(1920-1940): Slater, Di, 66 (1970), 121-42; (1940-1960):
Collins, Di, 66 (1970), 143-61; (1958-1968): Lane, SNNTS,
1 (1969), 240-53; (1960's): Ford, Di, 66 (1970), 163-82;
(1963-1967): Vann, SNNTS, 1 (1969), 255-78; (1967): Slater,
Di, 64 (1968), 178-83; (1968): Di, 65 (1969), 192-98; (1969):
Di, 66 (1970), 225-30; (1969-1970): Cohn and Denning, DSN,
1 (Sept. 1970), 22-25; 1 (Dec. 1970), 26-29; (1970): Andrews,
Di, 67 (1971), 162-67; Lane, DR, 54 (1974), 130-35; (1970-
1971): Cohn and Denning, DSN, 2 (1971), 28-30, 58-62, 92-96;
Cohn and Faulhaber, DSN, 2 (1971), 123-26; (1970, books):
Lane, SNNTS, 5 (1973), 125-38; (1970, source studies): Lane,
DSN, 4 (1973), 34-39; (1971): Andrews, Di, 68 (1972), 180-85;
(1971-1972): Cohn and Faulhaber, DSN, 3 (1972), 29-32, 62-64,
93-96, 124-26; (1972): Andrews, Di, 69 (1973), 176-81; (1972-
1973): Cohn and Faulhaber, DSN, 4 (1973), 29-32, 61-64,
93-96; Cohn and Kasel, DSN, 4 (1973), 123-26; (1973): Andrews,
Di, 70 (1974), 205-208; (1973-1974): Cohn and Griffith, DSN,

5 (1974), 91-95, 124-26; Cohn and Kasel, DSN, 5 (1974), 29-32, 61-64; (1974): Andrews, Di, 71 (1975), 164-68; (1974-1975): Cohn and Griffith, DSN, 6 (1975), 32-36, 66-68, 99-101; Cohn and Jones, DSN, 6 (1975), 129-32.

Dickens and role of literature: Stone, Di, 69 (1973), 139-47.

Dickens as critical realist in popular tradition: Kettle, Zeitschrift für Anglistik und Americanistik, 9 (1961), 231-52.

Dickens as humorist: Ganz, DSA, 1 (1970), 23-40.

Dickens vs. Arnoldian criteria for art: Lucas, RMS, 16 (1972), 87-111.

Dickens's double literary standard (Household Words vs. the novels): Easson, Di, 60 (1964), 104-14.

Dickens's position in history of novel: Stevenson, UTQ, 14 (1945), 371-72.

Dickens's relation to his age: Howarth, UTQ, 41 (1972), 155-59, 160-62; Johnson, Bibliotheca Bucnellensis, 4 (1966), 1-13.

Dickens's theory of fiction: Engel, MP, 53 (1955), 25-38; Marlow, NCF, 30 (1975), 20-32.

Research in progress (1971): Meckier, DSN, 2 (1971), 111-21.

EXPLANATORY NOTES, HISTORICAL BACKGROUND, and SOURCES

General: Levine, SNNTS, 1 (1969), 173-74.

Alcoholic beverages and public houses: Wilson, Di, 63 (1967), 46-61.

Amusements for poor: Collins, Di, 61 (1965), 8-18.

Bluebooks and statistics generally: Brantlinger, Criticism, 14 (1972), 328-44; Smith, RES, N.S. 21 (1970), 23-29.

Chimney-sweeps: Phillips, Di, 59 (1963), 28-44.

City in nineteenth century: Welsh, VS, 11 (1968), 388-400.

Dickens's political attitudes: Goldberg, JHI, 33 (1972), 61-76; (class structure): Engel, PMLA, 71 (1956), 952-56; (finance and industry): ibid., 964-72; (the poor): ibid., 957-64; (radicalism and subversion): ibid., 972-74; (representative government): ibid., 947-51.

Dickens's reading: Collins, Di, 60 (1964), 136-51; Hill, Di, 45 (1948/49), 81-90, 201-207; (childhood): Stedman, Di, 61 (1965), 150-54; Stone, Horn Book Magazine, 39 (1963), 306-21.

Novels

Education (for girls): Collins, Di, 57 (1961), 86-96; (rote learning): Shatto, Di, 70 (1974), 113-20.

Hats: Gibson, Di, 51 (1954/55), 108-10.

Jews, attitude toward: Lane, PMLA, 73 (1958), 94-100; Stone, VS, 2 (1959), 223-53.

Military, the: Sullivan, Di, 46 (1949/50), 138-43.

Names: Pechey, Di, 52 (1955/56), 180-82.

Prisons: Scrutton, Di, 62 (1966), 112-17.

Speech: R., N&Q, 195 (1950), 279.

Transportation, modes of: Lascelles, Di, 58 (1962), 75-86, 152-60.

ILLUSTRATIONS

General: Bentley, Di, 65 (1969), 148-62; Lane, DR, 54 (1974), 132-35; Steig, Criticism, 11 (1969), 220-33; Thomas, DSN, 4 (1973), 5-7.

Background: Steig, DSA, 2 (1972), 120-23.

Emblematic details: Steig, HLQ, 36 (1972), 55-67.

Peacock feathers showing pride or imminent misfortune: Steig, Ariel, 4 (1973), 49-51.

INFLUENCES (See also LITERARY PARALLELS)

(Dickens on) Conrad: Karl, N&Q, 202 (1957), 398-400; Walton, NCF, 23 (1969), 446-62; Dostoevsky: Futrell, EM, 7 (1956), 41-89; Hulse, Di, 51 (1954/55), 66-71; Dutch literature: Verkoren, Di, 55 (1959), 45; Eisenstein (montage): Zambrano, Style, 9 (1975), 471-79; Gogol (Dead Souls): Futrell, SEER, 34 (1956), 443-59; Howells: Gardner, MFS, 16 (1970), 323-43; Kafka: Pascal, Listener, 55 (1956), 504-506; Spilka, CL, 11 (1959), 289-90, 298-307; Lawson, Henry: Gerson, Di, 68 (1972), 77-89; Lewis, Sinclair: Fleissner, BNYPL, 74 (1970), 607-16; Mann: Riley, CL, 17 (1965), 61-62; modern comic writers: Howarth, UTQ, 41 (1972), 159-60; Norwegian writers in the nineteenth century: Brown, EDDA, 5 (1970), 66-82; Poe: Grubb, NCF, 5 (1950), 209-15; Raabe, Wilhelm: Klieneberger, OGS, 4 (1969), 90-117; Shaw: Brooks, Di, 59 (1963), 93-99; Johnson, VQR, 33 (1957), 66-79; Thackeray (theatrical analogy): Stevens, NCF, 22 (1968), 391-97; Trollope: Boll, Trollopian, 1 (Sept. 1946), 11-24.

(on Dickens) General: Churchill, <u>Scrutiny</u>, 10 (1942), 368-71;
  Wilson, <u>The Month</u>, 189 (May 1950), 353-55; Bentham: Goldberg,
  <u>JHI</u>, 33 (1972), 61-62; <u>Blackwood's</u>, Tale of Terror: Sucksmith, <u>NCF</u>, 26 (1971), 146-57; Burdett-Coutts, Miss: Fielding, <u>Di</u>, 51 (1954/55), 30-32; Carlyle: Christian, <u>Trollopian</u>,
  1 (Mar. 1947), 27-35; 2 (June 1947), 11-26; Dickins, <u>Di</u>, 53
  (1957), 102-106; Goldberg, <u>JHI</u>, 33 (1972), 62-76; Collins,
  Wilkie: Ashley, <u>Di</u>, 49 (1952/53), 59-65; Davis, <u>The Municipal</u>
  <u>University of Wichita Bulletin</u>, 16 (1945), 10-24; Fielding,
  <u>Di</u>, 49 (1952/53), 130-36; eighteenth-century fiction: Pritchett, <u>Listener</u>, 51 (1954), 970; Walker, <u>Di</u>, 51 (1954/55),
  102-104; Elizabethan and Jacobean dramatists (and irrational
  villains): Howarth, <u>UTQ</u>, 41 (1972), 154-55; Fielding (humor):
  Coolidge, <u>VN</u>, 18 (Fall 1960), 8-9, 12-13; Hazlitt (humor):
  ibid., 8, 12-13; Hazlitt (sympathetic imagination): Coolidge,
  <u>Mississippi Quarterly</u>, 15 (Spring 1962), 70-73; Hogarth (spatiotemporalization of form): Marten, <u>SNNTS</u>, 6 (1974), 145-62;
  Irving: Boll, <u>MLQ</u>, 5 (1944), 454-67; Wegelin, <u>MLQ</u>, 7 (1946),
  83-91; Longfellow: Wagenknecht, <u>Di</u>, 52 (1955/56), 18-19;
  Mathews, Charles (technique and characters): Zambrano, <u>MSpr</u>,
  66 (1972), 235-42; <u>The Portfolio</u>: Thomas, <u>Di</u>, 68 (1972),
  167-72; psychopathological theory: Manheim, <u>DSA</u>, 2 (1972),
  69-97; Radcliffe, Mrs.: Coolidge, <u>Di</u>, 58 (1962), 112-16;
  Theater: Churchill, <u>Scrutiny</u>, 10 (1942), 362-67.

LANGUAGE and STYLE (<u>See also</u> TECHNIQUES, VARIOUS)

General: Brook, <u>BJRL</u>, 49 (Autumn 1966), 47-68; Miller, <u>NCF</u>, 24
  (1970), 473-76; Quirk, <u>REL</u>, 2 (July 1961), 20-28; Ward,
  <u>Listener</u>, 69 (1963), 871, 874; (two voices): Ford, <u>NCF</u>, 24
  (1970), 430-48.

Animism: Gibson, <u>NCF</u>, 7 (1953), 283-91; Sipe, <u>NCF</u>, 30 (1975),
  1-14; Thale, <u>NCF</u>, 22 (1967), 141-43.

Archness: Parker, <u>Di</u>, 67 (1971), 149-58.

Dialect: Brook, <u>BJRL</u>, 47 (1964), 32-48.

Hyperbole: Thale, <u>NCF</u>, 22 (1967), 133-34.

Imagery: Smith, <u>RMS</u>, 3 (1959), 131-42; (animal): McMaster, <u>UTQ</u>,
  31 (1962), 354-61; (river): Robison, <u>ES</u>, 53 (1972), 436-39,
  441-42.

Malapropisms: Gerson, <u>Di</u>, 61 (1965), 40-45.

Metaphor: Thale, <u>NCF</u>, 22 (1967), 132-33; Van Ghent, <u>SR</u>, 58
  (1950), 419-38; (of transformation): Sipe, <u>NCF</u>, 30 (1975),
  1-19.

Novels

Metrical prose: Honan, <u>VN</u>, 28 (Fall 1965), 1-3.

Monologue (interior): Kelty, <u>Di</u>, 57 (1961), 160-65; Stone, <u>PQ</u>, 38 (1959), 52-59, 64-65.

Speech: Brook, <u>BJRL</u>, 49 (Autumn 1966), 62-67; Quirk, <u>REL</u>, 2 (July 1961), 20-22, 25-26; Roll-Hansen, <u>Norwegian Studies in English</u>, 9 (1963), 211-15.

Symbolism: Bodelsen, <u>ES</u>, 40 (1959), 420-31; Marlow, <u>NCF</u>, 30 (1975), 20-32; (the dandy and Regency values): McMaster, <u>SNNTS</u>, 1 (1969), 133-45; (names): Bodelsen, <u>REL</u>, 2 (July 1961), 42-48; (nature): McMaster, <u>SNNTS</u>, 1 (1969), 134-45; (use of double): Lane, <u>Di</u>, 55 (1959), 47-55.

LITERARY PARALLELS (<u>See also</u> INFLUENCES)

Balzac: Schilling, <u>Adam</u>, 331-33 (1969), 111-22; (character types): Wenger, <u>PMLA</u>, 62 (1947), 213-32.

Brontë, <u>Jane Eyre</u>: Mason, <u>Di</u>, 43 (1946/47), 122-24; 43 (1946/47), 173-78.

Chaucer: Davids, <u>Di</u>, 39 (1942/43), 70-74.

DeQuincey (theme of divided self): Herbert, <u>VS</u>, 17 (1974), 257-63; (theme of guilt): <u>ibid</u>., 252-57; (theme of loss): <u>ibid</u>., 251-56; (theme of memory): <u>ibid</u>., 248-50.

Faulkner: Fiedler, <u>Commentary</u>, 10 (1950), 385-86; Gold, <u>DR</u>, 49 (1969), 69-79.

Hoffmann, E. T. A. (animism): Viebrock, <u>ES</u>, 43 (1962), 396-402.

Irving: Boll, <u>MLQ</u>, 5 (1944), 456-67; Wegelin, <u>MLQ</u>, 7 (1946), 83-91.

James: Hall, <u>UTQ</u>, 39 (1970), 242-56; Rouse, <u>NCF</u>, 5 (1950), 151-57.

Jonson (London comedy): Simpson, <u>E&S</u>, 29 (1943), 85-92.

Kafka (grotesque): Spilka, <u>MinnR</u>, 1 (1961), 441-58.

Marryat: Hawes, <u>DSA</u>, 2 (1972), 46-54, 66-68.

Mayhew (description of the poor): Humpherys, <u>DSA</u>, 4 (1975), 78-90.

Melville (background, subject, method): Lane, <u>DR</u>, 51 (1971), 316-20.

"Mudfog Papers": Chaudhry, <u>Di</u>, 70 (1974), 104-12.

Proust (and imagery): Bizam, <u>NHQ</u>, 6 (Summer 1965), 174-80.

Scott (character types): Wenger, PMLA, 62 (1947), 213-32; (differences): Johnson, VN, 27 (Spring 1965), 9-11.

Shakespeare (characterization): Stoll, RES, 18 (1942), 264-68.

Shaw: Johnson, VQR, 33 (1957), 66-79.

Terrific Register: McMaster, DR, 38 (1958), 19-24.

West, Nathanael: Pinsker, Topic, 18 (1969), 40-52.

Wordsworth (on feeling): Donoghue, NCF, 24 (1970), 393-94.

Zola (character types): Wenger, PMLA, 62 (1947), 215-32.

PLOT (See also STRUCTURE/UNITY)

General: Coolidge, Di, 57 (1961), 174-82; 58 (1962), 112-16; Morse, PR, 16 (1949), 280-81.

Endings in the novels: Kennedy, SNNTS, 6 (1974), 280-86.

Fairy tale elements: Grob, TSLL, 5 (1964), 567-79.

Folktale elements: Briggs, JFI, 7 (1970), 3-20.

Foreshadowing: Gadd, Di, 36 (1939/40), 181-85.

Guiding Providence, presence of: Nelson, VN, 19 (Spring 1961), 11-14.

Moral growth: Wall, REL, 6 (Jan. 1965), 56-67.

Mystery, use of: Gibson, Di, 56 (1960), 176-78.

Static situation of danger: Coolidge, North Dakota Quarterly, 30 (Jan. 1962), 8-13.

POINT OF VIEW

General: Boege, PMLA, 65 (1950), 90-105.

Authorial intrusion: Levine, SNNTS, 1 (1969), 165-69.

Retrospective: Coolidge, North Dakota Quarterly, 30 (Jan. 1962), 12.

Stream-of-consciousness: Dobie, NCF, 25 (1971), 405-409.

Theatrical analogy in address to reader: Stevens, NCF, 22 (1968), 391-97.

Novels

PUBLICATION (See also COMPOSITION and TEXT)

   Serialization (monthly): Fielding, Di, 54 (1958), 4-11; (number
      divisions of monthly parts): ibid., 8-11; (number divisions
      of weekly parts): ibid., 140-41; (weekly): ibid., 134-41;
      Grubb, ELH, 9 (1942), 141-56.

SETTING

   Description: Thale, NCF, 22 (1967), 127-43; (atmospheric):
      ibid., 132; (enumerative): ibid., 129-30; (reportorial):
      ibid., 128-29; (selective): ibid., 130-31.

   Gothic elements: Kirkpatrick, VN, 31 (Spring 1967), 20-24.

   Pastoral, use of (later novels): Burgan, MLQ, 36 (1975), 293-315.

   Sea, use of: Rigg, Di, 40 (1943/44), 89-96, 151-58.

   Weather, use of: McNulty, Di, 41 (1944/45), 138-42.

   World of novels: Allen, Listener, 43 (1950), 302; Dunn, DiS,
      1 (1965), 33-39; Holloway, Listener, 73 (1965), 287-89; Morse,
      PR, 16 (1949), 277-82, 286-89; Spilka, MinnR, 1 (1961),
      441-58; Tick, BuR, 16 (1968), 85-95; Van Ghent, SR, 58 (1950),
      419-38; (man-made environment): Sipe, NCF, 30 (1975), 1-19;
      (society): Winner, DSA, 3 (1974), 101-108.

STRUCTURE/UNITY (See also PLOT)

   General: Coolidge, North Dakota Quarterly, 31 (Jan. 1963), 8-10.

   "keystone episode": Axton, UTQ, 37 (1967), 34-49.

   Serial publication: Axton, UTQ, 37 (1967), 31-49.

   Spatiotemporalization of form: Marten, SNNTS, 6 (1974), 145-62.

TECHNIQUES, VARIOUS

   General: Burns, CE, 18 (1956), 148-49; Churchill, Scrutiny, 10
      (1942), 358-67; Clarke, QQ, 52 (1945), 280-87; Cox, E&S,
      N.S. 11 (1958), 87-100; Dunn, DiS, 1 (1965), 33-39; Holloway,
      Listener, 73 (1965), 287-89; Morse, PR, 16 (1949), 277-82,
      286-89; Williams, CritQ, 6 (1964), 218-27; Wilson, AM, 165
      (1940), 683-91; CritQ, 2 (1960), 101-108.

   America, use of (New World): Heilman, Trollopian, 1 (Sept.
      1946), 36-43; 1 (Mar. 1947), 11-26.

Autobiography, use of: Stone, <u>ES</u>, 47 (1966), 11-16.

Autoplagiarism (borrowings from his other books): Brumleigh, <u>Di</u>, 39 (1942/43), 115-18, 169-73; 40 (1943/44), 9-11.

City, use of: Raleigh, <u>VS</u>, 11 (1968), 298-300, 322-24; Welsh, <u>VS</u>, 11 (1968), 380-400.

Comedy/humor: Coolidge, <u>VN</u>, 18 (Fall 1960), 8-15; Cox, <u>E&S</u>, N.S. 11 (1958), 87-92; Cross, <u>WHR</u>, 17 (1963), 143-49; Ganz, <u>DSA</u>, 1 (1970), 23-40; Monod, <u>REL</u>, 2 (July 1961), 29-38; Pritchett, <u>Listener</u>, 51 (1954), 970-73; Smith, <u>RMS</u>, 3 (1959), 131-42; Spilka, <u>MinnR</u>, 1 (1961), 441-58; Tomlin, <u>EA</u>, 23 (1970), 116-20; Walker, <u>Di</u>, 51 (1954/55), 102-103.

Cruelty and violence, use of: House, <u>Listener</u>, 37 (1947), 147-48.

Death, use of: Clark, <u>Boston University Studies in English</u>, 2 (1956), 125-29; Walbank, <u>Di</u>, 57 (1961), 166-73; Winters, <u>L&P</u>, 6 (1966), 109-15.

Depersonalization: Sipe, <u>NCF</u>, 30 (1975), 14-15.

Disease symptoms, description of: Brain, <u>British Medical Journal</u>, 24 (Dec. 1955), 1553-56.

Domestic scenes, description of: Cox, <u>E&S</u>, N.S. 11 (1958), 95-98.

Dramatic: Clarke, <u>QQ</u>, 52 (1945), 280-84.

Dreams, use of: Winters, <u>PMLA</u>, 63 (1948), 991-1006.

Father/daughter motif: Manning, <u>Di</u>, 71 (1975), 70-72.

Fathers and sons, use of: Winters, <u>L&P</u>, 6 (1966), 109-15.

Female education, use of: Collins, <u>Di</u>, 57 (1961), 86-96.

Fires, use of: Greaves, <u>Di</u>, 41 (1944/45), 43-47.

Food and drink (oysters): Hill, <u>Di</u>, 36 (1939/40), 139-46; (preparation or consumption): Clark, <u>DR</u>, 36 (1956), 251-57; Hill, <u>Di</u>, 37 (1940/41), 145-51, 191-99; 38 (1941/42), 23-31, 95-101, 167-71, 197-205; 39 (1942/43), 5-15; Watt, <u>DSA</u>, 3 (1974), 165-73.

Grotesque, use of: Dunn, <u>SNNTS</u>, 1 (1969), 147-55; Marten, <u>SNNTS</u>, 6 (1974), 158-62; Spilka, <u>MinnR</u>, 1 (1961), 441-58.

Horror: McMaster, <u>DR</u>, 38 (1958), 25-27; (and terror): Dunn, <u>DiS</u>, 1 (1965), 33-39.

Idyllic, the, use of: Gibson, <u>Di</u>, 52 (1955/56), 59-64.

Interpolated tales: Gibson, <u>Di</u>, 59 (1963), 99-101.

January-May motif: Manning, <u>Di</u>, 71 (1975), 67-74.

Novels

Law as father-image: Manheim, <u>AI</u>, 12 (1955), 18-23.

Melodrama: Perry, <u>Carleton Miscellany</u>, 3 (Spring 1962), 106-10;
   Wilson, <u>New Republic</u>, 102 (4 Mar. 1940), 297; (philosophical
   basis): Coolidge, <u>VN</u>, 20 (Fall 1961), 1-4.

Moral conversion: Hardy, <u>VS</u>, 5 (1961), 49-67.

Murder, use of: Williams, <u>Di</u>, 41 (1944/45), 145-48.

Names: Bodelsen, <u>REL</u>, 2 (July 1961), 40-48.

Opening scenes: Williams, <u>Di</u>, 42 (1945/46), 99-101.

Oral context: Watt, <u>DSA</u>, 3 (1974), 175-81.

Pursuit, use of: Winters, <u>VN</u>, 23 (Spring 1963), 23-24.

Railway, use of: Atthill, <u>English</u>, 13 (1961), 130-33.

Satire (use of city): Welsh, <u>VS</u>, 11 (1968), 380-400.

Sensationalism (philosophical basis): Coolidge, <u>VN</u>, 20 (Fall
   1961), 6-11.

Sex, treatment of: Johnson, <u>West Virginia University Bulletin</u>,
   4 (1943), 15-21.

Smells, use of: Rigby, <u>Di</u>, 53 (1957), 36-38.

Tears, evocation of: Voss-Moeton, <u>Di</u>, 58 (1962), 183-87.

Time, use of: Ford, <u>NCF</u>, 24 (1970), 429-48; Franklin, <u>DSA</u>, 4
   (1975), 1-35; Raleigh, <u>NCF</u>, 13 (1958), 127-37.

Tragi-comedy: Dunn, <u>SNNTS</u>, 1 (1969), 147-55.

Visual details: Zambrano, <u>Style</u>, 9 (1975), 479-81.

TEXT (<u>See also</u> COMPOSITION and PUBLICATION)

Editing for the modern reader: Hargreaves, <u>TLS</u>, 11 June 1970,
   p. 638; Nowell-Smith, <u>TLS</u>, 4 June 1970, pp. 615-16.

Revisions: Butt, <u>Listener</u>, 47 (1952), 342.

THEMES

General: Cox, <u>E&S</u>, N.S. 11 (1958), 98-100; Morse, <u>PR</u>, 16 (1949),
   282-83, 286-89; Wilson, <u>AM</u>, 165 (1940), 475-83, 681-91;
   <u>Susquehanna University Studies</u>, 6 (Apr.-June 1959), 422-57.

Amusements for poor: Collins, <u>Di</u>, 61 (1965), 7-19.

Anti-mechanism: Smith, <u>RMS</u>, 3 (1959), 134-42.

Childhood/children: Banta, Di, 63 (1967), 166–75; Fiedler, New Leader, 41 (14 Apr. 1958), 22–23; Van Ghent, SR, 58 (1950), 431–38.

Christmas, attitude toward: Carolan, DR, 52 (1972), 381–82.

Conventional tastes and moral standards: Milner, Philologica, 9 (1957), 61–67.

Crime/guilt: Van Ghent, SR, 58 (1950), 426–35.

Criminals and rebels: Wilson, AM, 165 (1940), 477–83.

Death (and river imagery): Robison, ES, 53 (1972), 436–39, 441–42.

Disciplined liberation (of character): Reed, DSA, 1 (1970), 41–54.

Evil: Cox, E&S, N.S. 11 (1958), 92–95; Wilson, KR, 29 (1967), 184–85, 194.

Fancy and imagination: Collins, ES, 42 (1961), 79–90.

Fathers and daughters: Rooke, E&S, N.S. 4 (1951), 55.

Fathers and sons: Rooke, E&S, N.S. 4 (1951), 54–69.

Forgiveness: Madden, CLS, 3 (1966), 144–45.

Individual possibility: Levine, SNNTS, 1 (1969), 169–72, 174–75.

Industrialism: Brantlinger, NCF, 26 (1971), 270–85.

Initiation (of child): Fiedler, New Leader, 41 (26 May 1958), 20.

Love (vs. self-interest): Lamb, Paunch, 33 (Dec. 1968), 33–46; (vs. self-mutilation): Dennis, TSLL, 11 (1969), 1237–46.

Moral conversion: Hardy, VS, 5 (1961), 49–67.

Moral values: Perry, Carleton Miscellany, 3 (Spring 1962), 106–10.

Mothers and daughters: Rooke, E&S, N.S. 4 (1951), 56.

Mothers and sons: Rooke, E&S, N.S. 4 (1951), 54–55.

Nihilism: Miller, CLS, 3 (1966), 110–11.

Parent/child relationships: Adrian, Di, 67 (1971), 3–11.

Pastoral primitivism: McMaster, SNNTS, 1 (1969), 133–45.

Political and social attitudes: Engel, PMLA, 71 (1956), 945–74; Goldberg, JHI, 33 (1972), 61–76; Johnson, Bibliotheca Bucnellensis, 4 (1966), 1–13; Kettle, Zeitschrift für Anglistik und Americanistik, 9 (1961), 237–52; (Christian Socialism): Peyrouton, Di, 58 (1962), 96–109.

Novels

Religion (general religious position): Bowkett, <u>Di</u>, 56 (1960), 182-84; Coolidge, <u>Di</u>, 59 (1963), 57-60.

Self-discovery: Fielding, <u>Aryan Path</u>, 33 (May 1962), 210-14.

Self-salvation: Wilson, <u>SAQ</u>, 73 (1974), 528-40.

Social criticism: Allen, <u>Listener</u>, 43 (1950), 302-303; Aydelotte, <u>The Tasks of Economic History</u>, 8 (1948), 42-58; Churchill, <u>Scrutiny</u>, 10 (1942), 371-75; Cooperman, <u>CE</u>, 22 (1960), 156-60; House, <u>Listener</u>, 37 (1947), 147-48; Van Ghent, <u>SR</u>, 58 (1950), 431-38; Williams, <u>CritQ</u>, 6 (1964), 214-27; Wilson, <u>AM</u>, 165 (1940), 479-83, 681-91; (society as abstraction): McMaster, <u>EA</u>, 23 (1970), 126-35; (the Two Nations): Levine, <u>SNNTS</u>, 1 (1969), 157-75.

Social unity: Dennis, <u>TSLL</u>, 11 (1969), 1243-46.

Time: Ford, <u>NCF</u>, 24 (1970), 428-48; Franklin, <u>DSA</u>, 4 (1975), 1-35.

Value of being "old fashioned": Nelson, <u>DSA</u>, 3 (1974), 44-47.

Bibliography for Novels

ADRIAN, ARTHUR A. "Dickens and Inverted Parenthood." _Di_, 67 (1971), 3-11.

_____. "Dickens and the Brick-and-Mortar Sects." _NCF_, 10 (1955), 188-201.

ALLEN, WALTER. "The World of Dickens' Imagination." _Listener_, 43 (1950), 302-303.

ANDREWS, MALCOLM. "The Year's Work in Dickens Studies 1970." _Di_, 67 (1971), 162-67.

_____. "The Year's Work in Dickens Studies 1971." _Di_, 68 (1972), 180-85.

_____. "The Year's Work in Dickens Studies 1972." _Di_, 69 (1973), 176-81.

_____. "The Year's Work in Dickens Studies 1973." _Di_, 70 (1974), 205-208.

_____. "The Year's Work in Dickens Studies 1974." _Di_, 71 (1975), 164-68.

ANIKST, ALEXANDER. "Dickens in Russia." _TLS_, 4 June 1970, p. 617.

ASHLEY, ROBERT P. "Wilkie Collins and the Dickensians." _Di_, 49 (1952/53), 59-65.

ATTHILL, ROBIN. "Dickens and the Railway." _English_, 13 (1961), 130-35.

AXTON, WILLIAM F. "'Keystone' Structure in Dickens' Serial Novels." _UTQ_, 37 (1967), 31-50.

_____ and ROBERT L. PATTEN. "Opportunities for Research." _DSN_, 2 (1971), 106-11.

AYDELOTTE, WILLIAM O. "The England of Marx and Mill as Reflected in Fiction." _The Tasks of Economic History_, 8 (1948), 42-58.

BANTA, MARTHA. "Charles Dickens's Warning to England." _Di_, 63 (1967), 166-75.

Novels

BENNETT, JOSEPH T. "A Note on Lord Acton's View of Charles Dickens." <u>ELN</u>, 7 (1970), 282-85.

BENTLEY, NICOLAS. "Dickens and His Illustrators." <u>Di</u>, 65 (1969), 148-62.

BIZAM, LENKE. "The Imagery of Dickens and Proust." <u>NHQ</u>, 6 (Summer 1965), 174-80.

BLOUNT, TREVOR. "The Chadbands and Dickens' View of Dissenters." <u>MLQ</u>, 25 (1964), 295-307.

_____. "The Lessons of G. K. Chesterton." <u>DSN</u>, 6 (1975), 15-16.

BODELSEN, C. A. "'The Physiognomy of the Name.'" <u>REL</u>, 2 (July 1961), 39-48.

_____. "Some Notes on Dickens' Symbolism." <u>ES</u>, 40 (1959), 420-31.

BOEGE, FRED W. "Point of View in Dickens." <u>PMLA</u>, 65 (1950), 90-105.

_____. "Recent Criticism of Dickens." <u>NCF</u>, 8 (1953), 171-87.

BOLL, ERNEST. "Charles Dickens and Washington Irving." <u>MLQ</u>, 5 (1944), 453-67.

_____. "The Infusions of Dickens in Trollope." <u>Trollopian</u>, 1 (Sept. 1946), 11-24.

BOWKETT, C. E. "Charles Dickens Commemoration Sermon." <u>Di</u>, 56 (1960), 182-84.

BRAIN, RUSSELL. "Dickensian Diagnoses." <u>British Medical Journal</u>, 24 (Dec. 1955), 1553-56.

BRANTLINGER, PATRICK. "Bluebooks, the Social Organism, and the Victorian Novel." <u>Criticism</u>, 14 (1972), 328-44.

_____. "Dickens and the Factories." <u>NCF</u>, 26 (1971), 270-85.

BRAYBROOKE, PATRICK. "Chesterton and Charles Dickens." <u>Di</u>, 41 (1944/45), 77-80.

BRICE, ALEC W. "The Compilation of the Critical Commentary in Forster's <u>Life of Charles Dickens</u>." <u>Di</u>, 70 (1974), 185-90.

_____. "Reviewers of Dickens in the <u>Examiner</u>: Fonblanque, Forster, Hunt, and Morley." <u>DSN</u>, 3 (1972), 68-80.

BRIGGS, KATHARINE M. "The Folklore of Charles Dickens." <u>JFI</u>, 7 (1970), 3-20.

BROMHILL, KENTLEY. "Names and Labels." <u>Di</u>, 41 (1944/45), 92-93.

BROOK, G. L. "Dickens as a Literary Craftsman." <u>BJRL</u>, 49 (Autumn 1966), 47-68.

_____. "The Language of Dickens." <u>BJRL</u>, 47 (1964), 32-48.

BROOKS, HAROLD F. and JEAN R. BROOKS. "Dickens in Shaw." Di, 59 (1963), 93-99.

BROWN, JAMES WESLEY. "Charles Dickens and Norwegian Belles-Lettres in the Nineteenth Century." EDDA, 5 (1970), 65-84.

BRUMLEIGH, T. KENT. "Autoplagiarism." Di, 39 (1942/43), 115-18, 169-73; 40 (1943/44), 9-11.

_____. "Relicts and Relics." Di, 38 (1941/42), 103-12.

BURGAN, WILLIAM. "Tokens of Winter in Dickens's Pastoral Settings." MLQ, 36 (1975), 293-315.

BURNS, WAYNE. "The Genuine and Counterfeit: A Study in Victorian and Modern Fiction." CE, 18 (1956), 143-50.

BUTT, JOHN E. "Dickens's Manuscripts." YULG, 36 (1962), 149-61.

_____. "Dickens's Notes for His Serial Parts." Di, 45 (1948/49), 129-38.

_____. "New Light on Charles Dickens." Listener, 47 (1952), 341-42.

CAROLAN, KATHERINE. "Dickens' Last Christmases." DR, 52 (1972), 373-83.

CARY, RICHARD. "Robinson on Dickens." AN&Q, 2 (1963), 35-36.

CHAUDHRY, G. A. "The Mudfog Papers." Di, 70 (1974), 104-12.

CHRISTIAN, MILDRED. "Carlyle's Influence Upon the Social Theory of Dickens." Trollopian, 1 (Mar. 1947), 27-35; 2 (June 1947), 11-26.

CHURCHILL, R. C. "Chesterton on Dickens: The Legend and the Reality." DSN, 5 (1974), 34-38.

_____. "Dickens, Drama, and Tradition." Scrutiny, 10 (1942), 358-75.

_____. "Dickensian Criticism." TLS, 23 July 1970, p. 814.

_____. "Dickensiana." TLS, 21 Aug. 1970, p. 927.

CLARK, WILLIAM ROSS. "The Hungry Mr. Dickens." DR, 36 (1956), 250-57.

_____. "The Rationale of Dickens' Death Rate." Boston University Studies in English, 2 (1956), 125-39.

CLARKE, GEORGE HERBERT. "Dickens Now." QQ, 52 (1945), 280-87.

COHN, ALAN M. and GEORGE V. GRIFFITH. "The Dickens Checklist." DSN, 5 (1974), 124-26.

_____. "The Dickens Checklist." DSN, 6 (1975), 32-36, 66-68, 99-101.

Novels

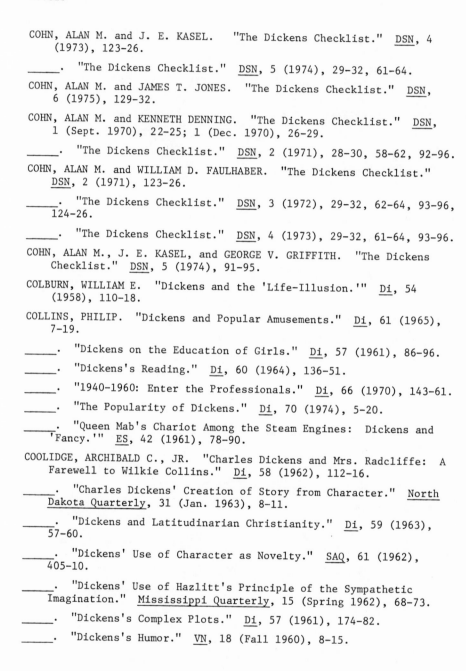

COHN, ALAN M. and J. E. KASEL. "The Dickens Checklist." DSN, 4 (1973), 123-26.

_____. "The Dickens Checklist." DSN, 5 (1974), 29-32, 61-64.

COHN, ALAN M. and JAMES T. JONES. "The Dickens Checklist." DSN, 6 (1975), 129-32.

COHN, ALAN M. and KENNETH DENNING. "The Dickens Checklist." DSN, 1 (Sept. 1970), 22-25; 1 (Dec. 1970), 26-29.

_____. "The Dickens Checklist." DSN, 2 (1971), 28-30, 58-62, 92-96.

COHN, ALAN M. and WILLIAM D. FAULHABER. "The Dickens Checklist." DSN, 2 (1971), 123-26.

_____. "The Dickens Checklist." DSN, 3 (1972), 29-32, 62-64, 93-96, 124-26.

_____. "The Dickens Checklist." DSN, 4 (1973), 29-32, 61-64, 93-96.

COHN, ALAN M., J. E. KASEL, and GEORGE V. GRIFFITH. "The Dickens Checklist." DSN, 5 (1974), 91-95.

COLBURN, WILLIAM E. "Dickens and the 'Life-Illusion.'" Di, 54 (1958), 110-18.

COLLINS, PHILIP. "Dickens and Popular Amusements." Di, 61 (1965), 7-19.

_____. "Dickens on the Education of Girls." Di, 57 (1961), 86-96.

_____. "Dickens's Reading." Di, 60 (1964), 136-51.

_____. "1940-1960: Enter the Professionals." Di, 66 (1970), 143-61.

_____. "The Popularity of Dickens." Di, 70 (1974), 5-20.

_____. "Queen Mab's Chariot Among the Steam Engines: Dickens and 'Fancy.'" ES, 42 (1961), 78-90.

COOLIDGE, ARCHIBALD C., JR. "Charles Dickens and Mrs. Radcliffe: A Farewell to Wilkie Collins." Di, 58 (1962), 112-16.

_____. "Charles Dickens' Creation of Story from Character." North Dakota Quarterly, 31 (Jan. 1963), 8-11.

_____. "Dickens and Latitudinarian Christianity." Di, 59 (1963), 57-60.

_____. "Dickens' Use of Character as Novelty." SAQ, 61 (1962), 405-10.

_____. "Dickens' Use of Hazlitt's Principle of the Sympathetic Imagination." Mississippi Quarterly, 15 (Spring 1962), 68-73.

_____. "Dickens's Complex Plots." Di, 57 (1961), 174-82.

_____. "Dickens's Humor." VN, 18 (Fall 1960), 8-15.

_____. "Two Commentaries on Dickens: A. Dickens and the Philosophic Basis of Melodrama. B. Dickens and the Heart as the Hope for Heaven: A Study of the Philosophic Basis of Sensational Literary Technique." VN, 20 (Fall 1961), 1-6, 6-13.

_____. "The Unremoved Thorn: A Study in Dickens' Narrative Methods." North Dakota Quarterly, 30 (Jan. 1962), 8-13.

COOPERMAN, STANLEY. "Dickens and the Secular Blasphemy: Social Criticism in Hard Times, Little Dorrit, and Bleak House." CE, 22 (1960), 156-60.

COX, C. B. "In Defence of Dickens." E&S, N.S. 11 (1958), 86-100.

CROSS, BARBARA M. "Comedy and Drama in Dickens." WHR, 17 (1963), 143-49.

DAVIDS, E. I. GORE. "A Fourteenth Century Dickens." Di, 39 (1942/43), 70-74.

DAVIS, EARLE R. "Charles Dickens and Wilkie Collins." The Municipal University of Wichita Bulletin, 16 (1945), 3-26.

DENNIS, CARL. "Dickens' Moral Vision." TSLL, 11 (1969), 1237-46.

DICKINS, LOUIS G. "The Friendship of Dickens and Carlyle." Di, 53 (1957), 98-106.

DOBIE, ANN B. "Early Stream-of-Consciousness Writing: Great Expectations." NCF, 25 (1971), 405-16.

DONOGHUE, DENIS. "The English Dickens and Dombey and Son." NCF, 24 (1970), 383-403.

DUNN, RICHARD J. "Dickens and the Tragi-Comic Grotesque." SNNTS, 1 (1969), 147-56.

_____. "Dickens's Mastery of the Macabre." DiS, 1 (1965), 33-39.

DUNSTAN, J. LESLIE. "The Ministers in Dickens." Di, 56 (1960), 103-13.

EASSON, ANGUS. "Dickens, Household Words, and a Double Standard." Di, 60 (1964), 104-14.

EASTON, EDWARD RAYMOND. "Doctors in Dickens." Di, 41 (1944/45), 150-56.

ENGEL, MONROE. "Dickens on Art." MP, 53 (1955), 25-38.

_____. "The Politics of Dickens' Novels." PMLA, 71 (1956), 945-74.

FIEDLER, LESLIE A. "From Redemption to Initiation." New Leader, 41 (26 May 1958), 20-23.

_____. "Good Good Girl and Good Bad Boy." New Leader, 41 (14 Apr. 1958), 22-25.

_____. "William Faulkner: An American Dickens." Commentary, 10 (1950), 384-87.

Novels

FIELDING, K. J. "Chesterton Revisited." DSN, 6 (1975), 14-15.

_____. "Dickens and Wilkie Collins: A Reply." Di, 49 (1952/53), 130-36.

_____. "Dickens' Novels and the Discovery of Soul." Aryan Path, 33 (May 1962), 210-14.

_____. "Dickens's Novels and Miss Burdett-Coutts." Di, 51 (1954/55), 30-34.

_____. "1870-1900: Forster and Reaction." Di, 66 (1970), 85-100.

_____. "Forster: Critic of Fiction." Di, 70 (1974), 159-70.

_____. "The Monthly Serialization of Dickens's Novels." Di, 54 (1958), 4-11.

_____. "The Weekly Serialization of Dickens's Novels." Di, 54 (1958), 134-41.

FLEISSNER, ROBERT F. "'Something out of Dickens' in Sinclair Lewis." BNYPL, 74 (1970), 607-16.

FLIBBERT, JOSEPH T. "Dickens and the French Debate over Realism: 1838-1856." CL, 23 (1971), 18-31.

FORD, GEORGE H. "Dickens and the Voices of Time." NCF, 24 (1970), 428-48.

_____. "Dickens in the 1960s." Di, 66 (1970), 163-82.

FRANKLIN, STEPHEN L. "Dickens and Time: The Clock without Hands." DSA, 4 (1975), 1-35.

FUTRELL, MICHAEL H. "Dostoevsky and Dickens." EM, 7 (1956), 41-89.

_____. "Gogol and Dickens." SEER, 34 (1956), 443-59.

GADD, W. LAURENCE. "The Dickens Touch." Di, 36 (1939/40), 181-85.

GANZ, MARGARET. "The Vulnerable Ego: Dickens' Humor in Decline." DSA, 1 (1970), 23-40.

GARDNER, JOSEPH H. "Howells: The 'Realist' as Dickensian." MFS, 16 (1970), 323-43.

_____. "Mark Twain and Dickens." PMLA, 84 (1969), 90-101.

GARLEY, GRANVILLE. "Small Fry Folk: Tributes to Some of the Less Famous." Di, 39 (1942/43), 147-48, 203-204; 40 (1943/44), 45-46, 64, 159-60.

GERSON, STANLEY. "Dickens's Use of Malapropisms." Di, 61 (1965), 40-45.

_____. "A Great Australian Dickensian." Di, 68 (1972), 75-89.

Bibliography

GIBSON, FRANK A. "Dickens and Germany." <u>Di</u>, 43 (1946/47), 69–74.

_____. "Dogs in Dickens." <u>Di</u>, 53 (1957), 145–52.

_____. "Hats in Dickens." <u>Di</u>, 51 (1954/55), 108–10.

_____. "The Idyllic in Dickens." <u>Di</u>, 52 (1955/56), 59–64.

_____. "Mysteries in Dickens." <u>Di</u>, 56 (1960), 176–78.

_____. "Why Those 'Papers'?" <u>Di</u>, 59 (1963), 99–101.

GIBSON, PRISCILLA. "Dickens's Uses of Animism." <u>NCF</u>, 7 (1953), 283–91.

GIDDINGS, ROBERT. "A Cockney in the Court of Uncle Sam." <u>DSN</u>, 6 (1975), 47–55.

GIFFORD, HENRY. "Dickens in Russia: The Initial Phase." <u>FMLS</u>, 4 (1968), 48–52.

GILENSON, BORIS. "Dickens in Russia." <u>Di</u>, 57 (1961), 56–58.

GOLD, JOSEPH. "Charles Dickens and Today's Reader." <u>EJ</u>, 58 (1969), 205–11.

_____. "Dickens and Faulkner: The Uses of Influence." <u>DR</u>, 49 (1969), 69–79.

GOLDBERG, MICHAEL. "From Bentham to Carlyle: Dickens' Political Development." <u>JHI</u>, 33 (1972), 61–76.

GOODHEART, EUGENE. "Dickens's Method of Characterization." <u>Di</u>, 54 (1958), 35–37.

GREAVES, JOHN. "Fireside Reflections." <u>Di</u>, 41 (1944/45), 43–47.

GREEN, ROGER LANCELYN. "Andrew Lang: Critic and Dickensian." <u>Di</u>, 41 (1944/45), 10–14.

GROB, SHIRLEY. "Dickens and Some Motifs of the Fairy Tale." <u>TSLL</u>, 5 (1964), 567–79.

GRUBB, GERALD GILES. "Dickens's Pattern of Weekly Serialization." <u>ELH</u>, 9 (1942), 141–56.

_____. "The Personal and Literary Relationships of Dickens and Poe (Part One: From <u>Sketches by Boz</u> through <u>Barnaby Rudge</u>; Part Two: 'English Notes' and 'The Poets of America'; Part Three: Poe's Literary Debt to Dickens)." <u>NCF</u>, 5 (1950), 1–22, 101–20, 209–21.

HAIGHT, GORDON S. "Dickens and Lewes." <u>PMLA</u>, 71 (1956), 166–79.

HALL, WILLIAM F. "Caricature in Dickens and James." <u>UTQ</u>, 39 (1970), 242–57.

HAMILTON, ROBERT. "Dickens in His Characters." <u>Nineteenth Century</u>, 142 (1947), 40–49.

Novels

HARDER, KELSIE B. "Charles Dickens Names His Characters." Names, 7 (Mar. 1959), 35-42.

HARDY, BARBARA. "The Change of Heart in Dickens' Novels." VS, 5 (1961), 49-67.

_____. "Dickens and the Passions." NCF, 24 (1970), 449-66.

_____. "Dickens's Storytellers." Di, 69 (1973), 71-78.

HARGREAVES, GEOFFREY D. "Editing Dickens." TLS, 11 June 1970, p. 638.

HARVEY, WILLIAM R. "Charles Dickens and the Byronic Hero." NCF, 24 (1969), 305-16.

HAWES, DONALD. "Marryat and Dickens: A Personal and Literary Relationship." DSA, 2 (1972), 39-68.

HEILMAN, ROBERT B. "The New World in Charles Dickens' Writings." Trollopian, 1 (Sept. 1946), 25-43; 1 (Mar. 1947), 11-26.

HERBERT, CHRISTOPHER. "DeQuincey and Dickens." VS, 17 (1974), 247-63.

HILL, T. W. "Books That Dickens Read." Di, 45 (1948/49), 81-90, 201-207.

_____. "The Dickens Dietary." Di, 37 (1940/41), 145-51, 191-99; 38 (1941/42), 23-31, 95-101, 167-71, 197-205; 39 (1942/43), 5-15.

_____. "Dickensian Biography from Forster to the Present Day." Di, 47 (1950/51), 10-15, 72-79.

_____. "The Oyster; A Close-Up." Di, 36 (1939/40), 139-46.

HOLLOWAY, JOHN. "Dickens's Vision of Society." Listener, 73 (1965), 287-89.

HONAN, PARK. "Metrical Prose in Dickens." VN, 28 (Fall 1965), 1-3.

HOUSE, HUMPHRY. "Two Aspects of Charles Dickens." Listener, 37 (1947), 147-48.

HOWARTH, HERBERT. "Voices of the Past in Dickens and Others." UTQ, 41 (1972), 151-62.

HULSE, BRYAN F. "Dostoevsky for Dickensians." Di, 51 (1954/55), 66-71.

HUMPHERYS, ANNE. "Dickens and Mayhew on the London Poor." DSA, 4 (1975), 78-90.

J., W. H. "Dickens in the 'D. N. B.'" N&Q, 184 (1943), 92-93.

JOHNSON, DAVID DALE. "'Without Benefit of Clergy' in Victorian Fiction." West Virginia University Bulletin: Philological Studies, 4 (1943), 15-21.

Bibliography

JOHNSON, EDGAR. "Dickens and His Critics." SatR, 10 Feb. 1962,
pp. 31, 69.

_____. "Dickens and Shaw: Critics of Society." VQR, 33 (1957),
66-79.

_____. "Dickens and the Spirit of the Age." Bibliotheca Bucnellen-
sis, 4 (1966), 1-13.

_____. "Dickens, Fagin, and Mr. Riah: The Intention of the Novel-
ist." Commentary, 9 (1950), 47-50.

_____. "The Present State of Dickensian Studies." VN, 7 (Apr. 1955),
4-9.

_____. "Scott and Dickens: Realist and Romantic." VN, 27 (Spring
1965), 9-11.

JUMP, JOHN D. "Dickens and His Readers." BJRL, 54 (1972), 384-97.

KARL, FREDERICK R. "Conrad's Debt to Dickens." N&Q, 202 (1957),
398-400.

KELLY, THOMAS. "Character in Dickens' Late Novels." MLQ, 30 (1969),
386-401.

KELTY, JEAN McCLURE. "The Modern Tone of Charles Dickens." Di, 57
(1961), 160-65.

KENNEDY, G. W. "Dickens's Endings." SNNTS, 6 (1974), 280-87.

KETTLE, ARNOLD. "Dickens and the Popular Tradition." Zeitschrift
für Anglistik und Americanistik, 9 (1961), 229-52.

KIRKPATRICK, LARRY. "The Gothic Flame of Charles Dickens." VN, 31
(Spring 1967), 20-24.

KLIENEBERGER, H. R. "Charles Dickens and Wilhelm Raabe." OGS, 4
(1969), 90-117.

KREUTZ, IRVING W. "Sly of Manner, Sharp of Tooth: A Study of Dickens's Villains." NCF, 22 (1968), 331-48.

LAMB, CEDRIC. "Love and Self-Interest in Dickens' Novels." Paunch,
33 (Dec. 1968), 32-47.

LANE, LAURIAT, JR. "Dickens and Melville: Our Mutual Friends." DR,
51 (1971), 315-31.

_____. "Dickens and the Double." Di, 55 (1959), 47-55.

_____. "Dickens' Archetypal Jew." PMLA, 73 (1958), 94-100.

_____. "Dickens Studies 1958-1968: An Overview." SNNTS, 1 (1969),
240-54.

_____. "Dickensian Iconography: 1970." DR, 54 (1974), 130-35.

Novels

_____. "Satire, Society, and Symbol in Recent Dickens Criticism." SNNTS, 5 (1973), 125-38.

_____. "Theory and Practice of Dickensian Source Study: 1970." DSN, 4 (1973), 34-39.

LASCELLES, T. S. "Transport in the Dickensian Era." Di, 58 (1962), 75-86, 152-60.

LEVIN, HARRY. "Charles Dickens (1812-1870)." ASch, 39 (1970), 670-76.

LEVINE, RICHARD A. "Dickens, the Two Nations, and Individual Possibility." SNNTS, 1 (1969), 157-80.

LUCAS, AUDREY. "Some Dickens Women." YR, 29 (1940), 706-28.

LUCAS, JOHN. "Dickens and Arnold." RMS, 16 (1972), 86-111.

MADDEN, WILLIAM A. "The Search for Forgiveness in Some Nineteenth Century English Novels." CLS, 3 (1966), 139-53.

MANHEIM, LEONARD F. "Dickens' Fools and Madmen." DSA, 2 (1972), 69-97.

_____. "The Dickens Hero as Child." SNNTS, 1 (1969), 189-95.

_____. "Floras and Doras: The Women in Dickens' Novels." TSLL, 7 (1965), 181-200.

_____. "The Law as 'Father.'" AI, 12 (1955), 17-23.

MANNING, SYLVIA. "Dickens, January, and May." Di, 71 (1975), 67-75.

MARCUS, STEVEN. "Dickens After One Hundred Years." NYTBR, 7 June 1970, pp. 1, 46-49, 51.

MARLOW, JAMES E. "Memory, Romance, and the Expressive Symbol in Dickens." NCF, 30 (1975), 20-32.

MARTEN, HARRY P. "The Visual Imaginations of Dickens and Hogarth: Structure and Scene." SNNTS, 6 (1974), 145-64.

MASON, LEO. "Charlotte Brontë and Charles Dickens." Di, 43 (1946/47), 118-24.

_____. "Jane Eyre and David Copperfield." Di, 43 (1946/47), 172-79.

_____. "Poe and the Messenger." Di, 36 (1939/40), 163-68.

MAUSKOPF, CHARLES. "Thackeray's Attitude Toward Dickens's Writings." NCF, 21 (1966), 21-33.

McMASTER, R. D. "Dickens and the Horrific." DR, 38 (1958), 18-28.

_____. "Dickens, the Dandy, and the Savage: A Victorian View of the Romantic." SNNTS, 1 (1969), 133-46.

_____. "Man into Beast in Dickensian Caricature." UTQ, 31 (1962), 354-61.

_____. "'Society (whatever that was)': Dickens and Society as Abstraction." EA, 23 (1970), 125-35.

McNULTY, J. H. "The Weather." Di, 41 (1944/45), 138-42.

MECKIER, JEROME. "Charles Dickens: Research in Progress (1971)." DSN, 2 (1971), 111-21.

MILLER, J. HILLIS. "Some Implications of Form in Victorian Fiction." CLS, 3 (1966), 109-18.

_____. "The Sources of Dickens's Comic Art: From American Notes to Martin Chuzzlewit." NCF, 24 (1970), 467-76.

MILLER, JONATHAN. "In Praise of Fear." Listener, 83 (1970), 704-705.

MILLER, WILLIAM. "Contemporary Views of Dickens." Di, 43 (1946/47), 200-202.

MILNER, IAN. "The Nature of the Hero in Dickens and the Eighteenth Century Tradition." Philologica, 9 (1957), 57-67.

MONOD, SYLVÈRE. "Confessions of an Unrepentant Chestertonian." DSA, 3 (1974), 214-28.

_____. "A French View of Dickens's Humour." REL, 2 (July 1961), 29-38.

_____. "1900-1920: The Age of Chesterton." Di, 66 (1970), 101-20.

MORSE, ROBERT. "Our Mutual Friend." PR, 16 (1949), 277-89.

NELSON, HARLAND S. "Dickens' Plots: 'The Ways of Providence' or the Influence of Collins?" VN, 19 (Spring 1961), 11-14.

_____. "Staggs's Gardens: The Railway Through Dickens' World." DSA, 3 (1974), 41-53.

NISBET, ADA. "Foreword." NCF, 24 (1970), 379-82.

NOWELL-SMITH, SIMON. "Editing Dickens: For Which Reader? From Which Text?" TLS, 4 June 1970, pp. 615-16.

PAGE, NORMAN. "Forms of Address in Dickens." Di, 67 (1971), 16-20.

PARKER, DAVID. "Dickens's Archness." Di, 67 (1971), 149-58.

PASCAL, ROY. "Dickens and Kafka." Listener, 55 (1956), 504-506.

PEARSON, GABRIEL. "Dickens and His Readers." Universities and Left Review, 1 (Spring 1957), 52-56.

PECHEY, R. F. "Dickensian Nomenclature." Di, 52 (1955/56), 180-82.

Novels

PERRY, JOHN OLIVER. "The Popular Tradition of Melodrama in Dickens." Carleton Miscellany, 3 (Spring 1962), 105-10.

PEYROUTON, N. C. "Charles Dickens and the Christian Socialists: The Kingsley-Dickens Myth." Di, 58 (1962), 96-109.

_____. "Dickens and the Chartists." Di, 60 (1964), 78-88, 152-61.

PHILLIPS, GEORGE LEWIS. "Dickens and the Chimney-Sweepers." Di, 59 (1963), 28-44.

PINSKER, SANFORD. "Charles Dickens and Nathanael West: Great Expectations Unfulfilled." Topic, 18 (1969), 40-52.

POPE, KATHERINE V. "Women in Dickens." DSN, 5 (1974), 4-7.

PRIESTLEY, J. B. "New Judgement." Di, 40 (1943/44), 61-63.

PRITCHETT, V. S. "The Humour of Charles Dickens." Listener, 51 (1954), 970-73.

QUIRK, RANDOLPH. "Some Observations on the Language of Dickens." REL, 2 (July 1961), 19-28.

R., V. "Dickens: Two Curious Idioms." N&Q, 195 (1950), 279.

RALEIGH, JOHN HENRY. "Dickens and the Sense of Time." NCF, 13 (1958), 127-37.

_____. "The Novel and the City: England and America in the Nineteenth Century." VS, 11 (1968), 291-328.

REED, JOHN R. "Confinement and Character in Dickens' Novels." DSA, 1 (1970), 41-54.

RIGBY, STEPHEN. "Olfactory Gleanings." Di, 53 (1957), 36-38.

RIGG, RONALD E. "The Fascination of the Sea." Di, 40 (1943/44), 89-96, 151-58.

RILEY, ANTHONY W. "Notes on Thomas Mann and English and American Literature." CL, 17 (1965), 57-72.

ROBISON, ROSELEE. "Time, Death and the River in Dickens' Novels." ES, 53 (1972), 436-54.

RODRIQUES, EUSEBIO L. "The Dickens of Great Expectations." Literary Criterion, 7 (1966), 41-53.

ROLL-HANSEN, DIDERIK. "Characters and Contrasts in Great Expectations." Norwegian Studies in English, 9 (1963), 197-226.

ROOKE, ELEANOR. "Fathers and Sons in Dickens." E&S, N.S. 4 (1951), 53-69.

ROUSE, H. BLAIR. "Charles Dickens and Henry James: Two Approaches to the Art of Fiction." NCF, 5 (1950), 151-57.

RUFF, LILLIAN M. "How Musical Was Charles Dickens?" Di, 68 (1972), 31-42.

SCHILLING, BERNARD N. "Balzac, Dickens and 'This Harsh World.'" Adam, 331-33 (1969), 109-22.

SCHOECK, R. J. "Acton on Dickens." Di, 52 (1955/56), 77-80.

SCRUTTON, T. B. "'The State of the Prisons' as Seen by John Howard and Charles Dickens." Di, 62 (1966), 112-17.

SENELICK, LAURENCE. "'Charl'z Dikkens' and the Russian Encyclopedias." DiS, 1 (1965), 129-44.

SHATTO, SUSAN. "'A complete course, according to question and answer.'" Di, 70 (1974), 113-20.

SHAW, GEORGE BERNARD. "Shaw on Dickens." Di, 69 (1973), 44-45.

SHUCKBURGH, JOHN. "The Villain of the Piece." Di, 46 (1949/50), 18-23.

SIMPSON, EVELYN M. "Jonson and Dickens: A Study in the Comic Genius of London." E&S, 29 (1943), 82-92.

SIPE, SAMUEL M. "The Intentional World of Dickens's Fiction." NCF, 30 (1975), 1-19.

SLATER, MICHAEL. "Dickensian Criticism." TLS, 7 Aug. 1970, p. 878.

_____. "1920-1940: 'Superior-Folk' and Scandalmongers." Di, 66 (1970), 121-42.

_____. "The Year's Work in Dickens Studies 1967." Di, 64 (1968), 178-83.

_____. "The Year's Work In Dickens Studies 1968." Di, 65 (1969), 192-98.

_____. "The Year's Work in Dickens Studies 1969." Di, 66 (1970), 225-30.

SMITH, SHEILA M. "Anti-Mechanism and the Comic in the Writings of Charles Dickens." RMS, 3 (1959), 131-44.

_____. "Blue Books and Victorian Novelists." RES, N.S. 21 (1970), 23-40.

SNOW, C. P. "The Case of Leavis and the Serious Case." TLS, 9 July 1970, pp. 737-40.

SPILKA, MARK. "Dickens and Kafka: 'The Technique of the Grotesque.'" MinnR, 1 (1961), 441-58.

_____. "Kafka's Sources for The Metamorphosis." CL, 11 (1959), 289-307.

STEDMAN, JANE W. "Child-Wives of Dickens." Di, 59 (1963), 112-18.

Novels

_____. "Good Spirits: Dickens's Childhood Reading." Di, 61 (1965), 150-54.

STEIG, MICHAEL. "The Critic and the Illustrated Novel." HLQ, 36 (1972), 55-67.

_____. "Cruikshank's Peacock Feathers in Oliver Twist." Ariel, 4 (1973), 49-53.

_____. "Dickens, Hablot Browne, and the Tradition of English Carica-ture." Criticism, 11 (1969), 219-33.

_____. "Martin Chuzzlewit's Progress by Dickens and Phiz." DSA, 2 (1972), 119-49.

STEVENS, JOAN. "A Note on Thackeray's 'Manager of the Performance.'" NCF, 22 (1968), 391-97.

STEVENSON, LIONEL. "The Second Birth of the English Novel." UTQ, 14 (1945), 366-74.

STOLL, ELMER E. "Heroes and Villains: Shakespeare, Middleton, Byron, and Dickens." RES, 18 (1942), 257-69.

STONE, HARRY. "Dark Corners of the Mind: Dickens' Childhood Read-ing." Horn Book Magazine, 39 (1963), 306-21.

_____. "Dickens and Interior Monologue." PQ, 38 (1959), 52-65.

_____. "Dickens and the Jews." VS, 2 (1959), 223-53.

_____. "Dickens and the Uses of Literature." Di, 69 (1973), 139-47.

_____. "A Note on 'Dickens' Archetypal Jew.'" VS, 3 (1960), 459-60.

_____. "The Novel as Fairy Tale: Dickens' Dombey and Son." ES, 47 (1966), 1-27.

SUCKSMITH, HARVEY PETER. "The Secret of Immediacy: Dickens' Debt to the Tale of Terror in Blackwood's." NCF, 26 (1971), 145-57.

SULLIVAN, A. E. "Soldiers of the Queen--and of Charles Dickens." Di, 46 (1949/50), 138-43.

THALE, JEROME. "The Imagination of Charles Dickens: Some Prelimi-nary Discriminations." NCF, 22 (1967), 127-43.

THOMAS, DEBORAH A. "Dickens and Carlyle." DSN, 6 (1975), 5-7.

_____. "Dickens and the Graphic Arts." DSN, 4 (1973), 5-7.

THOMAS, GILLIAN. "Dickens and The Portfolio." Di, 68 (1972), 167-72.

THOMAS, L. H. C. "Otto Ludwig and Charles Dickens: A German Reading of Great Expectations and Other Novels." Hermathena, 111 (1971), 35-50.

TICK, STANLEY. "On Not Being Charles Dickens." BuR, 16 (1968), 85-95.

TOMLIN, E. W. F. "The Englishness of Dickens." <u>EA</u>, 23 (1970), 113-24.

TOMLINSON, T. B. "Dickens and Individualism: <u>Dombey and Son</u>, <u>Bleak House</u>." <u>Critical Review</u>, 15 (1972), 64-81.

VAN GHENT, DOROTHY. "The Dickens World: A View from Todgers's." <u>SR</u>, 58 (1950), 419-38.

VANN, J. DON. "A Checklist of Dickens Criticism, 1963-1967." <u>SNNTS</u>, 1 (1969), 255-78.

VERKOREN, L. "Dickens in Holland." <u>Di</u>, 55 (1959), 44-46.

VIEBROCK, HELMUT. "The Knocker: Physiognomical Aspects of a Motif in Hoffmann and Dickens." <u>ES</u>, 43 (1962), 396-402.

VOSS-MOETON, J. F. G. VAN. "Tears in Literature: Particularly in Dickens." <u>Di</u>, 58 (1962), 182-87.

WAGENKNECHT, EDWARD. "Dickens in Longfellow's Letters and Journals." <u>Di</u>, 52 (1955/56), 7-19.

WALBANK, ALAN. "With a Blush Retire." <u>Di</u>, 57 (1961), 166-73.

WALKER, SAXON. "The Artistry of Dickens as an English Novelist." <u>Di</u>, 51 (1954/55), 102-108.

WALL, STEPHEN. "Dickens's Plot of Fortune." <u>REL</u>, 6 (Jan. 1965), 56-67.

WALTON, JAMES. "Conrad, Dickens, and the Detective Novel." <u>NCF</u>, 23 (1969), 446-62.

WARD, J. A. "Dining with the Novelists." <u>Personalist</u>, 45 (1964), 399-411.

WARD, W. A. "Language and Charles Dickens." <u>Listener</u>, 69 (1963), 870-71, 874.

WARNCKE, WAYNE. "George Orwell's Dickens." <u>SAQ</u>, 69 (1970), 373-81.

WATT, IAN. "Oral Dickens." <u>DSA</u>, 3 (1974), 165-81.

WEGELIN, CHRISTOF. "Dickens and Irving: The Problem of Influence." <u>MLQ</u>, 7 (1946), 83-91.

WELSH, ALEXANDER. "Satire and History: The City of Dickens." <u>VS</u>, 11 (1968), 379-400.

WENGER, JARED. "Character-Types of Scott, Balzac, Dickens, Zola." <u>PMLA</u>, 62 (1947), 213-32.

WILLIAMS, P. C. "In The Beginning..." <u>Di</u>, 42 (1945/46), 99-101.

_____. "Murder Most Foul." <u>Di</u>, 41 (1944/45), 145-48.

_____. "The Soldiers in Dickens." <u>Di</u>, 41 (1944/45), 48-51.

Novels

WILLIAMS, RAYMOND. "Social Criticism in Dickens: Some Problems of Method and Approach." CritQ, 6 (1964), 214-27.

WILSON, ANGUS. "Charles Dickens: A Haunting." CritQ, 2 (1960), 101-108.

_____. "Dickens and the Divided Conscience." The Month, 189 (May 1950), 349-60.

_____. "Evil in the English Novel." KR, 29 (1967), 167-94.

_____. "The Heroes and Heroines of Dickens." REL, 2 (July 1961), 9-18.

_____. "Light and Dark in Dickens." Listener, 83 (1970), 701-703.

WILSON, ARTHUR H. "The Great Theme in Charles Dickens." Susquehanna University Studies, 6 (Apr.-June 1959), 422-57.

WILSON, EDMUND. "Dickens and the Marshalsea Prison." AM, 165 (1940), 473-83, 681-91.

_____. "Dickens: The Two Scrooges." New Republic, 102 (4 Mar. 1940), 297-300, 339-42.

WILSON, JOHN R. "Dickens and Christian Mystery." SAQ, 73 (1974), 528-40.

WILSON, ROSS. "The Dickens of a Drink." Di, 63 (1967), 46-61.

WINNER, ANTHONY. "Character and Knowledge in Dickens: The Enigma of Jaggers." DSA, 3 (1974), 100-21.

WINTERS, WARRINGTON. "Charles Dickens: The Pursuers and the Pursued." VN, 23 (Spring 1963), 23-24.

_____. "The Death Hug in Charles Dickens." L&P, 6 (1966), 109-15.

_____. "Dickens and the Psychology of Dreams." PMLA, 63 (1948), 984-1006.

WOOLLEN, C. J. "Some Thoughts on Dickens's Women." Di, 36 (1939/40), 178-80.

ZABEL, MORTON DAUWEN. "Dickens: The Reputation Revised." Nation, 169 (Sept. 1949), 279-81.

ZAMBRANO, ANA LAURA. "Charles Dickens and Sergei Eisenstein: The Emergence of Cinema." Style, 9 (1975), 469-87.

_____. "Dickens and Charles Mathews." MSpr, 66 (1972), 235-42.

Pickwick Papers

Pickwick Papers

Pickwick Papers

188, 190-91, 194-96, 200; Reed, DSA, 1 (1970), 42-43; Rogers, NCF, 27 (1972), 21-37; Welsh, NCF, 22 (1967), 21-30; (prototype): Saywood, Di, 66 (1970), 24-29.

Sawyer, Bob: Ganz, DSA, 4 (1975), 53.

Slammer, Dr. (prototype): Carter, Di, 62 (1966), 147, 150.

Smorltork, Count (prototype): Tillotson, TLS, 22 Nov. 1957, p. 712.

Stiggins: Dunstan, Di, 56 (1960), 110; (prototype): Clinton-Baddeley, Di, 50 (1953/54), 53-56.

Weller, Sam: Axton, SEL, 5 (1965), 666-71; Colwell, DiS, 3 (1967), 104-105; Daniels, DSA, 4 (1975), 61-62, 65, 71-73; Ganz, DSA, 4 (1975), 46-52; Kincaid, NCF, 24 (1969), 131-41; Marcus, Daedalus, 101 (1972), 199; Rogers, NCF, 27 (1972), 31-32; Welsh, NCF, 22 (1967), 27-29; Williams, Trivium, 1 (1966), 88-100; (language): Page, ES, 51 (1970), 340-42.

Weller, Tony: Axton, SEL, 5 (1965), 667-70; Bovill, N&Q, 201 (1956), 324-26; Ganz, DSA, 4 (1975), 51-52; Marcus, Daedalus, 101 (1972), 197-98.

Winkle: Colwell, DiS, 3 (1967), 107-108.

COMPOSITION (See also TEXT)

General: Marcus, Daedalus, 101 (1972), 183-201.

Interpolated tales: Patten, DiS, 1 (1965), 86-89; (dating): Patten, DSN, 1 (Mar. 1970), 7-10.

CRITICAL ASSESSMENT

General: Fadiman, AM, 184 (Dec. 1949), 25-29; Wilson, Susquehanna University Studies, 6 (Apr.-June 1959), 426-27.

Anticipation of later themes: McNulty, Di, 37 (1940/41), 141-43.

Contemporary reaction (American): Mason, Di, 36 (1939/40), 164-65; (first five numbers): Vann, Di, 70 (1974), 49-52.

Position in career: Hamilton, Di, 36 (1939/40), 242-44.

EXPLANATORY NOTES, HISTORICAL BACKGROUND, and SOURCES

"Bold Turpin" (Chapter 14): Yarre, Di, 43 (1946/47), 12-13.

Bramah locks: Horn, Di, 62 (1966), 100-105.

Dispute between Pickwick and Blotton: Patten, <u>Di</u>, 66 (1970), 218.

"...the gentleman <u>IS</u> awake. Hem, Shakespeare!": H., <u>N&Q</u>, 195 (1950), 372; R., <u>N&Q</u>, 195 (1950), 372.

Hypocritical clergyman (Stiggins): Clinton-Baddeley, <u>Di</u>, 50 (1953/54), 54-56.

Miscellaneous annotations: Hill, <u>Di</u>, 44 (1947/48), 29-36, 81-88, 105, 145-52, 193-98; 45 (1948/49), 27-33, 110.

Name Sam Weller: Stone, <u>Di</u>, 56 (1960), 48-49.

"a red-faced Nixon" (Chapter 42): B., <u>N&Q</u>, 179 (1940), 197; C., <u>N&Q</u>, 179 (1940) 358-59; Ignoto, <u>N&Q</u>, 179 (1940), 137; Senex, <u>N&Q</u>, 179 (1940), 302-303.

Serial publication: Patten, <u>RUS</u>, 61 (Winter 1975), 51-71.

Tony Weller's trade: Bovill, <u>N&Q</u>, 201 (1956), 324-28, 527-31; 202 (1957), 155-59, 260-63, 451-53.

ILLUSTRATIONS

General: Patten, <u>Di</u>, 66 (1970), 205-208.

Frontispiece: Patten, <u>ELH</u>, 34 (1967), 354-66.

Mr. Pott: Patten, <u>Di</u>, 66 (1970), 211-23.

Plate 14 ("Mrs. Leo Hunter's Fancy dress dejeune"): Patten, <u>Di</u>, 66 (1970), 206-24.

INFLUENCES (<u>See also</u> LITERARY PARALLELS)

(Dickens on) Dutch literature: Finlay, <u>Di</u>, 53 (1957), 40, 42; Marryat, <u>Japhet, in Search of a Father</u>, and Jingle: Hawes, <u>DSA</u>, 2 (1972), 65-66.

(on Dickens): eighteenth-century fiction: Dunn, <u>Di</u>, 62 (1966), 53-55; Irving: Carolan, <u>DSN</u>, 4 (1973), 41-45; <u>5</u> (1974), 104-106; Mathews, Charles (technique and characters): Zambrano, <u>MSpr</u>, 66 (1972), 236-40; penny-a-liners: Gill, <u>MLR</u>, 63 (1968), 33-36; police reports: Penner, <u>Di</u>, 64 (1968), 158-62; psychopathological theory: Manheim, <u>DSA</u>, 2 (1972), 74-77, 78-79; Sterne (<u>Tristram Shandy</u>): Robison, <u>UTQ</u>, 39 (1970), 258-72.

LANGUAGE and STYLE (<u>See also</u> TECHNIQUES, VARIOUS)

Pickwick Papers

General: Marcus, Daedalus, 101 (1972), 183-201.

Allusion (Dr. Johnson): Savage, Di, 48 (1951/52), 42.

Eighteenth-century models: Dunn, Di, 62 (1966), 53-55.

Imagery (labyrinth): Herbert, NCF, 27 (1972), 8-10.

Literary parody (Cervantes): Welsh, NCF, 22 (1967), 19-30;
    (Scott): ibid., 21-30.

"penny-a-line" rhetoric: Gill, MLR, 63 (1968), 33-36.

Speech (Cockney dialect): Page, ES, 51 (1970), 340-42; (Wellers):
    Gerson, Di, 62 (1966), 138-46; Williams, Trivium, 1 (1966),
    92-95; Wood, N&Q, 190 (1946), 234-35.

LITERARY PARALLELS (See also INFLUENCES)

Bucket and Sam Weller: Steig, PMASAL, 50 (1965), 579-80.

Cervantes, Don Quixote: Welsh, NCF, 22 (1967), 19-30.

Combe, Dr. Syntax's Tour: Saywood, Di, 66 (1970), 24-29.

Forebears of Jingle: Davis, PMLA, 55 (1940), 231-40.

Forerunners and imitations: James, DSA, 1 (1970), 65-80.

Irving ("Rip Van Winkle" and tale of Gabriel Grub): Carolan,
    DSN, 5 (1974), 104-106; (The Sketch Book and Christmas
    scenes): ibid., DSN, 4 (1973), 41-45.

Jonson, Bartholomew Fair, and Stiggins: Clinton-Baddeley, Di, 50
    (1953/54), 53-54.

Master Humphrey's Clock: Saint Victor, TSLL, 10 (1969), 569-70,
    577-84.

Scott's romances: Welsh, NCF, 22 (1967), 21-30.

Shakespeare, 1 Henry IV, Act 3, and Chapter 32: Nicholas, Di, 62
    (1966), 55-56.

Shaw, opening of Pygmalion, and Chapter 2: Drew, N&Q, 200
    (1955), 221-22.

Skimpole and Pickwick: Rogers, NCF, 27 (1972), 35-37.

PLOT (See also STRUCTURE/UNITY)

End of novel: Kennedy, SNNTS, 6 (1974), 281.

POINT OF VIEW

General: Axton, <u>SEL</u>, 5 (1965), 665-76.

SETTING

World of novel: Daniels, <u>DSA</u>, 4 (1975), 69-77; Ganz, <u>DSA</u>, 4
(1975), 37-55; Herbert, <u>NCF</u>, 27 (1972), 2-20; Kincaid, <u>NCF</u>,
24 (1969), 127-41.

STRUCTURE/UNITY (<u>See also</u> PLOT)

General: Axton, <u>SEL</u>, 5 (1965), 663-76; Colwell, <u>DiS</u>, 3 (1967),
90-110; Daniels, <u>DSA</u>, 4 (1975), 56-77; Herbert, <u>NCF</u>, 27
(1972), 1-20; Marcus, <u>Daedalus</u>, 101 (1972), 183-201.

Comic prose epic: Kestner, <u>University of Dayton Review</u>, 9 (Summer 1972), 15-23.

"keystone episode": Axton, <u>UTQ</u>, 37 (1967), 35-38.

Time, use of: Bevington, <u>NCF</u>, 16 (1961), 219-30.

TECHNIQUES, VARIOUS

General: Kincaid, <u>NCF</u>, 24 (1969), 127-41; Williams, <u>Trivium</u>,
1 (1966), 88-100.

Comedy/humor: Ganz, <u>DSA</u>, 4 (1975), 36-55; Welsh, <u>NCF</u>, 22 (1967),
22-24; Williams, <u>Trivium</u>, 1 (1966), 93-97.

Fathers and sons, use of: Winters, <u>L&P</u>, 6 (1966), 110-11.

Fires, use of: Greaves, <u>Di</u>, 41 (1944/45), 43-46.

Food and drink (preparation or consumption): Watt, <u>DSA</u>, 3
(1974), 165-66.

Interpolated tales: Axton, <u>SEL</u>, 5 (1965), 666, 674-76; Colwell,
<u>DiS</u>, 3 (1967), 102-105; Herbert, <u>NCF</u>, 27 (1972), 1, 7-20;
Levy and Ruff, <u>DiS</u>, 3 (1967), 122-25; Marcus, <u>Daedalus</u>, 101
(1972), 196-97; Patten, <u>DiS</u>, 1 (1965), 86-89; <u>ELH</u>, 34 (1967),
349-66; Reinhold, <u>Di</u>, 64 (1968), 141-43; Rogers, <u>NCF</u>, 27
(1972), 32-33; Saint Victor, <u>TSLL</u>, 10 (1969), 572-74; Wilson,
<u>AM</u>, 165 (1940), 475-76; Winters, <u>L&P</u>, 6 (1966), 110-11; ("A
Madman's Manuscript"): Easson, <u>Di</u>, 60 (1964), 105-107;
Manheim, <u>DSA</u>, 2 (1972), 75-77; ("Old Man's Tale about the
Queer Client"): Easson, <u>Di</u>, 64 (1968), 105-106, 108; Levy and
Ruff, <u>Di</u>, 64 (1968), 19-21; ("The Parish Clerk"): Lougy, <u>NCF</u>,

Pickwick Papers

25 (1970), 100-104; ("Story of the Goblin Who Stole a Sexton"): Carolan, DSN, 4 (1973), 46; 5 (1974), 104-106; Patten, ELH, 34 (1967), 362-65; ("The Stroller's Tale"): Lane, NCF, 14 (1959), 171-72; Patten, ELH, 34 (1967), 356-58; Reinhold, Di, 64 (1968), 143-51; ("The True Legend of Prince Bladud"): Levy and Ruff, DiS, 3 (1967), 122-24; Patten, DiS, 1 (1965), 87-89.

Mob, use of: Herbert, NCF, 27 (1972), 11-12.

Theatrical: James, DSA, 1 (1970), 70-72.

TEXT (See also COMPOSITION)

Footnote in first edition (chap. 2): Tillotson, TLS, 1 Apr. 1960, p. 214.

THEMES

General: Maclean, NCF, 8 (1953), 198-212; McNulty, Di, 37 (1940/41), 141-43.

Anger: Maclean, NCF, 8 (1953), 208-209.

Appearance/reality: Axton, SEL, 5 (1965), 664-76.

Avarice: Maclean, NCF, 8 (1953), 205-206.

Benevolence: Dunn, Di, 62 (1966), 53-54.

Chancery abuses: Rogers, NCF, 27 (1972), 33-34.

Christmas, meaning of: Brown, Di, 60 (1964), 17-18; Carolan, DSN, 4 (1973), 41-47.

Confinement: Reed, DSA, 1 (1970), 41-43.

Education: Kincaid, NCF, 24 (1969), 127-41.

Freedom: Herbert, NCF, 27 (1972), 5-7.

Gluttony and sloth: Maclean, NCF, 8 (1953), 209-10.

Imprisonment: Wilson, AM, 165 (1940), 476-77; (for debt): Easson, Di, 64 (1968), 105-12.

Innocence: Rogers, NCF, 27 (1972), 23-37.

Language: Saint Victor, TSLL, 10 (1969), 570-76.

Law: Easson, Di, 64 (1968), 109-12; Welsh, NCF, 22 (1967), 25-27.

Lust or lechery: Maclean, NCF, 8 (1953), 210-11.

Malice: Maclean, NCF, 8 (1953), 207-208.

Subject Index

Marriage and family: Rogers, <u>NCF</u>, 27 (1972), 29-33.

Money: Rogers, <u>NCF</u>, 27 (1972), 23-25.

Pride: Maclean, <u>NCF</u>, 8 (1953), 206-207.

Reason and responsibility: Kaplan, <u>VN</u>, 37 (Spring 1970), 18-21.

Revenge: Herbert, <u>NCF</u>, 27 (1972), 12-17.

Suffering, unrelieved: Herbert, <u>NCF</u>, 27 (1972), 17-20.

Time: Rogers, <u>NCF</u>, 27 (1972), 28-29.

Bibliography for
Pickwick Papers

AXTON, WILLIAM F. "'Keystone' Structure in Dickens' Serial Novels."
UTQ, 37 (1967), 31–50.

_____. "Unity and Coherence in the Pickwick Papers." SEL, 5 (1965),
663–76.

B., E. G. "Pickwick: Two Queries." N&Q, 179 (1940), 197.

BEVINGTON, DAVID M. "Seasonal Relevance in The Pickwick Papers."
NCF, 16 (1961), 219–30.

BLOUNT, TREVOR. "The Documentary Symbolism of Chancery in Bleak
House." Di, 62 (1966), 47–52, 106–11, 167–74.

BOVILL, E. W. "Tony Weller's Trade." N&Q, 201 (1956), 324–28,
527–31; 202 (1957), 155–59, 260–63, 451–53.

BROWN, F. J. "Those Dickens Christmases." Di, 60 (1964), 17–20.

C., T. C. "Pickwick: Two Queries." N&Q, 179 (1940), 358–59.

CARLTON, W. J. "Mr. Blackmore Engages an Office Boy." Di, 48
(1951/52), 162–67.

_____. "Serjeant Buzfuz." Di, 45 (1948/49), 21–22.

CAROLAN, KATHERINE. "The Dingley Dell Christmas." DSN, 4 (1973),
41–48.

_____. "The Dingley Dell Christmas Continued: 'Rip Van Winkle' and
the Tale of Gabriel Grub." DSN, 5 (1974), 104–106.

CARTER, JOHN ARCHER, JR. "Memories of 'Charley Wag.'" Di, 62
(1966), 147–51.

CLINTON-BADDELEY, V. C. "Stiggins." Di, 50 (1953/54), 53–56.

COLWELL, MARY. "Organization in Pickwick Papers." DiS, 3 (1967),
90–110.

COX, C. B. "In Defence of Dickens." E&S, N.S. 11 (1958), 86–100.

DANIELS, STEVEN V. "Pickwick and Dickens: Stages of Development."
DSA, 4 (1975), 56–77.

Pickwick Papers

DAVIS, EARLE R. "Dickens and the Evolution of Caricature." PMLA, 55 (1940), 231-40.

DREW, ARNOLD P. "Pygmalion and Pickwick." N&Q, 200 (1955), 221-22.

DUNN, RICHARD J. "'But We Grow Affecting: Let Us Proceed.'" Di, 62 (1966), 53-55.

DUNSTAN, J. LESLIE. "The Ministers in Dickens." Di, 56 (1960), 103-13.

EASSON, ANGUS. "Dickens, Household Words, and a Double Standard." Di, 60 (1964), 104-14.

_____. "Imprisonment for Debt in Pickwick Papers." Di, 64 (1968), 105-12.

FADIMAN, CLIFTON. "Pickwick Lives Forever." AM, 184 (Dec. 1949), 23-29.

FINLAY, IAN F. "Dickens's Influence on Dutch Literature." Di, 53 (1957), 40-42.

GANZ, MARGARET. "Pickwick Papers: Humor and the Refashioning of Reality." DSA, 4 (1975), 36-55.

GERSON, STANLEY. "'I Spells it with a "V."'" Di, 62 (1966), 138-46.

GILL, STEPHEN C. "Pickwick Papers and the 'Chroniclers by the Line': A Note on Style." MLR, 63 (1968), 33-36.

GREAVES, JOHN. "Fireside Reflections." Di, 41 (1944/45), 43-47.

H., A. "Dickens: A Curious Idiom." N&Q, 195 (1950), 372.

HAMILTON, ROBERT. "Dickens and Boz." Di, 36 (1939/40), 242-44.

_____. "Dickens in His Characters." Nineteenth Century, 142 (1947), 40-49.

HARDY, BARBARA. "Dickens's Storytellers." Di, 69 (1973), 71-78.

HAWES, DONALD. "Marryat and Dickens: A Personal and Literary Relationship." DSA, 2 (1972), 39-68.

HERBERT, CHRISTOPHER. "Converging Worlds in Pickwick Papers." NCF, 27 (1972), 1-20.

HILL, T. W. "Notes on the Pickwick Papers." Di, 44 (1947/48), 29-36, 81-88, 105, 145-52, 193-98; 45 (1948/49), 27-33, 110.

HORN, ROBERT D. "Dickens and the Patent Bramah Lock." Di, 62 (1966), 100-105.

IGNOTO. "Pickwick: Two Queries." N&Q, 179 (1940), 137.

JAMES, LOUIS. "Pickwick in America!" DSA, 1 (1970), 65-80.

KAPLAN, FRED. "Pickwick's 'Magnanimous Revenge': Reason and Responsibility in the Pickwick Papers." VN, 37 (Spring 1970), 18-21.

KENNEDY, G. W. "Dickens's Endings." SNNTS, 6 (1974), 280-87.

KESTNER, JOSEPH. "Elements of Epic in The Pickwick Papers." University of Dayton Review, 9 (Summer 1972), 15-24.

KINCAID, JAMES R. "The Education of Mr. Pickwick." NCF, 24 (1969), 127-41.

LANE, LAURIAT, JR. "Mr. Pickwick and The Dance of Death." NCF, 14 (1959), 171-72.

LEVY, HERMAN M., JR. and WILLIAM RUFF. "The Interpolated Tales in Pickwick Papers, a Further Note." DiS, 3 (1967), 122-25.

_____. "Who Tells the Story of a Queer Client?" Di, 64 (1968), 19-21.

LEWIS, E. A. "A Defense of Mrs. Bardell." Di, 38 (1941/42), 208-209.

LOUGY, ROBERT E. "Pickwick and 'The Parish Clerk.'" NCF, 25 (1970), 100-104.

MACLEAN, H. N. "Mr. Pickwick and the Seven Deadly Sins." NCF, 8 (1953), 198-212.

MANHEIM, LEONARD F. "Dickens' Fools and Madmen." DSA, 2 (1972), 69-97.

MARCUS, STEVEN. "Language into Structure: Pickwick Revisited." Daedalus, 101 (1972), 183-202.

MASON, LEO. "Poe and the Messenger." Di, 36 (1939/40), 163-68.

McNULTY, J. H. "The Overture." Di, 37 (1940/41), 141-44.

NICHOLAS, CONSTANCE. "Mrs. Raddle and Mistress Quickly." Di, 62 (1966), 55-56.

PAGE, NORMAN. "Convention and Consistency in Dickens's Cockney Dialect." ES, 51 (1970), 339-44.

PATTEN, ROBERT L. "The Art of Pickwick's Interpolated Tales." ELH, 34 (1967), 349-66.

_____. "The Interpolated Tales in Pickwick Papers." DiS, 1 (1965), 86-89.

_____. "Pickwick and the Development of Serial Fiction." RUS, 61 (Winter 1975), 51-74.

_____. "Portraits of Pott: Lord Brougham and the Pickwick Papers." Di, 66 (1970), 205-24.

_____. "The Unpropitious Muse: Pickwick's 'Interpolated' Tales." DSN, 1 (Mar. 1970), 7-10.

Pickwick Papers

PENNER, TALBOT. "Dickens: An Early Influence." Di, 64 (1968), 157-62.

R., V. "Dickens: Two Curious Idioms." N&Q, 195 (1950), 279.

REED, JOHN R. "Confinement and Character in Dickens' Novels." DSA, 1 (1970), 41-54.

REINHOLD, HEINZ. "'The Stroller's Tale' in Pickwick." Di, 64 (1968), 141-51.

ROBISON, ROSELEE. "Dickens and the Sentimental Tradition: Mr. Pickwick and My Uncle Toby." UTQ, 39 (1970), 258-73.

ROGERS, PHILIP. "Mr. Pickwick's Innocence." NCF, 27 (1972), 21-37.

SAINT VICTOR, CAROL de. "Master Humphrey's Clock: Dickens' 'Lost' Book." TSLL, 10 (1969), 569-84.

SAVAGE, OLIVER D. "Johnson and Dickens: A Comparison." Di, 48 (1951/52), 42-44.

SAYWOOD, B. C. "Dr. Syntax: A Pickwickian Prototype?" Di, 66 (1970), 24-29.

SENEX. "Pickwick: Two Queries." N&Q, 179 (1940), 302-303.

STEIG, MICHAEL. "The Whitewashing of Inspector Bucket: Origins and Parallels." PMASAL, 50 (1965), 575-84.

STONE, HARRY. "Dickens and the Naming of Sam Weller." Di, 56 (1960), 47-49.

SUCKSMITH, HARVEY PETER. "The Identity and Significance of the Mad Huntsman in Pickwick Papers." Di, 68 (1972), 109-14.

TILLOTSON, KATHLEEN. "Dickens's Count Smorltork." TLS, 22 Nov. 1957, p. 712.

_____. "Pickwick and Edward Jesse." TLS, 1 Apr. 1960, p. 214.

VANN, J. DON. "Pickwick in the London Newspapers." Di, 70 (1974), 49-52.

WATT, IAN. "Oral Dickens." DSA, 3 (1974), 165-81.

WELSH, ALEXANDER. "Waverly, Pickwick, and Don Quixote." NCF, 22 (1967), 19-30.

WILLIAMS, GWENLLIAN L. "Sam Weller." Trivium, 1 (1966), 88-101.

WILSON, ARTHUR H. "The Great Theme in Charles Dickens." Susquehanna University Studies, 6 (Apr.-June 1959), 422-57.

WILSON, EDMUND. "Dickens and the Marshalsea Prison." AM, 165 (1940), 473-83, 681-91.

WINTERS, WARRINGTON. "The Death Hug in Charles Dickens." L&P, 6 (1966), 109-15.

WOOD, FREDERICK T. "Sam Weller's Cockneyisms." N&Q, 190 (1946), 234-35.

YARRE, d'A. P. "The Bold Turpin." Di, 43 (1946/47), 12-13.

ZAMBRANO, ANA LAURA. "Dickens and Charles Mathews." MSpr, 66 (1972), 235-42.

Oliver Twist

Oliver Twist

CHARACTERIZATION

General: Bishop, VN, 15 (Spring 1959), 14-16; Brogan, Listener,
40 (1948), 310-11; Cranfield, NSN, N.S. 29 (1945), 95-96;
Duffy, ELH, 35 (1968), 404-11, 416-19; Gold, Mosaic, 2 (Fall
1968), 79-89; Kincaid, PMLA, 83 (1968), 66-70; Patten, SNNTS,
1 (1969), 207-20; Tillotson, E&S, N.S. 12 (1959), 91-101;
Westburg, SNNTS, 6 (1974), 28-36.

Comic: Kincaid, PMLA, 83 (1968), 64-70.

Devil archetype: Lane, Di, 52 (1955/56), 132-36.

"Good People": Slater, Di, 70 (1974), 80-81.

CHARACTERS

Artful Dodger: Kincaid, PMLA, 83 (1968), 69; Slater, Di, 70
(1974), 79; Steig, PMASAL, 50 (1965), 580.

Brownlow: Duffy, ELH, 35 (1968), 416-19.

Bumble: Gold, Mosaic, 2 (Fall 1968), 79-87; Kincaid, PMLA, 83
(1968), 66-69; Schlicke, Di, 71 (1975), 149-55.

Fagin: Brogan, Listener, 40 (1948), 311; Duffy, ELH, 35 (1968),
416-17; Gold, Mosaic, 2 (Fall 1968), 79-80, 84-87; Johnson,
Commentary, 9 (1950), 47-50; Kreutz, NCF, 22 (1968), 331-34;
Lane, TLS, 20 July 1951, p. 460; Di, 52 (1955/56), 132-36;
Manheim, DSA, 2 (1972), 81-82; Patten, SNNTS, 1 (1969),
214-17; Shuckburgh, Di, 46 (1949/50), 19-20; Slater, Di, 70
(1974), 77-81; Stone, VS, 2 (1959), 233-35, 245-46, 251-53;
Westburg, SNNTS, 6 (1974), 33-36; (as Jew): Lane, PMLA, 73
(1958), 94-96, 99-100; Stone, VS, 3 (1960), 460; (genesis):
Marcus, Commentary, 34 (1962), 48-59; McLean, Lock Haven Review, 9 (1967), 29-35; (prototype): Tobias, Di, 65 (1969),
171-75.

Gamfield: Kincaid, PMLA, 83 (1968), 65.

Oliver Twist

Losberne, Dr.: Williamson, NCF, 22 (1967), 225-26, 228-29, 232-33.

Maylie, Harry: Williamson, NCF, 22 (1967), 229, 231-34.

Maylie, Rose: Brogan, Listener, 40 (1948), 311; (prototype): Boll, PsyR, 27 (1940), 136-42.

Maylies: Gold, Mosaic, 2 (Fall 1968), 88-89.

Monks: Kreutz, NCF, 22 (1968), 334-35; Westburg, SNNTS, 6 (1974), 33.

Nancy: Brogan, Listener, 40 (1948), 311; Manheim, DSA, 2 (1972), 80-81; Patten, SNNTS, 1 (1969), 218-20; Slater, Di, 70 (1974), 79-80.

Sikes, Bill: Bishop, VN, 15 (Spring 1959), 15-16; Ferns, QQ, 79 (1972), 90-91; Hardy, NCF, 24 (1970), 453-57; Kreutz, NCF, 22 (1968), 331-34; Shuckburgh, Di, 46 (1949/50), 19; Slater, Di, 70 (1974), 79.

Twist, Oliver: Bishop, VN, 15 (Spring 1959), 14-16; Boll, PsyR, 27 (1940), 134-35; Duffy, ELH, 35 (1968), 404-11, 415; Eoff, SP, 54 (1957), 442-47; Kincaid, PMLA, 83 (1968), 64-70; Page, Di, 65 (1969), 100-101; Slater, Di, 70 (1974), 75-77; Wilson, SAQ, 73 (1974), 528-32.

COMPOSITION (See also PUBLICATION and TEXT)

Serialization: Schachterle, DSA, 3 (1974), 1-13.

CRITICAL ASSESSMENT

General: Wilson, Susquehanna University Studies, 6 (Apr.-June 1959), 427-28.

Contemporary reaction (American): Mason, Di, 36 (1939/40), 165-66.

EXPLANATORY NOTES, HISTORICAL BACKGROUND, and SOURCES

Bluebooks and statistics generally: Brantlinger, Criticism, 14 (1972), 328-44.

"brought up by hand" (definition): Finkel, NCF, 20 (1966), 389-90.

Jews, attitude toward: Lane, PMLA, 73 (1958), 94-100; Stone, VS, 2 (1959), 223-53.

Oliver Twist

Magazine serialization of fiction: Schachterle, DSA, 3 (1974), 1-13.

Miscellaneous annotations: Hill, Di, 46 (1949/50), 146-56, 213.

Parish orphans: Williams, Listener, 94 (1975), 819-20.

Political context: Rice, DSN, 4 (1973), 11-14.

Poor Law: Schlicke, Di, 71 (1975), 149-52.

ILLUSTRATIONS

General: Cohen, HLB, 17 (1969), 179-87; Robb, Listener, 74 (1965), 130-31; (Cruikshank's prototypes): Vogler, DSA, 2 (1972), 98-116.

Bates, Charley (prototype): Vogler, DSA, 2 (1972), 113.

Bull's Eye (prototype): Vogler, DSA, 2 (1972), 108.

Bumble (prototype): Vogler, DSA, 2 (1972), 114.

Fagin (prototype): Vogler, DSA, 2 (1972), 108-12.

Fireside Plate (deleted from Chapter LIII): Steig, Ariel, 4 (1973), 49, 51-53.

Nancy (prototype): Vogler, DSA, 2 (1972), 112-13.

"Oliver recovering from the fever" (Chapter XII): Steig, Ariel, 4 (1973), 49, 51-53.

Origin and composition: Vogler, PULC, 35 (1973/74), 61-91.

Plate 11 ("Mr. Bumble and Mrs. Corney taking tea"): Steig, DSA, 2 (1972), 120-21.

Sikes (prototype): Vogler, DSA, 2 (1972), 101-108.

INFLUENCES (See also LITERARY PARALLELS)

(Dickens on) Marryat, Joseph Rushbrook, Poor Jack, and Snarleyyow: Hawes, DSA, 2 (1972), 60-65.

(on Dickens) Blackwood's, Tale of Terror (and Chapter 52): Sucksmith, NCF, 26 (1971), 151-55; Cruikshank: Vogler, DSA, 2 (1972), 98-116; police reports: Penner, Di, 64 (1968), 158-62; psychopathological theory: Manheim, DSA, 2 (1972), 80-82.

Oliver Twist

LANGUAGE and STYLE (See also TECHNIQUES, VARIOUS)

    Allusion (Charles I--Cromwell--Charles II): Westburg, SNNTS, 6
      (1974), 28-36; (names): ibid., 28-33.

    Imagery (faces): Herbert, VS, 17 (1974), 256-57.

    Speech: Page, Di, 65 (1969), 100-101.

    Symbolism (handkerchief): Patten, SNNTS, 1 (1969), 219-20.

LITERARY PARALLELS (See also INFLUENCES)

    Artful Dodger and Bucket: Steig, PMASAL, 50 (1965), 580.

    Barnaby Rudge: Rice, DSN, 4 (1973), 10-14.

    Mayhew (description of Jacob's Island): Humpherys, DSA, 4
      (1975), 79-81.

    Shakespeare, Othello (and murder of Nancy): Senelick, Di, 70
      (1974), 97-102.

    Sketches by Boz: Tillotson, E&S, N.S. 12 (1959), 90-91.

    Thompson, "Le Revenant" (Blackwood's) and Chapter 52: Sucksmith,
      NCF, 26 (1971), 151-55.

    Twain, Huckleberry Finn (contrast): Auden, Listener, 50 (1953),
      540-41.

PLOT (See also STRUCTURE/UNITY)

    General: Williamson, NCF, 22 (1967), 225-34.

    End of novel: Kennedy, SNNTS, 6 (1974), 285.

    Inconsistencies: Gibson, Di, 50 (1953/54), 86-87.

    Suspense: Schachterle, DSA, 3 (1974), 10-13.

POINT OF VIEW

    Subversion of humor: Kincaid, PMLA, 83 (1968), 64-70.

PUBLICATION (See also COMPOSITION and TEXT)

    History: Tillotson, Library, ser. 5, 18 (1953), 113-32.

    Serialization: Grubb, MLN, 56 (1941), 290-94.

Oliver Twist

SETTING

City vs. country: Duffy, ELH, 35 (1968), 408-15.

World of novel: Cranfield, NSN, N.S. 29 (1945), 95-96; Freder-
    ick, CE, 27 (1966), 465-70; Kincaid, PMLA, 83 (1968), 64-70;
    Patten, SNNTS, 1 (1969), 207-20.

STRUCTURE/UNITY (See also PLOT)

"keystone episode": Axton, UTQ, 37 (1967), 38-41.

Picaresque tradition, use of: Eoff, SP, 54 (1957), 440-47.

TECHNIQUES, VARIOUS

General: Duffy, ELH, 35 (1968), 404-19; Patten, SNNTS, 1 (1969),
    207-20; Slater, Di, 70 (1974), 75-81; Tillotson, E&S, N.S. 12
    (1959), 91-101, 103-105.

Autobiography, use of: Marcus, Commentary, 34 (1962), 57-59.

Comedy/humor: Bishop, VN, 15 (Spring 1959), 14-15; Kincaid,
    PMLA, 83 (1968), 63-70.

Dreams, use of: Duffy, ELH, 35 (1968), 409-10.

Fathers and sons, use of: Winters, L&P, 6 (1966), 111-14.

Idyllic, the, use of: Gibson, Di, 52 (1955/56), 60.

Newgate fiction, methods of: Lucas, DR, 34 (1954), 381-87.

TEXT (See also COMPOSITION and PUBLICATION)

Chapter variations: Schweitzer, PBSA, 60 (1966), 337-43.

Variant (description of Fagin): Lane, TLS, 20 July 1951, p. 460.

THEMES

General: Duffy, ELH, 35 (1968), 419-21; Frederick, CE, 27
    (1966), 466-70; Tillotson, E&S, N.S. 12 (1959), 101-103.

Alienation: Gold, Mosaic, 2 (Fall 1968), 77-89.

Benthamite and Malthusian philosophy: Patten, SNNTS, 1 (1969),
    207-20.

Compassion: Patten, SNNTS, 1 (1969), 209-20.

Oliver Twist

Death (and river imagery): Robison, ES, 53 (1972), 439.

Family: Frederick, CE, 27 (1966), 466-70.

Good vs. evil: Tillotson, E&S, N.S. 12 (1959), 91-95.

Passivity: Wilson, SAQ, 73 (1974), 529-32.

Self-salvation: Wilson, SAQ, 73 (1974), 528-32.

Social criticism: Brogan, Listener, 40 (1948), 310-11; Churchill, Scrutiny, 10 (1942), 372-74; Frederick, CE, 27 (1966),
469-70; Slater, Di, 70 (1974), 75-81; (Poor Law): Schlicke,
Di, 71 (1975), 149-55; (world of affection vs. world of depri-
vation): Ferns, QQ, 79 (1972), 87-92.

Violence: Williamson, NCF, 22 (1967), 229-34.

Bibliography for *Oliver Twist*

AUDEN, W. H. "Huck and Oliver." Listener, 50 (1953), 540-41.

AXTON, WILLIAM F. "'Keystone' Structure in Dickens' Serial Novels." UTQ, 37 (1967), 31-50.

BISHOP, JONATHAN. "The Hero-Villain of Oliver Twist." VN, 15 (Spring 1959), 14-16.

BOLL, ERNEST. "Charles Dickens in Oliver Twist." PsyR, 27 (1940), 133-43.

BRANTLINGER, PATRICK. "Bluebooks, the Social Organism, and the Victorian Novel." Criticism, 14 (1972), 328-44.

BROGAN, COLIN. "Oliver Twist Re-Examined." Listener, 40 (1948), 310-11.

CHURCHILL, R. C. "Dickens, Drama, and Tradition." Scrutiny, 10 (1942), 358-75.

COHEN, JANE RABB. "'All-of-a Twist': The Relationship of George Cruikshank and Charles Dickens." HLB, 17 (1969), 169-94.

CRANFIELD, LIONEL. "Books in General." NSN, N.S. 29 (1945), 95-96.

DUFFY, JOSEPH M., JR. "Another Version of Pastoral: Oliver Twist." ELH, 35 (1968), 403-21.

EOFF, SHERMAN. "Oliver Twist and the Spanish Picaresque Novel." SP, 54 (1957), 440-47.

FERNS, JOHN. "Oliver Twist: Destruction of Love." QQ, 79 (1972), 87-92.

FINKEL, ROBERT J. "Another Boy Brought Up 'By Hand.'" NCF, 20 (1966), 389-90.

FREDERICK, KENNETH C. "The Cold, Cold Hearth: Domestic Strife in Oliver Twist." CE, 27 (1966), 465-70.

GIBSON, FRANK A. "Discomforts in Dickens." Di, 50 (1953/54), 86-89.

_____. "The Idyllic in Dickens." Di, 52 (1955/56), 59-64.

GOLD, JOSEPH. "Dickens' Exemplary Aliens: Bumble the Beadle and Fagin the Fence." Mosaic, 2 (Fall 1968), 77-89.

Oliver Twist

GRUBB, GERALD GILES. "On the Serial Publication of Oliver Twist."
MLN, 56 (1941), 290-94.

HARDY, BARBARA. "Dickens and the Passions." NCF, 24 (1970), 449-66.

HAWES, DONALD. "Marryat and Dickens: A Personal and Literary Relationship." DSA, 2 (1972), 39-68.

HERBERT, CHRISTOPHER. "DeQuincey and Dickens." VS, 17 (1974),
247-63.

HILL, T. W. "Notes on Oliver Twist." Di, 46 (1949/50), 146-56, 213.

HUMPHERYS, ANNE. "Dickens and Mayhew on the London Poor." DSA, 4
(1975), 78-90.

JOHNSON, EDGAR. "Dickens, Fagin, and Mr. Riah: The Intention of the
Novelist." Commentary, 9 (1950), 47-50.

KENNEDY, G. W. "Dickens's Endings." SNNTS, 6 (1974), 280-87.

KINCAID, JAMES R. "Laughter and Oliver Twist." PMLA, 83 (1968),
63-70.

KREUTZ, IRVING W. "Sly of Manner, Sharp of Tooth: A Study of Dickens's Villains." NCF, 22 (1968), 331-48.

LANE, LAURIAT, JR. "The Devil in Oliver Twist." Di, 52 (1955/56),
132-36.

_____. "Dickens' Archetypal Jew." PMLA, 73 (1958), 94-100.

_____. "Oliver Twist: A Revision." TLS, 20 July 1951, p. 460.

LUCAS, ALEC. "Oliver Twist and the Newgate Novel." DR, 34 (1954),
381-87.

MANHEIM, LEONARD F. "Dickens' Fools and Madmen." DSA, 2 (1972),
69-97.

MARCUS, STEVEN. "Who is Fagin?" Commentary, 34 (1962), 48-59.

MASON, LEO. "Poe and the Messenger." Di, 36 (1939/40), 163-68.

McLEAN, ROBERT SIMPSON. "Fagin: An Early View of Evil." Lock Haven
Review, 9 (1967), 29-36.

PAGE, NORMAN. "'A Language Fit for Heroes': Speech in Oliver Twist
and Our Mutual Friend." Di, 65 (1969), 100-107.

PATTEN, ROBERT L. "Capitalism and Compassion in Oliver Twist."
SNNTS, 1 (1969), 207-21.

PENNER, TALBOT. "Dickens: An Early Influence." Di, 64 (1968),
157-62.

RICE, THOMAS JACKSON. "Oliver Twist and the Genesis of Barnaby
Rudge." DSN, 4 (1973), 10-15.

ROBB, BRIAN. "George Cruikshank's Etchings for Oliver Twist." Listener, 74 (1965), 130-31.

ROBISON, ROSELEE. "Time, Death and the River in Dickens' Novels." ES, 53 (1972), 436-54.

SCHACHTERLE, LANCE. "Oliver Twist and Its Serial Predecessors." DSA, 3 (1974), 1-13.

SCHLICKE, PAUL. "Bumble and the Poor Law Satire of Oliver Twist." Di, 71 (1975), 149-56.

SCHWEITZER, JOAN. "The Chapter Numbering in Oliver Twist." PBSA, 60 (1966), 337-43.

SENELICK, LAURENCE. "Traces of Othello in Oliver Twist." Di, 70 (1974), 97-102.

SHUCKBURGH, JOHN. "The Villain of the Piece." Di, 46 (1949/50), 18-23.

SLATER, MICHAEL. "On Reading Oliver Twist." Di, 70 (1974), 75-81.

STEIG, MICHAEL. "Cruikshank's Peacock Feathers in Oliver Twist." Ariel, 4 (1973), 49-53.

_____. "Martin Chuzzlewit's Progress by Dickens and Phiz." DSA, 2 (1972), 119-49.

_____. "The Whitewashing of Inspector Bucket: Origins and Parallels." PMASAL, 50 (1965), 575-84.

STONE, HARRY. "Dickens and the Jews." VS, 2 (1959), 223-53.

_____. "A Note on 'Dickens' Archetypal Jew.'" VS, 3 (1960), 459-60.

SUCKSMITH, HARVEY PETER. "The Secret of Immediacy: Dickens' Debt to the Tale of Terror in Blackwood's." NCF, 26 (1971), 145-57.

TILLOTSON, KATHLEEN. "Oliver Twist." E&S, N.S. 12 (1959), 87-105.

_____. "Oliver Twist in Three Volumes." Library, ser. 5, 18 (1953), 113-32.

TOBIAS, J. J. "Ikey Solomons--a Real-Life Fagin." Di, 65 (1969), 171-75.

VOGLER, RICHARD A. "Cruikshank and Dickens: A Reassessment of the Role of the Artist and the Author." PULC, 35 (1973/74), 61-91.

_____. "Oliver Twist: Cruikshank's Pictorial Prototypes." DSA, 2 (1972), 98-118.

WESTBURG, BARRY. "'His Allegorical Way of Expressing It': Civil War and Psychic Conflict in Oliver Twist and A Child's History." SNNTS, 6 (1974), 27-37.

Oliver Twist

WILLIAMS, NIGEL. "The Parish Boy's Progress." Listener, 94 (1975), 819-20.

WILLIAMSON, COLIN. "Two Missing Links in Oliver Twist." NCF, 22 (1967), 225-34.

WILSON, ARTHUR H. "The Great Theme in Charles Dickens." Susquehanna University Studies, 6 (Apr.-June 1959), 422-57.

WILSON, JOHN R. "Dickens and Christian Mystery." SAQ, 73 (1974), 528-40.

WINTERS, WARRINGTON. "The Death Hug in Charles Dickens." L&P, 6 (1966), 109-15.

Nicholas Nickleby

Nicholas Nickleby

CHARACTERIZATION

General: Hannaford, Criticism, 16 (1974), 247-59; Meckier, DSA, 1 (1970), 136-46; Reed, PLL, 3 (1967), 135-47; Roulet, Di, 60 (1964), 120-23.

Melodramatic: Purton, EA, 28 (1975), 23-24.

Minor characters: Reed, PLL, 3 (1967), 136-41.

CHARACTERS

Bray, Madeline: Hannaford, Criticism, 16 (1974), 251-52.

Cheeryble brothers: Graham, Di, 45 (1948/49), 23-25; Hannaford, Criticism, 16 (1974), 253-54; (prototype): Adrian, MLN, 64 (1949), 269-70.

Crummles, Vincent: Carter, Di, 58 (1962), 50-53; (prototype): Morley, Di, 58 (1962), 25-27; 59 (1963), 51-56.

Infant Phenomenon (prototype): Disher, TLS, 6 May 1944, p. 228; 27 May 1944, p. 259.

La Creevy, Miss (prototype): Shyvers, Di, 44 (1947/48), 91-93.

Nickleby, Kate: Reed, PLL, 3 (1967), 141-42.

Nickleby, Mrs.: Hannaford, Criticism, 16 (1974), 257-59; Manheim, DSA, 2 (1972), 86-87; Slater, Di, 71 (1975), 136-39; Thompson, SNNTS, 1 (1969), 222-28.

Nickleby, Nicholas: Lucas, RMS, 16 (1972), 99-101; Reed, PLL, 3 (1967), 141-47.

Nickleby, Ralph: Kreutz, NCF, 22 (1968), 335-37; Meckier, SAQ, 71 (1972), 78-80; Noffsinger, DSN, 5 (1974), 112-14; Reed, PLL, 3 (1967), 142-46; Wing, Di, 64 (1968), 10-19.

Noggs, Newman (prototype): Carlton, Di, 48 (1951/52), 165.

Smike: Ball, Di, 62 (1966), 125-28; Manheim, DSA, 2 (1972), 85-86.

Nicholas Nickleby

Snevellicci, Miss: Clinton-Baddeley, <u>Di</u>, 57 (1961), 43-44, 50-52.

Squeers, Wackford: Paterson, <u>Di</u>, 39 (1942/43), 95-97; Shuckburgh, <u>Di</u>, 46 (1949/50), 18-19; (prototype): Clinton-Baddeley, <u>Cornhill</u>, 169 (1957), 369.

CRITICAL ASSESSMENT

General: Wilson, <u>Susquehanna University Studies</u>, 6 (Apr.-June 1959), 429-30.

EXPLANATORY NOTES, HISTORICAL BACKGROUND, and SOURCES

Crummles' company: Clinton-Baddeley, <u>Di</u>, 57 (1961), 45-52; (prototype): <u>ibid</u>., 45-47.

Dotheboys Hall: Clinton-Baddeley, <u>Cornhill</u>, 169 (1957), 362-82.

Miscellaneous annotations: Hill, <u>Di</u>, 45 (1948/49), 98-102, 163-66; 46 (1949/50), 42-48, 99-104.

Old Portsmouth Theatre: Olle, <u>Di</u>, 47 (1950/51), 143-47.

Squeers as schoolmaster: Paterson, <u>Di</u>, 39 (1942/43), 96.

"Thirsty Woman of Tutbury": Greaves, <u>Di</u>, 61 (1965), 51-52; Slater, <u>Di</u>, 61 (1965), 181.

ILLUSTRATIONS

Plates 1 and 22 (peacock feathers indicate pride or misfortune): Steig, <u>Ariel</u>, 4 (1973), 50.

INFLUENCES (<u>See also</u> LITERARY PARALLELS)

(on Dickens) Hogarth (spatiotemporalization of form): Marten, <u>SNNTS</u>, 6 (1974), 153-57; melodrama (theatrical): Purton, <u>EA</u>, 28 (1975), 22-24, 25-26; psychopathological theory: Manheim, <u>DSA</u>, 2 (1972), 85-87.

LANGUAGE and STYLE (<u>See also</u> TECHNIQUES, VARIOUS)

Monologue (interior): Kelty, <u>Di</u>, 57 (1961), 160-61.

Nicholas Nickleby

LITERARY PARALLELS

Meredith, Evan Harrington and Cheeryble brothers: Graham, Di, 45 (1948/49), 23-25.

PLOT (See also STRUCTURE/UNITY)

End of novel: Kennedy, SNNTS, 6 (1974), 282.

Fairy tale elements: Hannaford, Criticism, 16 (1974), 247-59.

PUBLICATION (See also TEXT)

Monthly number divisions: Levy, Di, 63 (1967), 41.

SETTING

World of novel: Carter, Di, 58 (1962), 50-53; Hannaford, Criticism, 16 (1974), 254-59; Meckier, DSA, 1 (1970), 130-46.

STRUCTURE/UNITY (See also PLOT)

General: Carter, Di, 58 (1962), 50-53; Meckier, DSA, 1 (1970), 129-46; Roulet, Di, 60 (1964), 117-24.

Moral form: Reed, PLL, 3 (1967), 134.

Spatiotemporalization of form: Marten, SNNTS, 6 (1974), 153-57.

TECHNIQUES, VARIOUS

General: Meckier, DSA, 1 (1970), 129-46; Reed, PLL, 3 (1967), 134-47.

Idyllic, the, use of: Gibson, Di, 52 (1955/56), 59-61.

Interpolated tales: Meckier, DSA, 1 (1970), 134-35; Reed, PLL, 3 (1967), 134-35.

Melodrama: Purton, EA, 28 (1975), 22-24, 25-26.

TEXT (See also PUBLICATION)

Variants in first edition and National Edition: R., Di, 41 (1944/45), 84-86.

Nicholas Nickleby

THEMES

Charity: Reed, <u>PLL</u>, 3 (1967), 138–41, 146–47.

Education (reform): Adrian, <u>NCF</u>, 4 (1949), 237–41.

Good vs. evil: Reed, <u>PLL</u>, 3 (1967), 134–47.

Optimism vs. pessimism: Thompson, <u>SNNTS</u>, 1 (1969), 222–28.

Selfishness: Reed, <u>PLL</u>, 3 (1967), 136–38, 145–47.

Social criticism: Carter, <u>Di</u>, 58 (1962), 50–53.

Bibliography for
Nicholas Nickleby

ADRIAN, ARTHUR A. "The Cheeryble Brothers: A Further Note." MLN, 64 (1949), 269-70.

_____. "Nicholas Nickleby and Educational Reform." NCF, 4 (1949), 237-41.

BALL, ROY A. "The Development of Smike." Di, 62 (1966), 125-28.

CARLTON, W. J. "Mr. Blackmore Engages an Office Boy." Di, 48 (1951/52), 162-67.

CARTER, JOHN ARCHER, JR. "The World of Squeers and the World of Crummles." Di, 58 (1962), 50-53.

CLINTON-BADDELEY, V. C. "Benevolent Teachers of Youth." Cornhill, 169 (1957), 361-82.

_____. "Snevellicci." Di, 57 (1961), 43-52.

DISHER, M. WILLSON. "The Crummleses." TLS, 27 May 1944, p. 259.

_____. "Playbills of the Crummleses." TLS, 6 May 1944, p. 228.

GIBSON, FRANK A. "The Idyllic in Dickens." Di, 52 (1955/56), 59-64.

GRAHAM, W. H. "The Cheerybles and the Cogglesbys." Di, 45 (1948/49), 23-25.

GREAVES, JOHN. "The Thirsty Woman of Tutbury." Di, 61 (1965), 51-52.

HANNAFORD, RICHARD. "Fairy-Tale Fantasy in Nicholas Nickleby." Criticism, 16 (1974), 247-59.

HILL, T. W. "Notes on Nicholas Nickleby." Di, 45 (1948/49), 98-102, 163-66; 46 (1949/50), 42-48, 99-104.

KELTY, JEAN McCLURE. "The Modern Tone of Charles Dickens." Di, 57 (1961), 160-65.

KENNEDY, G. W. "Dickens's Endings." SNNTS, 6 (1974), 280-87.

KREUTZ, IRVING W. "Sly of Manner, Sharp of Tooth: A Study of Dickens's Villains." NCF, 22 (1968), 331-48.

Nicholas Nickleby

LEVY, HERMAN M., JR. "An Omission Unnoticed: Nickleby Forgotten." Di, 63 (1967), 41.

LUCAS, JOHN. "Dickens and Arnold." RMS, 16 (1972), 86-111.

MANHEIM, LEONARD F. "Dickens' Fools and Madmen." DSA, 2 (1972), 69-97.

MARTEN, HARRY P. "The Visual Imaginations of Dickens and Hogarth: Structure and Scene." SNNTS, 6 (1974), 145-64.

MECKIER, JEROME. "Dickens and King Lear: A Myth for Victorian England." SAQ, 71 (1972), 75-90.

_____. "The Faint Image of Eden: The Many Worlds of Nicholas Nickleby." DSA, 1 (1970), 129-46.

MORLEY, MALCOLM. "More about Crummles." Di, 59 (1963), 51-56.

_____. "Where Crummles Played." Di, 58 (1962), 23-29.

NOFFSINGER, JOHN W. "The Complexity of Ralph Nickleby." DSN, 5 (1974), 112-14.

OLLE, JAMES G. "Where Crummles Played." Di, 47 (1950/51), 143-47.

PATERSON, ANDREW. "A Word for Wackford Squeers." Di, 39 (1942/43), 95-97.

PURTON, VALERIE. "Dickens and 'Cheap Melodrama.'" EA, 28 (1975), 22-26.

R., D. A. P. "Nicholas Slips." Di, 41 (1944/45), 84-86.

REED, JOHN R. "Some Indefinable Resemblance: Moral Form in Dickens' Nicholas Nickleby." PLL, 3 (1967), 134-47.

ROULET, ANN. "A Comparative Study of Nicholas Nickleby and Bleak House." Di, 60 (1964), 117-24.

SHUCKBURGH, JOHN. "The Villain of the Piece." Di, 46 (1949/50), 18-23.

SHYVERS, W. GIBSON. "'Positively the First Appearance.'" Di, 44 (1947/48), 89-93.

SLATER, MICHAEL. "Appreciating Mrs. Nickleby." Di, 71 (1975), 136-39.

_____. "The Thirsty Woman of Tutbury." Di, 61 (1965), 181.

STEIG, MICHAEL. "Cruikshank's Peacock Feathers in Oliver Twist." Ariel, 4 (1973), 49-53.

THOMPSON, LESLIE M. "Mrs. Nickleby's Monologue: The Dichotomy of Pessimism and Optimism in Nicholas Nickleby." SNNTS, 1 (1969), 222-29.

Subject Index

WILSON, ARTHUR H. "The Great Theme in Charles Dickens." <u>Susquehanna</u> <u>University Studies</u>, 6 (Apr.-June 1959), 422-57.

WING, G. D. "A Part to Tear a Cat in." <u>Di</u>, 64 (1968), 10-19.

The Old Curiosity Shop

The Old Curiosity Shop

CHARACTERIZATION

General: Cranfield, NSN, N.S. 29 (1945), 95-96; Dyson, CritQ, 8
(1966), 111-12, 114-28; Gibson, Di, 60 (1964), 178-83;
Meckier, JNT, 2 (1972), 200-205.

Sexual: Pratt, HSL, 6 (1974), 131-34.

CHARACTERS

Bachelor: Rogers, NCF, 28 (1973), 136-37, 139.

Brass, Sally: Bennett, RES, N.S. 22 (1971), 433; Senelick, DiS,
3 (1967), 157-58.

Brass, Sampson (as Jew): Lane, PMLA, 73 (1958), 97.

Garland, Abel: Rogers, NCF, 28 (1973), 143-44.

Humphrey, Master: Rogers, NCF, 28 (1973), 129-33.

Marchioness: Diskin, N&Q, 219 (1974), 212; Easson, MLR, 65
(1970), 517-18; Steig, L&P, 15 (1965), 168-69; DiS, 2 (1966),
141-46; (parentage): Bennett, Di, 36 (1939/40), 205-208;
Grubb, MLN, 68 (1953), 162-64.

Nell's Grandfather: Brumleigh, Di, 38 (1941/42), 14-15; Dyson,
CritQ, 8 (1966), 126-28; Gottshall, NCF, 16 (1961), 135-37;
Manheim, DSA, 2 (1972), 90; Meckier, SAQ, 71 (1972), 82-84;
Rogers, NCF, 28 (1973), 139-40; (name of): Steig, DSN, 4
(1973), 40; Walder, DSN, 4 (1973), 123; (prototype): Diskin,
N&Q, 219 (1974), 210-11.

Nubbles, Kit: Dyson, CritQ, 8 (1966), 118-21, 124-25; Senelick,
DiS, 3 (1967), 156-57.

Quilp, Daniel: Bennett, RES, N.S. 22 (1971), 428-32; Dunn,
SNNTS, 1 (1969), 147-48; Dyson, CritQ, 8 (1966), 114-18,
124-25; Franklin, DSA, 4 (1975), 11-12; Hamilton, Nineteenth
Century, 142 (1947), 47-48; Howarth, UTQ, 41 (1972), 151-52;
McLean, VN, 34 (Fall 1968), 29-33; Pratt, HSL, 6 (1974),

The Old Curiosity Shop

129-44; Rogers, NCF, 28 (1973), 134-35; Senelick, DiS, 3
(1967), 157; Spilka, PMASAL, 45 (1960), 428-30; Steig, L&P,
15 (1965), 164-70; CLS, 6 (1969), 170, 173-77; Winters, Di,
63 (1967), 176-79; (prototype): Cotterell, Di, 43 (1946/47),
39-40; McLean, NCF, 26 (1971), 337-39; Olshin, NCF, 25 (1970),
97-99; Watkins, N&Q, 216 (1971), 411-13.

Schoolmaster: Rogers, NCF, 28 (1973), 138, 139-40.

Scott, Tom: Pratt, HSL, 6 (1974), 134-35.

Sexton: Rogers, NCF, 28 (1973), 137-38, 139.

Swiveller, Dick: Bennett, RES, N.S. 22 (1971), 434; Dyson,
CritQ, 8 (1966), 121-23, 124-25; Franklin, DSA, 4 (1975),
11-13; Hamilton, Nineteenth Century, 142 (1947), 43-45;
Rogers, NCF, 28 (1973), 140-42; S., TLS, 6 Apr. 1940, p. 167;
Senelick, DiS, 3 (1967), 156; Steig, L&P, 15 (1965), 168-69.

Trent, Nell (Little Nell): Bennett, RES, N.S. 22 (1971), 423-27;
Blount, MP, 62 (1965), 325; Boll, PsyR, 27 (1940), 141-42;
Brumleigh, Di, 38 (1941/42), 14; Burgan, MLQ, 36 (1975),
303-305; Cranfield, NSN, N.S. 29 (1945), 95-96; Field, RLV, 35
(1969), 615-21; Franklin, DSA, 4 (1975), 7-11; Gibson, Di, 60
(1964), 179-82; Meckier, JNT, 2 (1972), 199-205; SAQ, 71
(1972), 80-83; Pickering, Illinois Quarterly, 36 (Sept. 1973),
12, 14-17; Pratt, HSL, 6 (1974), 136-37, 140-43; Rogers, NCF,
28 (1973), 127-44; Senelick, DiS, 3 (1967), 149-59; Spilka,
PMASAL, 45 (1960), 427-37; Steig, L&P, 15 (1965), 163-70;
Winters, Di, 63 (1967), 179-80.

COMPOSITION (See also TEXT)

Background: Andrews, Di, 67 (1971), 70-86.

CRITICAL ASSESSMENT

General: Wilson, Susquehanna University Studies, 6 (Apr.-June
1959), 430-32.

Contemporary reaction: S., TLS, 6 Apr. 1940, p. 167; (American):
Mason, Di, 39 (1942/43), 24-26; (Bulwer-Lytton): Flower, Di,
69 (1973), 82; (Poe): Grubb, NCF, 5 (1950), 3-8.

Position in career: Dyson, CritQ, 8 (1966), 112-14.

EXPLANATORY NOTES, HISTORICAL BACKGROUND, and SOURCES

Child prostitution: Senelick, DiS, 3 (1967), 154-56.

Death of Nell: Senelick, DiS, 3 (1967), 151-54.

Miscellaneous annotations: Brumleigh, Di, 37 (1940/41), 231-35; 38 (1941/42), 14-16; Hill, Di, 49 (1952/53), 86-93, 137-42, 183-91.

Quilp: Watkins, N&Q, 216 (1971), 411-13.

State Trials (conspiracy of Quilp and Brass against Kit): Gibson, Di, 53 (1957), 12-15.

"The Yellow Dwarf": Olshin, NCF, 25 (1970), 96-99.

ILLUSTRATIONS

General: Stevens, SB, 20 (1967), 114-24, 127-33.

Marchioness: Steig, DiS, 2 (1966), 143-46.

Nell: Cohen, DSA, 1 (1970), 85.

INFLUENCES (See also LITERARY PARALLELS)

(Dickens on) Frith, Derby Day: Wilson, DSN, 2 (1971), 88-89.

(on Dickens) DeQuincey, Confessions (and Marchioness): Diskin, N&Q, 219 (1974), 212; DeQuincey, "The Household Wreck" (and Kit): ibid., 212; Hoffmann, "Spielergluck" (and opening chapters): ibid., 210-11; Mrs. Radcliffe (plot): Coolidge, Di, 58 (1962), 114; psychopathological theory: Manheim, DSA, 2 (1972), 90; religious tracts: Pickering, Illinois Quarterly, 36 (Sept. 1973), 6-19; Rogers, Analysis of the First Part of the Pleasures of Memory (and Chapter 1): Andrews, N&Q, 216 (1971), 410-11; Schiller, "The German Brothers" (and Nell's Grandfather): Diskin, N&Q, 219 (1974), 211; Shakespeare, King Lear: Meckier, SAQ, 71 (1972), 75-76, 80-84; Wordsworth, The Excursion (and Nell's later adventures): Diskin, N&Q, 219 (1974), 212-13; Wordsworth, "Resolution and Independence" (and Chapter 72): ibid., 213; Wordsworth, "The Revenge of Poor Susan" (and Chapter 1): ibid., 213; Wordsworth, "Westminster Bridge" (and Chapter 12): ibid., 213.

The Old Curiosity Shop

LITERARY PARALLELS (See also INFLUENCES)

Bunyan, The Pilgrim's Progress: Bennett, RES, N.S. 22 (1971), 423-27.

Carroll, Lewis, Alice in Wonderland: Field, RLV, 35 (1969), 612-13, 618-20.

Punch (the marionette): Bennett, RES, N.S. 22 (1971), 427-34.

Quilp and Bucket: Steig, PMASAL, 50 (1965), 580-81.

Richmond, The Dairyman's Daughter and The Young Cottager (latitudinarian morality): Pickering, Illinois Quarterly, 36 (Sept. 1973), 11-18.

Shakespeare, Richard III: Howarth, UTQ, 41 (1972), 151-52; King Lear: Fleissner, Di, 58 (1962), 125-27.

Sterne, Tristram Shandy Book 5, and Chapter 49: Barnett, N&Q, 200 (1955), 403-404.

PLOT (See also STRUCTURE/UNITY)

Fantasy, use of: Field, RLV, 35 (1969), 609-21.

Folk motifs, use of: Pratt, HSL, 6 (1974), 137-39.

Inconsistencies: Gibson, Di, 50 (1953/54), 87-88.

SETTING

General: Bennett, RES, N.S. 22 (1971), 424-27.

Gothic elements: Kirkpatrick, VN, 31 (Spring 1967), 20-21.

Pastoral, use of: Burgan, MLQ, 36 (1975), 303-305.

World of novel: Cranfield, NSN, N.S. 29 (1945), 95-96; Dyson, CritQ, 8 (1966), 126-28; (Industrial Midlands): ibid., 128-29.

STRUCTURE/UNITY (See also PLOT)

General: Bennett, RES, N.S. 22 (1971), 423-34.

Allegory: Gibson, Di, 60 (1964), 178-83.

Serialization (final eleven numbers): Meckier, JNT, 2 (1972), 199-205.

TECHNIQUES, VARIOUS

    General: Senelick, DiS, 3 (1967), 147-59; Spilka, PMASAL, 45 (1960), 427-37; Steig, L&P, 15 (1965), 163-70.

    Death of Nell: Blount, MP, 62 (1965), 325; Meckier, JNT, 2 (1972), 199-205; Pickering, Illinois Quarterly, 36 (Sept. 1973), 14-16.

    Grotesque, use of: Dunn, SNNTS, 1 (1969), 147-48; Dyson, CritQ, 8 (1966), 111-12, 114-30.

    Idyllic, the, use of: Gibson, Di, 52 (1955/56), 62-63.

    Sentimentality: Cockshut, TC, 161 (1957), 354-56, 361-64.

    Time, use of: Franklin, DSA, 4 (1975), 7-14.

TEXT (See also COMPOSITION)

    Changes (manuscript to print): Easson, DSA, 1 (1970), 93-128.

    Unpublished material (from corrected proofs): Staples, Di, 50 (1953/54), 17-23, 63-66, 132-36.

THEMES

    General: Dyson, CritQ, 8 (1966), 119-20.

    Industrialism: Brantlinger, NCF, 26 (1971), 271-72, 273-74.

    Latitudinarian morality: Pickering, Illinois Quarterly, 36 (Sept. 1973), 6-19.

    Parent/child relationships: Adrian, Di, 67 (1971), 5-6.

    Sexuality: Steig, L&P, 15 (1965), 163-70.

    Social criticism: Gibson, Di, 60 (1964), 178-83.

    Time: Franklin, DSA, 4 (1975), 7-14; (growth and decay): Rogers, NCF, 28 (1973), 127-44.

    Youth vs. age: Senelick, DiS, 3 (1967), 148-50.

Bibliography for
The Old Curiosity Shop

ADRIAN, ARTHUR A. "Dickens and Inverted Parenthood." Di, 67 (1971), 3-11.

ANDREWS, MALCOLM. "Dickens, Samuel Rogers, and The Old Curiosity Shop." N&Q, 216 (1971), 410-11.

_____. "Introducing Master Humphrey." Di, 67 (1971), 70-86.

BARNETT, GEORGE L. "Corporal Trim's Hat." N&Q, 200 (1955), 403-404.

BENNETT, RACHEL. "Punch vs. Christian in The Old Curiosity Shop." RES, N.S. 22 (1971), 423-34.

BENNETT, WILLIAM CROSBY. "The Mystery of the Marchioness." Di, 36 (1939/40), 205-208.

BLOUNT, TREVOR. "Poor Jo, Education, and the Problem of Juvenile Delinquency in Dickens' Bleak House." MP, 62 (1965), 325-39.

BOLL, ERNEST. "Charles Dickens in Oliver Twist." PsyR, 27 (1940), 133-43.

BRANTLINGER, PATRICK. "Dickens and the Factories." NCF, 26 (1971), 270-85.

BRUMLEIGH, T. KENT. "On the Road with the Trents." Di, 37 (1940/41), 231-35; 38 (1941/42), 14-16.

BURGAN, WILLIAM. "Tokens of Winter in Dickens's Pastoral Settings." MLQ, 36 (1975), 293-315.

COCKSHUT, A. O. J. "Sentimentality in Fiction." TC, 161 (1957), 354-64.

COHEN, JANE RABB. "Strained Relations: Charles Dickens and George Cattermole." DSA, 1 (1970), 81-92.

COOLIDGE, ARCHIBALD C., JR. "Charles Dickens and Mrs. Radcliffe: A Farewell to Wilkie Collins." Di, 58 (1962), 112-16.

COTTERELL, T. STURGE. "The Original of Quilp?" Di, 43 (1946/47), 39-40.

CRANFIELD, LIONEL. "Books in General." NSN, N.S. 29 (1945), 95-96.

The Old Curiosity Shop

DISKIN, PATRICK. "The Literary Background of The Old Curiosity Shop." N&Q, 219 (1974), 210-13.

DUNN, RICHARD J. "Dickens and the Tragi-Comic Grotesque." SNNTS, 1 (1969), 147-56.

DYSON, A. E. "The Old Curiosity Shop: Innocence and the Grotesque." CritQ, 8 (1966), 111-30.

EASSON, ANGUS. "Dickens's Marchioness Again." MLR, 65 (1970), 517-18.

_____. "The Old Curiosity Shop: From Manuscript to Print." DSA, 1 (1970), 93-128.

FIELD, J. C. "Fantasy and Flaw in The Old Curiosity Shop." RLV, 35 (1969), 609-22.

FLEISSNER, ROBERT F. "'Fancy's Knell.'" Di, 58 (1962), 125-27.

FLOWER, SIBYLLA JANE. "Charles Dickens and Edward Bulwer-Lytton." Di, 69 (1973), 79-89.

FRANKLIN, STEPHEN L. "Dickens and Time: The Clock Without Hands." DSA, 4 (1975), 1-35.

GIBSON, FRANK A. "Discomforts in Dickens." Di, 50 (1953/54), 86-89.

_____. "The Idyllic in Dickens." Di, 52 (1955/56), 59-64.

_____. "A 17th Century Kit Nubbles." Di, 53 (1957), 12-15.

GIBSON, JOHN W. "The Old Curiosity Shop: The Critical Allegory." Di, 60 (1964), 178-83.

GOTTSHALL, JAMES K. "Devils Abroad: The Unity and Significance of Barnaby Rudge." NCF, 16 (1961), 133-46.

GRUBB, GERALD GILES. "Dickens' Marchioness Identified." MLN, 68 (1953), 162-65.

_____. "The Personal and Literary Relationships of Dickens and Poe (Part One: From Sketches by Boz through Barnaby Rudge; Part Two: 'English Notes' and 'The Poets of America'; Part Three: Poe's Literary Debt to Dickens)." NCF, 5 (1950), 1-22, 101-20, 209-21.

HAMILTON, ROBERT. "Dickens in His Characters." Nineteenth Century, 142 (1947), 40-49.

HILL, T. W. "Notes on The Old Curiosity Shop." Di, 49 (1952/53), 86-93, 137-42, 183-91.

HOWARTH, HERBERT. "Voices of the Past in Dickens and Others." UTQ, 41 (1972), 151-62.

KIRKPATRICK, LARRY. "The Gothic Flame of Charles Dickens." VN, 31 (Spring 1967), 20-24.

Bibliography

LANE, LAURIAT, JR. "Dickens' Archetypal Jew." PMLA, 73 (1958), 94–100.

MANHEIM, LEONARD F. "Dickens' Fools and Madmen." DSA, 2 (1972), 69–97.

MASON, LEO. "More about Dickens and Poe." Di, 39 (1942/43), 21–28.

McLEAN, ROBERT SIMPSON. "Another Source for Quilp." NCF, 26 (1971), 337–39.

_____. "Putting Quilp To Rest." VN, 34 (Fall 1968), 29–33.

MECKIER, JEROME. "Dickens and King Lear: A Myth for Victorian England." SAQ, 71 (1972), 75–90.

_____. "Suspense in The Old Curiosity Shop: Dickens' Contrapuntal Artistry." JNT, 2 (1972), 199–207.

OLSHIN, TOBY A. "'The Yellow Dwarf' and The Old Curiosity Shop." NCF, 25 (1970), 96–99.

PICKERING, SAMUEL F., JR. "The Old Curiosity Shop––a Religious Tract?" Illinois Quarterly, 36 (Sept. 1973), 5–20.

PRATT, BRANWEN. "Sympathy for the Devil: A Dissenting View of Quilp." HSL, 6 (1974), 129–46.

ROGERS, PHILIP. "The Dynamics of Time in The Old Curiosity Shop." NCF, 28 (1973), 127–44.

S., D. M. "The Old Curiosity Shop: Dickens and Disney." TLS, 6 Apr. 1940, p. 167.

SENELICK, LAURENCE. "Little Nell and the Prurience of Sentimentality." DiS, 3 (1967), 146–59.

SPILKA, MARK. "Little Nell Revisited." PMASAL, 45 (1960), 427–37.

STAPLES, L. C. "Shavings from Dickens' Workshop: Unpublished Fragments from the Novels. IV. The Old Curiosity Shop." Di, 50 (1953/54), 17–23, 63–66, 132–36.

STEIG, MICHAEL. "The Central Action of Old Curiosity Shop: or Little Nell Revisited Again." L&P, 15 (1965), 163–70.

_____. "Ghosts in Master Humphrey's Clock: Two Notes on Scholarly Errors." DSN, 4 (1973), 40–41.

_____. "The Grotesque and the Aesthetic Response in Shakespeare, Dickens, and Gunter Grass." CLS, 6 (1969), 167–81.

_____. "Phiz's Marchioness." DiS, 2 (1966), 141–46.

_____. "The Whitewashing of Inspector Bucket: Origins and Parallels." PMASAL, 50 (1965), 575–84.

The Old Curiosity Shop

STEVENS, JOAN. "'Woodcuts dropped into the Text': The Illustrations in The Old Curiosity Shop and Barnaby Rudge." SB, 20 (1967), 113-33.

WALDER, DENNIS. "Letter to Editor." DSN, 4 (1973), 123.

WATKINS, G. M. "A Possible Source for Quilp." N&Q, 216 (1971), 411-13.

WILSON, ANGUS. "Little Nell and Derby Day." DSN, 2 (1971), 88-89.

WILSON, ARTHUR H. "The Great Theme in Charles Dickens." Susquehanna University Studies, 6 (Apr.-June 1959), 422-57.

WINTERS, WARRINGTON. "The Old Curiosity Shop: A Consummation Devoutly to be Wished." Di, 63 (1967), 176-80.

Barnaby Rudge

Barnaby Rudge

CHARACTERIZATION

General: Dyson, CritQ, 9 (1967), 144-60; Folland, PMLA, 74
(1959), 408-17; Gottshall, NCF, 16 (1961), 138-45; Monod,
DiS, 1 (1965), 6-26; Steele, Steinbeck Quarterly, 5 (Winter
1972), 9.

Grotesque: Dunn, SNNTS, 1 (1969), 148-49.

Groupings: Folland, PMLA, 74 (1959), 407.

Through analogies: Rice, NCF, 30 (1975), 174-77.

CHARACTERS

Chester, Sir John: Dyson, CritQ, 9 (1967), 156-57; Folland,
PMLA, 74 (1959), 411-12, 415-17; Graham, Contemporary Review,
194 (1958), 92; Postlethwaite, Di, 54 (1958), 83-87.

Dennis, Ned: Dunn, SNNTS, 1 (1969), 148-49; Dyson, CritQ, 9
(1967), 154-55; Folland, PMLA, 74 (1959), 412-14; O'Brien,
DiS, 5 (1969), 34-35; Wilson, AM, 165 (1940), 480; (prototype): Ziegler, Di, 54 (1958), 81-82.

Gashford: Dyson, CritQ, 9 (1967), 156-57; Folland, PMLA, 74
(1959), 408; (prototype): Gibson, Di, 44 (1947/48), 124-26.

Gordon, Lord George: Dyson, CritQ, 9 (1967), 155; Folland, PMLA,
74 (1959), 410; Gibson, Di, 44 (1947/48), 126-29; 57 (1961),
81-85; Graham, Contemporary Review, 194 (1958), 90-91; Manheim, DSA, 2 (1972), 83-85; O'Brien, DiS, 5 (1969), 33-34.

Haredale, Geoffrey: Folland, PMLA, 74 (1959), 415.

Hugh: Dyson, CritQ, 9 (1967), 152-54; Folland, PMLA, 74 (1959),
410-11, 416-17; Gottshall, NCF, 16 (1961), 144-45; McMaster,
UTQ, 31 (1962), 354-56; Monod, DiS, 1 (1965), 6-26; Rice, DSN,
4 (1973), 10-11; (prototype): Ziegler, Di, 54 (1958), 82.

Hugh's mother (prototype): Ziegler, Di, 54 (1958), 82.

Barnaby Rudge

Miggs, Miss: Folland, PMLA, 74 (1959), 414; (prototype): Robinson, AUMLA, 40 (1973), 191-92.

Rudge (Barnaby's father): Folland, PMLA, 74 (1959), 416.

Rudge, Barnaby: Dyson, CritQ, 9 (1967), 149-52; Folland, PMLA, 74 (1959), 410, 416-17; Gottshall, NCF, 16 (1961), 133-34, 141-45; Manheim, DSA, 2 (1972), 82-83; O'Brien, DiS, 5 (1969), 41-44; Ryan, English, 19 (1970), 43-44; Steele, Steinbeck Quarterly, 5 (Winter 1972), 9-14, 17.

Stagg: Dyson, CritQ, 9 (1967), 157.

Tappertit, Simon: Dyson, CritQ, 9 (1967), 148-49; Folland, PMLA, 74 (1959), 414; (prototype): Robinson, AUMLA, 40 (1973), 192; Steig, DSN, 4 (1973), 67-68.

Varden, Dolly: Folland, PMLA, 74 (1959), 414; Monod, DiS, 1 (1965), 19-20.

Varden, Gabriel: Dyson, CritQ, 9 (1967), 158-60.

Willet, John: Franklin, DSA, 4 (1975), 14-15; Manheim, DSA, 2 (1972), 89-90.

CRITICAL ASSESSMENT

General: Monod, DiS, 1 (1965), 4-6; Wilson, Susquehanna University Studies, 6 (Apr.-June 1959), 432-33.

Contemporary reaction (American): Mason, Di, 39 (1942/43), 23-24; (Bulwer-Lytton): Flower, Di, 69 (1973), 82-83; (Poe): Grubb, NCF, 5 (1950), 8-15, 209; Mason, Di, 36 (1939/40), 112-14.

Position in career: Dyson, CritQ, 9 (1967), 143-44; Gottshall, NCF, 16 (1961), 135-37; Lillishaw, Di, 44 (1947/48), 141-44.

EXPLANATORY NOTES, HISTORICAL BACKGROUND, and SOURCES

General: Graham, Contemporary Review, 194 (1958), 91-92; O'Brien, DiS, 5 (1969), 31-34, 36.

Gordon, depiction of: Gibson, Di, 42 (1945/46), 12-20; 57 (1961), 81-85.

Hanging of Mary Jones (Chapter 37): Ziegler, Di, 54 (1958), 80-82.

Military, the: Sullivan, Di, 46 (1949/50), 139-41.

86

Barnaby Rudge

Miscellaneous annotations: Hill, <u>Di</u>, 50 (1953/54), 91–94; 51 (1954/55), 93–96, 137–41; 52 (1955/56), 136–40, 185–88; 53 (1957), 52–57.

Poe, The Raven: Grubb, <u>NCF</u>, 5 (1950), 210–12.

Political context: Rice, <u>DSN</u>, 4 (1973), 11–14; Steig, <u>DSN</u>, 4 (1973), 67–68.

Scott, The Lady of the Lake, and Chapter 45: Lane, <u>NCF</u>, 6 (1951), 223–24.

Sim's 'prentice Knights: Brantlinger, <u>VS</u>, 13 (1969), 38, 40.

Sir John Fielding (absence of): Robinson, <u>AUMLA</u>, 40 (1973), 183–85.

ILLUSTRATIONS

General: Cohen, <u>DSA</u>, 1 (1970), 87–89; Stevens, <u>SB</u>, 20 (1967), 113–15, 124–33.

Dolly Varden (Chapter XX): Steig, <u>Ariel</u>, 4 (1973), 49–50.

INFLUENCES (<u>See also</u> LITERARY PARALLELS)

(Dickens on) Poe: Mason, <u>Di</u>, 36 (1939/40), 112–14, 116–17; Thackeray, <u>Vanity Fair</u>, Chapter 24: Steig, <u>NCF</u>, 25 (1970), 353–54.

(on Dickens) Fielding: Robinson, <u>AUMLA</u>, 40 (1973), 185–97; Mrs. Radcliffe (plot): Coolidge, <u>Di</u>, 58 (1962), 114–16; psycho-pathological theory: Manheim, <u>DSA</u>, 2 (1972), 82–83, 89–90, 92–95; Scott: O'Brien, <u>DiS</u>, 5 (1969), 27–28; Shakespeare, <u>Macbeth</u> and <u>Lear</u>: Ryan, <u>English</u>, 19 (1970), 43–48.

LANGUAGE and STYLE (<u>See also</u> TECHNIQUES, VARIOUS)

Imagery: Folland, <u>PMLA</u>, 74 (1959), 409; Gottshall, <u>NCF</u>, 16 (1961), 138–46.

LITERARY PARALLELS (<u>See also</u> INFLUENCES)

Barnaby and Fool in <u>Lear</u>: Ryan, <u>English</u>, 19 (1970), 43–44.

Eisenstein (structure and characterization): Zambrano, <u>Style</u>, 9 (1975), 482.

Barnaby Rudge

    Gaskell, <u>North and South</u>: Brantlinger, <u>VS</u>, 13 (1969), 44-45, 48-52.

    <u>Oliver Twist</u>: Rice, <u>DSN</u>, 4 (1973), 10-14.

    Steinbeck, <u>Of Mice and Men</u> (idiots and irrational characters): Steele, <u>Steinbeck Quarterly</u>, 5 (Winter 1972), 9-17.

    Warren, <u>Ten Thousand a-Year</u> (1839-1841): Steig, <u>DSN</u>, 4 (1973), 67-68.

PLOT (<u>See also</u> STRUCTURE/UNITY)

    End of novel: Kennedy, <u>SNNTS</u>, 6 (1974), 281, 283-84.

    Foreshadowing: Gadd, <u>Di</u>, 36 (1939/40), 184.

    Mob violence: Briggs, <u>JFI</u>, 7 (1970), 5-6; Folland, <u>PMLA</u>, 74 (1959), 408-10; Lucas, <u>SAQ</u>, 39 (1940), 448-52; Manheim, <u>DSA</u>, 2 (1972), 92-95; O'Brien, <u>DiS</u>, 5 (1969), 36-44; Robinson, <u>AUMLA</u>, 40 (1973), 193-96.

POINT OF VIEW

    Perspective of narrator: Rice, <u>NCF</u>, 30 (1975), 181.

PUBLICATION (<u>See also</u> TEXT)

    Background: Dyson, <u>CritQ</u>, 9 (1967), 142-43.

    Preface to Volume II of weekly numbers of <u>MHC</u>: Robinson, <u>AUMLA</u>, 40 (1973), 188-89.

STRUCTURE/UNITY (<u>See also</u> PLOT)

    General: Dyson, <u>CritQ</u>, 9 (1967), 144-45; Folland, <u>PMLA</u>, 74 (1959), 406-17; Gottshall, <u>NCF</u>, 16 (1961), 133-35, 137-46.

    Analogical: Rice, <u>NCF</u>, 30 (1975), 172-77.

    Time, use of: Rice, <u>NCF</u>, 30 (1975), 178-81.

TECHNIQUES, VARIOUS

    General: Folland, <u>PMLA</u>, 74 (1959), 406-17; Gibson, <u>Di</u>, 54 (1958), 21-23; Gottshall, <u>NCF</u>, 16 (1961), 133-35, 137-46;

Lillishaw, <u>Di</u>, 44 (1947/48), 143-44; O'Brien, <u>DiS</u>, 5 (1969), 26-41.

Historical novel: O'Brien, <u>DiS</u>, 5 (1969), 27-34.

Idyllic, the, use of: Gibson, <u>Di</u>, 52 (1955/56), 63-64.

Time, use of: Franklin, <u>DSA</u>, 4 (1975), 14-15.

TEXT (<u>See also</u> PUBLICATION)

Textual variation after first edition (gardener's remains): Westburg, <u>DSN</u>, 5 (1974), 38-40.

THEMES

General: Folland, <u>PMLA</u>, 74 (1959), 407-17.

Criminals and rebels: Wilson, <u>AM</u>, 165 (1940), 478-80.

Fathers and sons: Rooke, <u>E&S</u>, N.S. 4 (1951), 57-60.

Hatred: Dyson, <u>CritQ</u>, 9 (1967), 145-47, 157-60.

Love: Gibson, <u>Di</u>, 54 (1958), 21-22.

Responsibility: Folland, <u>PMLA</u>, 74 (1959), 408-17.

Social criticism: O'Brien, <u>DiS</u>, 5 (1969), 34-44; Steele, <u>Steinbeck Quarterly</u>, 5 (Winter 1972), 8, 16-17.

Time: Franklin, <u>DSA</u>, 4 (1975), 14-15.

Trade unionism: Brantlinger, <u>VS</u>, 13 (1969), 40.

Violence: Folland, <u>PMLA</u>, 74 (1959), 408-10; Lucas, <u>SAQ</u>, 39 (1940), 448-52; O'Brien, <u>DiS</u>, 5 (1969), 36-44.

Bibliography for *Barnaby Rudge*

BRANTLINGER, PATRICK. "The Case Against Trade Unions in Early Victorian Fiction." VS, 13 (1969), 37-52.

BRIGGS, KATHARINE M. "The Folklore of Charles Dickens." JFI, 7 (1970), 3-20.

COHEN, JANE RABB. "Strained Relations: Charles Dickens and George Cattermole." DSA, 1 (1970), 81-92.

COOLIDGE, ARCHIBALD C., JR. "Charles Dickens and Mrs. Radcliffe: A Farewell to Wilkie Collins." Di, 58 (1962), 112-16.

DUNN, RICHARD J. "Dickens and the Tragi-Comic Grotesque." SNNTS, 1 (1969), 147-56.

DYSON, A. E. "Barnaby Rudge: The Genesis of Violence." CritQ, 9 (1967), 142-60.

FLOWER, SIBYLLA JANE. "Charles Dickens and Edward Bulwer-Lytton." Di, 69 (1973), 79-89.

FOLLAND, HAROLD F. "The Doer and the Deed: Theme and Pattern in Barnaby Rudge." PMLA, 74 (1959), 406-17.

FRANKLIN, STEPHEN L. "Dickens and Time: The Clock Without Hands." DSA, 4 (1975), 1-35.

GADD, W. LAURENCE. "The Dickens Touch." Di, 36 (1939/40), 181-85.

GIBSON, FRANK A. "Gashford and Gordon." Di, 44 (1947/48), 124-29.

_____. "The Idyllic in Dickens." Di, 52 (1955/56), 59-64.

_____. "The Love Interest in Barnaby Rudge." Di, 54 (1958), 21-23.

_____. "A Note on George Gordon." Di, 57 (1961), 81-85.

_____. "The Trial of George Gordon." Di, 42 (1945/46), 12-20.

GOTTSHALL, JAMES K. "Devils Abroad: The Unity and Significance of Barnaby Rudge." NCF, 16 (1961), 133-46.

GRAHAM, W. H. "Notes on Barnaby Rudge." Contemporary Review, 194 (1958), 90-92.

Barnaby Rudge

GRUBB, GERALD GILES. "The Personal and Literary Relationships of Dickens and Poe (Part One: From Sketches by Boz through Barnaby Rudge; Part Two: 'English Notes' and 'The Poets of America'; Part Three: Poe's Literary Debt to Dickens)." NCF, 5 (1950), 1-22, 101-20, 209-21.

HILL, T. W. "Notes on Barnaby Rudge." Di, 50 (1953/54), 91-94; 51 (1954/55), 93-96, 137-41; 52 (1955/56), 136-40, 185-88; 53 (1957), 52-57.

KENNEDY, G. W. "Dickens's Endings." SNNTS, 6 (1974), 280-87.

LANE, LAURIAT, JR. "Dickens and Scott: An Unusual Borrowing." NCF, 6 (1951), 223-24.

LILLISHAW, A. M. "The Case of Barnaby Rudge." Di, 44 (1947/48), 141-44.

LUCAS, JOHN PAUL, JR. "To John Landseer, Esquire: A Note from Charles Dickens." SAQ, 39 (1940), 448-53.

MANHEIM, LEONARD F. "Dickens' Fools and Madmen." DSA, 2 (1972), 69-97.

MASON, LEO. "More about Dickens and Poe." Di, 39 (1942/43), 21-28.

_____. "A Tale of Three Authors." Di, 36 (1939/40), 109-19.

McMASTER, R. D. "Man into Beast in Dickensian Caricature." UTQ, 31 (1962), 354-61.

MONOD, SYLVÈRE. "Rebel with a Cause: Hugh of the Maypole." DiS, 1 (1965), 4-26.

O'BRIEN, ANTHONY. "Benevolence and Insurrection: The Conflicts of Form and Purpose in Barnaby Rudge." DiS, 5 (1969), 26-44.

POSTLETHWAITE, ANGELA. "Poor Sir John!" Di, 54 (1958), 83-87.

RICE, THOMAS JACKSON. "The End of Dickens's Apprenticeship: Variable Focus in Barnaby Rudge." NCF, 30 (1975), 172-84.

_____. "Oliver Twist and the Genesis of Barnaby Rudge." DSN, 4 (1973), 10-15.

ROBINSON, ROGER. "The Influence of Fielding on Barnaby Rudge." AUMLA, 40 (1973), 183-97.

ROOKE, ELEANOR. "Fathers and Sons in Dickens." E&S, N.S. 4 (1951), 53-69.

RYAN, SISTER M. ROSARIO. "Dickens and Shakespeare: Probable Sources of Barnaby Rudge." English, 19 (1970), 43-48.

STEELE, JOAN. "A Century of Idiots: Barnaby Rudge and Of Mice and Men." Steinbeck Quarterly, 5 (Winter 1972), 8-17.

STEIG, MICHAEL. "Barnaby Rudge and Vanity Fair: A Note on a Possible Influence." NCF, 25 (1970), 353-54.

_____. "Cruikshank's Peacock Feathers in Oliver Twist." Ariel, 4 (1973), 49-53.

_____. "Ten Thousand a-Year and the Political Content of Barnaby Rudge." DSN, 4 (1973), 67-68.

STEVENS, JOAN. "'Woodcuts dropped into the Text': The Illustrations in The Old Curiosity Shop and Barnaby Rudge." SB, 20 (1967), 113-33.

SULLIVAN, A. E. "Soldiers of the Queen--and of Charles Dickens." Di, 46 (1949/50), 138-43.

WESTBURG, BARRY. "How Poe Solved the Mystery of Barnaby Rudge." DSN, 5 (1974), 38-40.

WILSON, ARTHUR H. "The Great Theme in Charles Dickens." Susquehanna University Studies, 6 (Apr.-June 1959), 422-57.

WILSON, EDMUND. "Dickens and the Marshalsea Prison." AM, 165 (1940), 473-83, 681-91.

ZAMBRANO, ANA LAURA. "Charles Dickens and Sergei Eisenstein: The Emergence of Cinema." Style, 9 (1975), 469-87.

ZIEGLER, ARNOLD U. "A Barnaby Rudge Source." Di, 54 (1958), 80-82.

Martin Chuzzlewit

Martin Chuzzlewit

CHARACTERIZATION

General: Benjamin, PQ, 34 (1955), 42-47; Churchill, Scrutiny, 10
(1942), 358-62; Curran, NCF, 25 (1970), 52-67; Dyson, CritQ, 9
(1967), 236-50; Gold, DSA, 2 (1972), 158-62; McNulty, Di, 38
(1941/42), 144-46; Whitley, PMASAL, 50 (1965), 587-97.

Comic: Miller, NCF, 24 (1970), 471-73.

Grotesque: Dunn, SNNTS, 1 (1969), 149-50.

Satanic vs. virtuous: Curran, NCF, 25 (1970), 54-67.

Through illustrations: Steig, DSA, 2 (1972), 126-48.

CHARACTERS

Bailey: Pratt, NCF, 30 (1975), 185-99.

Chuffey: Manheim, DSA, 2 (1972), 90-91.

Chuzzlewit, Jonas: Brogunier, Di, 58 (1962), 165-70; Burke, DSA,
3 (1974), 20-21, 28-29, 37-39; Kreutz, NCF, 22 (1968), 337-41;
Lane, Di, 55 (1959), 47-50; Shuckburgh, Di, 46 (1949/50),
22-23.

Chuzzlewit, Martin, the elder: Curran, NCF, 25 (1970), 64-65,
66-67; Dyson, CritQ, 9 (1967), 236; Gold, DSA, 2 (1972),
154-55.

Chuzzlewit, Martin, the younger: Burke, DSA, 3 (1974), 18-19;
Christensen, SNNTS, 3 (1971), 19-20, 22-24; Curran, NCF, 25
(1970), 63-64; Gold, DSA, 2 (1972), 155-57; Hardy, VS, 5
(1961), 55-57; Whitley, PMASAL, 50 (1965), 587-89.

Gamp, Mrs.: Bligh, Di, 48 (1951/52), 40-42; Burke, DSA, 3
(1974), 21-23, 36; Colburn, Di, 54 (1958), 113; Dunn, SNNTS,
1 (1969), 149-50; Dyson, CritQ, 9 (1967), 242-45; Ganz, DSA,
1 (1970), 30-31; Hardy, Di, 69 (1973), 73; Kennedy, VN, 41
(Spring 1972), 1-5; Stuart, Contemporary Review, 192 (1957),

Martin Chuzzlewit

205-208; Tomlin, EA, 23 (1970), 116-18; (speech): Owen, Di, 67 (1971), 91-96; Page, ES, 51 (1970), 342-44.

Nadgett, Mr.: Burke, DSA, 3 (1974), 23; Curran, NCF, 25 (1970), 65; Winner, DSA, 3 (1974), 104.

Pecksniff, Charity: Ward, Listener, 69 (1963), 871.

Pecksniff, Mercy: Stedman, Di, 59 (1963), 113-16.

Pecksniff, Seth: Burke, DSA, 3 (1974), 16-18; Curran, NCF, 25 (1970), 58-59; Dyson, CritQ, 9 (1967), 238-41; Gold, DSA, 2 (1972), 151, 154; Hamilton, Nineteenth Century, 142 (1947), 45-46; Lansbury, DSN, 3 (1972), 41-42; Pritchett, Listener, 51 (1954), 971-72; Shuckburgh, Di, 46 (1949/50), 20; Steig, SNNTS, 1 (1969), 185-87; Ward, Listener, 69 (1963), 871, 874.

Pinch, Tom: Burke, DSA, 3 (1974), 18, 32; Dyson, CritQ, 9 (1967), 245-50; Gold, DSA, 2 (1972), 158-59; Hannaford, VN, 46 (Fall 1974), 27; Steig, SNNTS, 1 (1969), 181-85.

Sweedlepipe, Poll (prototype): Carlton, Di, 48 (1951/52), 9-12.

Tapley, Mark: Gold, DSA, 2 (1972), 158-59.

Tigg, Montague: Brogunier, Di, 58 (1962), 165-70; Curran, NCF, 25 (1970), 59-60.

CRITICAL ASSESSMENT

General: Churchill, Scrutiny, 10 (1942), 358-62; Dyson, CritQ, 9 (1967), 234-35, 251-53; Wilson, Susquehanna University Studies, 6 (Apr.-June 1959), 434-35.

EXPLANATORY NOTES, HISTORICAL BACKGROUND, and SOURCES

General: Gadd, Di, 38 (1941/42), 51-52.

American scenes: Lansbury, DSN, 3 (1972), 37-39; Stone, PMLA, 72 (1957), 464-78; Whitley, PMASAL, 50 (1965), 589-96.

Bramah locks: Horn, Di, 62 (1966), 100-105.

Eden: Baetzhold, Di, 55 (1959), 169-75; Grubb, SP, 48 (1951), 87-97.

"his owls was organs": Hill, N&Q, 196 (1951), 460.

Miscellaneous annotations: Hill, Di, 42 (1945/46), 141-48, 196-203; 43 (1946/47), 28-35.

Murder of Tigg: Williams, Di, 41 (1944/45), 145-46.

Subject Index

Martin Chuzzlewit

Watertoast Association of United Sympathizers: Fielding, <u>N&Q</u>,
198 (1953), 254–56.

ILLUSTRATIONS

Frontispiece: Steig, <u>DSA</u>, 2 (1972), 124–25, 143–45.

Monthly wrapper: Steig, <u>DSA</u>, 2 (1972), 124–25.

Plates 1–40: Steig, <u>DSA</u>, 2 (1972), 126–48.

"Thriving City of Eden": Butt, <u>REL</u>, 2 (July 1961), 49–50.

Title-page: Steig, <u>DSA</u>, 2 (1972), 145–48.

INFLUENCES (<u>See also</u> LITERARY PARALLELS)

(on Dickens) Carlyle, <u>Sartor Resartus</u> (bildungsroman pattern):
   Christensen, <u>SNNTS</u>, 3 (1971), 18–24; Hogarth (illustrations):
   Steig, <u>DSA</u>, 2 (1972), 123–48; psychopathological theory:
   Manheim, <u>DSA</u>, 2 (1972), 79, 90.

LANGUAGE and STYLE (<u>See also</u> TECHNIQUES, VARIOUS)

General: Ward, <u>Listener</u>, 69 (1963), 871.

Allusion (Book of Jonah): Gold, <u>DSA</u>, 2 (1972), 151–54.

Dialect (American): Pound, <u>AS</u>, 22 (1947), 125–29; (Cockney):
   Owen, <u>Di</u>, 67 (1971), 91–96; Page, <u>ES</u>, 51 (1970), 342–44.

Imagery: Marten, <u>SNNTS</u>, 6 (1974), 160–62; (architectural):
   Burke, <u>DSA</u>, 3 (1974), 14, 16–40; (garden of Eden): Curran,
   <u>NCF</u>, 25 (1970), 55–67; (labyrinth): Burke, <u>DSA</u>, 3 (1974),
   25–32; (Monument of the Great Fire): <u>ibid</u>., 14–16, 24–25,
   26–27, 33–39.

Symbolism (use of double): Lane, <u>Di</u>, 55 (1959), 47–50.

LITERARY PARALLELS (<u>See also</u> INFLUENCES)

Collins, <u>The Woman in White</u>: Tillotson, <u>Di</u>, 69 (1973), 173.

Twain, <u>The Gilded Age</u>: Hamblen, <u>MTJ</u>, 12 (Winter 1964), 9–11, 16.

West, Nathanael, <u>A Cool Million</u>: Pinsker, <u>Topic</u>, 18 (1969),
   47–51.

Martin Chuzzlewit

PLOT (See also STRUCTURE/UNITY)

    Foreshadowing: Gadd, <u>Di</u>, 36 (1939/40), 182-83.

    Martin and his grandfather: Christensen, <u>SNNTS</u>, 3 (1971), 18-24.

    Moral growth: Wall, <u>REL</u>, 6 (Jan. 1965), 58-60.

    Myth (loss of paradise): Curran, <u>NCF</u>, 25 (1970), 51-67.

POINT OF VIEW

    Hallucinatory: Van Ghent, <u>SR</u>, 58 (1950), 425-26.

SETTING

    American scenes: Burke, <u>DSA</u>, 3 (1974), 29-31; Gold, <u>DSA</u>, 2 (1972), 157-58; Pinsker, <u>Topic</u>, 18 (1969), 47-50; Stone, <u>PMLA</u>, 72 (1957), 466-78.

    Landscape, description of: Lansbury, <u>DSN</u>, 3 (1972), 41-45.

    Todgers: Burke, <u>DSA</u>, 3 (1974), 26-28; Van Ghent, <u>SR</u>, 58 (1950), 425-26, 434-35.

    World of novel: Burke, <u>DSA</u>, 3 (1974), 24-40.

STRUCTURE/UNITY (See also PLOT)

    General: Benjamin, <u>PQ</u>, 34 (1955), 39-47; Curran, <u>NCF</u>, 25 (1970), 51-67; Dyson, <u>CritQ</u>, 9 (1967), 235.

    Moral progress: Steig, <u>DSA</u>, 2 (1972), 124-48.

    Spiritual pilgrimage: Lansbury, <u>DSN</u>, 3 (1972), 40-45.

TECHNIQUES, VARIOUS

    General: Churchill, <u>Scrutiny</u>, 10 (1942), 358-62; Dyson, <u>CritQ</u>, 9 (1967), 234-53; McNulty, <u>Di</u>, 38 (1941/42), 143-44; Ward, <u>Listener</u>, 69 (1963), 871, 874; Whitley, <u>PMASAL</u>, 50 (1965), 587-97.

    Archetype, use of (Jung's Great Mother): Kennedy, <u>VN</u>, 41 (Spring 1972), 1-5.

    Autobiography, use of: Stone, <u>PMLA</u>, 72 (1957), 466-78.

    Comedy/humor: Dyson, <u>CritQ</u>, 9 (1967), 235-45; Miller, <u>NCF</u>, 24 (1970), 467-73.

Martin Chuzzlewit

Dreams, use of: Brogunier, <u>Di</u>, 58 (1962), 165-70.

First monthly number: Clayton, <u>Di</u>, 39 (1942/43), 166-68.

Food and drink (preparation or consumption): Watt, <u>DSA</u>, 3
(1974), 167-68.

Sentimentality (vs. irony): Hannaford, <u>VN</u>, 46 (Fall 1974), 26-28.

TEXT

Revision (Chapter 4): McNulty, <u>Di</u>, 36 (1939/40), 147-49.

THEMES

Fathers and sons: Rooke, <u>E&S</u>, N.S. 4 (1951), 60-61.

Freedom of the individual: Pratt, <u>NCF</u>, 30 (1975), 185-99.

Manhood, false ideals of: Christensen, <u>SNNTS</u>, 3 (1971), 19-20.

Moral progress: Steig, <u>DSA</u>, 2 (1972), 124-48.

Moral quest: Gold, <u>DSA</u>, 2 (1972), 158-62.

Pastoral romanticism: Lansbury, <u>DSN</u>, 3 (1972), 41-45.

Selfishness: Benjamin, <u>PQ</u>, 34 (1955), 40-47; Burke, <u>DSA</u>, 3
(1974), 14-16, 24, 39; Gold, <u>DSA</u>, 2 (1972), 150-62; McNulty,
<u>Di</u>, 38 (1941/42), 144.

Time: Burke, <u>DSA</u>, 3 (1974), 33-39.

Bibliography for
Martin Chuzzlewit

BAETZHOLD, HOWARD G. "What Place Was the Model for Martin Chuzzlewit's 'Eden'?: A Last Word on the 'Cairo Legend.'" Di, 55
   (1959), 169-75.

BENJAMIN, EDWIN B. "The Structure of Martin Chuzzlewit." PQ, 34
   (1955), 39-47.

BLIGH, EDWARD. "A Defence of Mrs. Gamp." Di, 48 (1951/52), 40-42.

BROGUNIER, JOSEPH. "The Dreams of Montague Tigg and Jonas Chuzzlewit." Di, 58 (1962), 165-70.

BURKE, ALAN R. "The House of Chuzzlewit and the Architectural City."
   DSA, 3 (1974), 14-40.

BUTT, JOHN E. "Dickens' Instructions for Martin Chuzzlewit,
   Plate XVIII." REL, 2 (July 1961), 49-50.

CARLTON, W. J. "The Barber of Dean Street." Di, 48 (1951/52), 8-12.

CHRISTENSEN, ALLAN C. "A Dickensian Hero Retailored: The Carlylean
   Apprenticeship of Martin Chuzzlewit." SNNTS, 3 (1971), 18-25.

CHURCHILL, R. C. "Dickens, Drama, and Tradition." Scrutiny, 10
   (1942), 358-75.

CLAYTON, J. K. "Martin Chuzzlewit--the First Monthly Number." Di,
   39 (1942/43), 166-68.

COLBURN, WILLIAM E. "Dickens and the 'Life-Illusion.'" Di, 54
   (1958), 110-18.

CURRAN, STUART. "The Lost Paradises of Martin Chuzzlewit." NCF, 25
   (1970), 51-67.

DUNN, RICHARD J. "Dickens and the Tragi-Comic Grotesque." SNNTS, 1
   (1969), 147-56.

DYSON, A. E. "Martin Chuzzlewit: Howls the Sublime." CritQ, 9
   (1967), 234-53.

FIELDING, K. J. "Martin Chuzzlewit and the Liberator." N&Q, 198
   (1953), 254-56.

Martin Chuzzlewit

GADD, W. LAURENCE. "The Dickens Touch." Di, 36 (1939/40), 181-85.

_____. "Fact and Fiction of America." Di, 38 (1941/42), 49-52.

GANZ, MARGARET. "The Vulnerable Ego: Dickens' Humor in Decline." DSA, 1 (1970), 23-40.

GOLD, JOSEPH. "'Living in a Wale': Martin Chuzzlewit." DSA, 2 (1972), 150-62.

GRUBB, GERALD GILES. "Dickens' Western Tour and the Cairo Legend." SP, 48 (1951), 87-97.

HAMBLEN, ABIGAIL ANN. "The American Scene: Dickens and Mark Twain." MTJ, 12 (Winter 1964), 9-11, 16.

HAMILTON, ROBERT. "Dickens in His Characters." Nineteenth Century, 142 (1947), 40-49.

HANNAFORD, RICHARD. "Irony and Sentimentality: Conflicting Modes in Martin Chuzzlewit." VN, 46 (Fall 1974), 26-28.

HARDY, BARBARA. "The Change of Heart in Dickens' Novels." VS, 5 (1961), 49-67.

_____. "Dickens's Storytellers." Di, 69 (1973), 71-78.

HILL, T. W. "Notes on Martin Chuzzlewit." Di, 42 (1945/46), 141-48, 196-203; 43 (1946/47), 28-35.

_____. "Organs." N&Q, 196 (1951), 460.

HORN, ROBERT D. "Dickens and the Patent Bramah Lock." Di, 62 (1966), 100-105.

KENNEDY, VERONICA M. S. "Mrs. Gamp as the Great Mother: A Dickensian Use of the Archetype." VN, 41 (Spring 1972), 1-5.

KREUTZ, IRVING W. "Sly of Manner, Sharp of Tooth: A Study of Dickens's Villains." NCF, 22 (1968), 331-48.

LANE, LAURIAT, JR. "Dickens and the Double." Di, 55 (1959), 47-55.

LANSBURY, CORAL. "Dickens' Romanticism Domesticated." DSN, 3 (1972), 36-46.

MANHEIM, LEONARD F. "Dickens' Fools and Madmen." DSA, 2 (1972), 69-97.

MARTEN, HARRY P. "The Visual Imaginations of Dickens and Hogarth: Structure and Scene." SNNTS, 6 (1974), 145-64.

McNULTY, J. H. "An Omitted Chapter." Di, 36 (1939/40), 147-49.

_____. "The Two Spirits of Fun and Beauty." Di, 38 (1941/42), 143-46.

Bibliography

MILLER, J. HILLIS. "The Sources of Dickens's Comic Art: From Ameri-can Notes to Martin Chuzzlewit." NCF, 24 (1970), 467-76.

OWEN, W. J. B. "Mrs. Gamp's Poetic Diction." Di, 67 (1971), 91-96.

PAGE, NORMAN. "Convention and Consistency in Dickens's Cockney Dia-lect." ES, 51 (1970), 339-44.

PINSKER, SANFORD. "Charles Dickens and Nathanael West: Great Expec-tations Unfulfilled." Topic, 18 (1969), 40-52.

POUND, LOUISE. "The American Dialect of Charles Dickens." AS, 22 (1947), 124-30.

PRATT, BRANWEN BAILEY. "Dickens and Freedom: Young Bailey in Martin Chuzzlewit." NCF, 30 (1975), 185-99.

PRITCHETT, V. S. "The Humour of Charles Dickens." Listener, 51 (1954), 970-73.

ROOKE, ELEANOR. "Fathers and Sons in Dickens." E&S, N.S. 4 (1951), 53-69.

SHUCKBURGH, JOHN. "The Villain of the Piece." Di, 46 (1949/50), 18-23.

STEDMAN, JANE W. "Child-Wives of Dickens." Di, 59 (1963), 112-18.

STEIG, MICHAEL. "Martin Chuzzlewit: Pinch and Pecksniff." SNNTS, 1 (1969), 181-88.

_____. "Martin Chuzzlewit's Progress by Dickens and Phiz." DSA, 2 (1972), 119-49.

STONE, HARRY. "Dickens' Use of His American Experience in Martin Chuzzlewit." PMLA, 72 (1957), 464-78.

STUART, DOROTHY MARGARET. "Sarah Gamp." Contemporary Review, 192 (1957), 205-208.

TILLOTSON, KATHLEEN. "Dickens, Wilkie Collins and the Sucicidal Curates." Di, 69 (1973), 173.

TOMLIN, E. W. F. "The Englishness of Dickens." EA, 23 (1970), 113-24.

VAN GHENT, DOROTHY. "The Dickens World: A View from Todgers's." SR, 58 (1950), 419-38.

WALL, STEPHEN. "Dickens's Plot of Fortune." REL, 6 (Jan. 1965), 56-67.

WARD, W. A. "Language and Charles Dickens." Listener, 69 (1963), 870-71, 874.

WATT, IAN. "Oral Dickens." DSA, 3 (1974), 165-81.

Martin Chuzzlewit

WHITLEY, JOHN S. "The Two Hells of Martin Chuzzlewit." PMASAL, 50 (1965), 585-97.

WILLIAMS, P. C. "Murder Most Foul." Di, 41 (1944/45), 145-48.

WILSON, ARTHUR H. "The Great Theme in Charles Dickens." Susquehanna University Studies, 6 (Apr.-June 1959), 422-57.

WINNER, ANTHONY. "Character and Knowledge in Dickens: The Enigma of Jaggers." DSA, 3 (1974), 100-21.

Dombey and Son

Dombey and Son

CHARACTERIZATION

General: Axton, PMLA, 78 (1963), 341-48; ELH, 31 (1964), 305-16;
   Butt and Tillotson, E&S, N.S. 4 (1951), 75-93; Cranfield, NSN,
   N.S. 30 (1945), 301-302; Donoghue, NCF, 24 (1970), 395-403;
   Leavis, SR, 70 (1962), 179-96; Pickering, GaR, 26 (1972),
   443-54; Stone, ES, 47 (1966), 2-27; Talon, DSA, 1 (1970),
   148-60.

Grotesque: Steig, CentR, 14 (1970), 315-24.

Illustrations: Steig, DSA, 1 (1970), 161-67.

Inner life: Milner, NCF, 24 (1970), 477-87.

Nautical characters: Lecker, Di, 67 (1971), 22-30.

CHARACTERS

Bagstock, Major: Levine, SNNTS, 1 (1969), 158-59.

Brown, Mrs.: Stone, ES, 47 (1966), 19-20, 22-24.

Carker, James: Butt and Tillotson, E&S, N.S. 4 (1951), 83-90;
   Hardy, NCF, 24 (1970), 458-60; Kreutz, NCF, 22 (1968), 341-47;
   McMaster, UTQ, 31 (1962), 356-58; Robison, ES, 53 (1972), 441;
   Stone, ES, 47 (1966), 22-24; Tick, MLQ, 36 (1975), 400; Zam-
   brano, Style, 9 (1975), 472-73.

Cuttle, Captain: Rosenberg, JEGP, 59 (1960), 11-12; Spilka,
   MinnR, 1 (1961), 445-49; (prototype): Carlton, Di, 64 (1968),
   152-56.

Diogenes: MacDonald, N&Q, 210 (1965), 59.

Dombey, Edith: Adamowski, SNNTS, 4 (1972), 383-84; Butt and
   Tillotson, E&S, N.S. 4 (1951), 83-90; Dyson, Novel, 2 (1969),
   132-33; Leavis, SR, 70 (1962), 193-94; Milner, NCF, 24 (1970),
   484-85; Stone, ES, 47 (1966), 9-10, 23-24.

Dombey, Florence: Adamowski, SNNTS, 4 (1972), 381; Cranfield,
   NSN, N.S. 30 (1945), 301; Donoghue, NCF, 24 (1970), 389-90,

Dombey and Son

399-403; Dyson, Novel, 2 (1969), 129-32; Milner, NCF, 24 (1970), 480-84, 486-87; Stone, CE, 25 (1963), 218-20; ES, 47 (1966), 11-13, 19-21, 25-26.

Dombey, Mr.: Adamowski, SNNTS, 4 (1972), 379-84; Carlisle, JNT, 1 (1971), 149-50; Cranfield, NSN, N.S. 30 (1945), 301; Donoghue, NCF, 24 (1970), 384-91; Dyson, Novel, 2 (1969), 123-34; Franklin, DSA, 4 (1975), 16-17; Hardy, NCF, 24 (1970), 457-58; Leavis, SR, 70 (1962), 179-94; Meckier, SAQ, 71 (1972), 85-88, 90; Milner, NCF, 24 (1970), 477-87; Reed, DSA, 1 (1970), 44-45; Sobel, RUS, 59 (Summer 1973), 72, 74-81; Steig, CentR, 14 (1970), 320-24; Stone, CE, 25 (1963), 218-20; ES, 47 (1966), 2-8; Tomlinson, Critical Review, 15 (1972), 66-68; (prototype): Partington, AM, 180 (Aug. 1947), 57-61.

Dombey, Paul: Adamowski, SNNTS, 4 (1972), 380-81; Blount, MP, 62 (1965), 325-26; Cranfield, NSN, N.S. 30 (1945), 301; Donoghue, NCF, 24 (1970), 390-91; Dyson, Novel, 2 (1969), 123; Manheim, SNNTS, 1 (1969), 191-94; Meckier, SAQ, 71 (1972), 78; Nelson, DSA, 3 (1974), 47-50; Robison, ES, 53 (1972), 440-41; Steig, CentR, 14 (1970), 316-20; Stone, ES, 47 (1966), 15-16.

Gay, Walter: Axton, PMLA, 78 (1963), 342-43; Lecker, Di, 67 (1971), 21-22, 25-30; Stone, ES, 47 (1966), 25-26; (proto-types): Axton, ELH, 31 (1964), 304-16.

Gills, Sol: Lecker, Di, 67 (1971), 22-30; Tick, MLQ, 36 (1975), 392-98.

Pipchin, Mrs.: Stone, ES, 47 (1966), 17-18.

Skewton, Mrs.: Donoghue, NCF, 24 (1970), 395; Dyson, Novel, 2 (1969), 133; McMaster, SNNTS, 1 (1969), 135-36; Robison, ES, 53 (1972), 441.

Toodles: Donoghue, NCF, 24 (1970), 384-88; Leavis, SR, 70 (1962), 183-90, 195; Stone, ES, 47 (1966), 5-7.

Toots: Robison, ES, 53 (1972), 440-41.

COMPOSITION (See also TEXT)

Initial intention: Butt and Tillotson, E&S, N.S. 4 (1951), 71-77.

Memoranda and number plans: Butt and Tillotson, E&S, N.S. 4 (1951), 77-93; Herring, MP, 68 (1970), 151-87.

CRITICAL ASSESSMENT

General: Wilson, <u>Susquehanna University Studies</u>, 6 (Apr.–June 1959), 438–40; (modern commentaries): Collins, <u>Di</u>, 63 (1967), 90–94.

Contemporary reaction: Collins, <u>Di</u>, 63 (1967), 83–90; (parody): Edminson, <u>Di</u>, 56 (1960), 50–59.

EXPLANATORY NOTES, HISTORICAL BACKGROUND, and SOURCES

Hogarth: Leavis, <u>SR</u>, 70 (1962), 196–97.

Miscellaneous annotations: Brumleigh, <u>Di</u>, 38 (1941/42), 211–17; 39 (1942/43), 31–39.

Popular theater: Axton, <u>ELH</u>, 31 (1964), 303–17.

Staggs's Gardens (source for name): Steig, <u>Di</u>, 67 (1971), 145–46.

"walking matching," Chapter XXII (definition): Fleissner, <u>Explicator</u>, 32 (Dec. 1973), 26.

ILLUSTRATIONS

General (plates throughout text): Bromhill, <u>Di</u>, 38 (1941/42), 48–51, 57–60.

Allegorical commentary: Steig, <u>DSA</u>, 1 (1970), 161–67.

"Coming home from Church": Steig, <u>ELN</u>, 7 (1969), 124–27.

Cover: Bromhill, <u>Di</u>, 38 (1941/42), 219–20; Butt and Tillotson, <u>E&S</u>, N.S. 4 (1951), 73–75.

Diogenes: MacDonald, <u>N&Q</u>, 210 (1965), 59.

Dombey: Reed, <u>DSA</u>, 1 (1970), 45.

Edith: Steig, <u>HLQ</u>, 36 (1972), 56–57.

Frontispiece: Bromhill, <u>Di</u>, 38 (1941/42), 220–21; Pickering, <u>GaR</u>, 26 (1972), 443–46.

"Mr. Dombey and the World": Steig, <u>Ariel</u>, 4 (1973), 50.

INFLUENCES (<u>See also</u> LITERARY PARALLELS)

(on Dickens) Shakespeare, <u>King Lear</u>: Meckier, <u>SAQ</u>, 71 (1972), 75–78, 84–88.

Dombey and Son

LANGUAGE and STYLE (See also TECHNIQUES, VARIOUS)

Grotesque exaggeration: Steig, CentR, 14 (1970), 313-14.

Imagery: Stone, ES, 47 (1966), 7-11; (sea): Axton, PMLA, 78
(1963), 342-48; ELH, 31 (1964), 314-16.

Poetic: Leavis, SR, 70 (1962), 196-201.

Rhetoric: Axton, PMLA, 78 (1963), 347-48.

Speech: Roll-Hansen, Norwegian Studies in English, 9 (1963), 212.

Symbolism: Axton, PMLA, 78 (1963), 341-48; Stone, ES, 47 (1966),
5-11; (Dombey and Midshipman): Talon, DSA, 1 (1970), 156-57;
(hand and face): ibid., 152-54; (house): Pickering, GaR, 26
(1972), 451-53; Talon, DSA, 1 (1970), 148-51; (meal): ibid.,
151-52; (music-staircase leitmotif): Stone, CE, 25 (1963),
218-20; (sea): Steig, CentR, 14 (1970), 324; (time): Talon,
DSA, 1 (1970), 154-56.

LITERARY PARALLELS (See also INFLUENCES)

Balzac, Le Père Goriot: Sobel, RUS, 59 (Summer 1973), 71-81.

Comic journals (railway mania): Steig, Di, 67 (1971), 145-48.

Faulkner, Absalom, Absalom! (theme of extreme individualism):
Adamowski, SNNTS, 4 (1972), 378-89.

Jerrold, Black-Ey'd Susan; or, All in the Downs: Axton, ELH, 31
(1964), 310-16.

Shakespeare, Macbeth (and Marwood plot): Howarth, UTQ, 41
(1972), 152-54.

Smith, Albert, Dick Whittington and His Cat: Axton, ELH, 31
(1964), 304-309.

Thackeray, Dr. Birch and His Young Friends, and Dr. Blimber's
Academy: Carolan, SSF, 11 (1974), 196-99.

PLOT (See also STRUCTURE/UNITY)

End of novel: Dyson, Novel, 2 (1969), 129-32; Kennedy, SNNTS, 6
(1974), 285-86.

Fairy tale elements: Lecker, Di, 67 (1971), 21-30; Stone, ES,
47 (1966), 11-27.

Folktale elements: Briggs, JFI, 7 (1970), 15-18; (and myth):
Axton, PMLA, 78 (1963), 342-43.

Foreshadowing: Gadd, <u>Di</u>, 36 (1939/40), 183.

Static situation of danger: Coolidge, <u>North Dakota Quarterly</u>, 30 (Jan. 1962), 8-9.

POINT OF VIEW

Authorial intrusion: Levine, <u>SNNTS</u>, 1 (1969), 166-67.

Narration (present tense): Carlisle, <u>JNT</u>, 1 (1971), 146-57.

SETTING

Staggs's Gardens: Nelson, <u>DSA</u>, 3 (1974), 42-44, 46-53.

World of novel: Carlisle, <u>JNT</u>, 1 (1971), 147-52, 153-57; Donoghue, <u>NCF</u>, 24 (1970), 384-91, 395-403; Lecker, <u>Di</u>, 67 (1971), 21-30; Stone, <u>ES</u>, 47 (1966), 4-27; Talon, <u>DSA</u>, 1 (1970), 157-60.

STRUCTURE/UNITY (<u>See also</u> PLOT)

General: Coolidge, <u>Mississippi Quarterly</u>, 14 (Fall 1961), 192-93.

Allegory: Dyson, <u>Novel</u>, 2 (1969), 132-34.

"keystone episode": Axton, <u>UTQ</u>, 37 (1967), 41-43.

Montage: Zambrano, <u>Style</u>, 9 (1975), 472-73.

Parable (Unitarian): Pickering, <u>GaR</u>, 26 (1972), 443-54.

Theme vs. portraiture: Tick, <u>MLQ</u>, 36 (1975), 390-402.

Tone: Axton, <u>PMLA</u>, 78 (1963), 341-48.

TECHNIQUES, VARIOUS

General: Axton, <u>ELH</u>, 31 (1964), 303-17; Bland, <u>Di</u>, 52 (1955/56), 142-43; Donoghue, <u>NCF</u>, 24 (1970), 384-91, 395-403; Leavis, <u>SR</u>, 70 (1962), 178-201; Milner, <u>NCF</u>, 24 (1970), 477-87; Stone, <u>ES</u>, 47 (1966), 2-27; Talon, <u>DSA</u>, 1 (1970), 148-60; Tillotson, <u>Di</u>, 47 (1950/51), 81-82; Tomlinson, <u>Critical Review</u>, 15 (1972), 65-68.

Appearance vs. reality: Levine, <u>SNNTS</u>, 1 (1969), 159-61.

Death of Carker: Robison, <u>ES</u>, 53 (1972), 441.

Death of Mrs. Skewton: Robison, <u>ES</u>, 53 (1972), 441.

Dombey and Son

Death of Paul: Blount, MP, 62 (1965), 325-26; Nelson, DSA, 3 (1974), 47-50; Robison, ES, 53 (1972), 440-41.

Food and drink (preparation or consumption): Watt, DSA, 3 (1974), 168-69.

Opening: Leavis, SR, 70 (1962), 179-82.

Railway, use of: Atthill, English, 13 (1961), 130-33; Axton, PMLA, 78 (1963), 346; Donoghue, NCF, 24 (1970), 387-88; Dyson, Novel, 2 (1969), 125; Hardy, NCF, 24 (1970), 457-60; Nelson, DSA, 3 (1974), 41-44, 48-53; Steig, CentR, 14 (1970), 325; Stone, ES, 47 (1966), 6-8; Tick, MLQ, 36 (1975), 399-400.

Time, use of: Franklin, DSA, 4 (1975), 16-17.

Title: Butt and Tillotson, E&S, N.S. 4 (1951), 72-73.

TEXT (See also COMPOSITION)

Cancelled passages of proofs: Staples, Di, 49 (1952/53), 37-43, 65-68.

Variant (end Chapter 16): Bland, Di, 52 (1955/56), 142-43; Tillotson, Di, 47 (1950/51), 81-82.

THEMES

General: Axton, PMLA, 78 (1963), 345-48; Leavis, SR, 70 (1962), 179-201; Sobel, RUS, 59 (Summer 1973), 74-81; Talon, DSA, 1 (1970), 147-57.

Benevolence: Pickering, GaR, 26 (1972), 450-54.

Business: Stone, ES, 47 (1966), 4-11.

Death (and water imagery): Robison, ES, 53 (1972), 440-41.

Dombeyism vs. values of Wooden Midshipman: Lecker, Di, 67 (1971), 22-30.

Domesticity: Talon, DSA, 1 (1970), 147-48.

Fathers and sons: Rooke, E&S, N.S. 4 (1951), 61-62.

Feeling: Donoghue, NCF, 24 (1970), 392-403.

Individualism, extreme: Adamowski, SNNTS, 4 (1972), 378-84.

Love: Dyson, Novel, 2 (1969), 128-34; Stone, ES, 47 (1966), 2-4; (brother/sister): ibid., 12-16.

Money: Stone, ES, 47 (1966), 2-4.

Pride: Butt and Tillotson, <u>E&S</u>, N.S. 4 (1951), 80; Leavis, <u>SR</u>, 70 (1962), 179-94.

Sexuality: Steig, <u>DSA</u>, 1 (1970), 161-67.

Social criticism: Dyson, <u>Novel</u>, 2 (1969), 124-28; Sobel, <u>RUS</u>, 59 (Summer 1973), 78-81; (abandoned by Dickens): Tick, <u>MLQ</u>, 36 (1975), 390-402; (the Two Nations): Donoghue, <u>NCF</u>, 24 (1970), 384-91; Levine, <u>SNNTS</u>, 1 (1969), 159-61, 166-67.

Time: Franklin, <u>DSA</u>, 4 (1975), 16-17.

Value of being "old fashioned": Nelson, <u>DSA</u>, 3 (1974), 44-47.

Bibliography for
Dombey and Son

ADAMOWSKI, THOMAS H. "Dombey and Son and Sutpen and Son." SNNTS, 4 (1972), 378-89.

ATTHILL, ROBIN. "Dickens and the Railway." English, 13 (1961), 130-35.

AXTON, WILLIAM F. "Dombey and Son: From Stereotype to Archetype." ELH, 31 (1964), 301-17.

_____. "'Keystone' Structure in Dickens' Serial Novels." UTQ, 37 (1967), 31-50.

_____. "Tonal Unity in Dombey and Son." PMLA, 78 (1963), 341-48.

BLAND, D. S. "The 'Lost' Sentence in Dombey and Son Once More." Di, 52 (1955/56), 142-43.

BLOUNT, TREVOR. "Poor Jo, Education, and the Problem of Juvenile Delinquency in Dickens' Bleak House." MP, 62 (1965), 325-39.

BRIGGS, KATHARINE M. "The Folklore of Charles Dickens." JFI, 7 (1970), 3-20.

BROMHILL, KENTLEY. "Phiz's Illustrations to Dombey and Son." Di, 38 (1941/42), 219-21; 39 (1942/43), 48-51, 57-60.

BRUMLEIGH, T. KENT. "Notes on Dombey and Son." Di, 38 (1941/42), 211-17; 39 (1942/43), 31-39.

BUTT, JOHN E. and KATHLEEN TILLOTSON. "Dickens at Work on Dombey and Son." E&S, N.S. 4 (1951), 70-93.

CARLISLE, JANICE. "Dombey and Son: The Reader and the Present Tense." JNT, 1 (1971), 146-57.

CARLTON, W. J. "A Note on Captain Cuttle." Di, 64 (1968), 152-56.

CAROLAN, KATHERINE. "Dickensian Echoes in a Thackeray Christmas Book." SSF, 11 (1974), 196-99.

COLLINS, PHILIP. "Dombey and Son--Then and Now." Di, 63 (1967), 82-94.

COOLIDGE, ARCHIBALD C., JR. "Great Expectations: The Culmination of a Developing Art." Mississippi Quarterly, 14 (Fall 1961), 190-96.

Dombey and Son

_____. "The Unremoved Thorn: A Study in Dickens' Narrative Methods." North Dakota Quarterly, 30 (Jan. 1962), 8-13.

CRANFIELD, LIONEL. "Books in General." NSN, N.S. 30 (1945), 301-302.

DONOGHUE, DENIS. "The English Dickens and Dombey and Son." NCF, 24 (1970), 383-403.

DYSON, A. E. "The Case for Dombey Senior." Novel, 2 (1969), 123-34.

EDMINSON, MARY. "Charles Dickens and The Man in the Moon." Di, 56 (1960), 50-59.

FLEISSNER, ROBERT F. "Dickens' Dombey and Son, Chapter XXII." Explicator, 32 (Dec. 1973), 26.

FRANKLIN, STEPHEN L. "Dickens and Time: The Clock Without Hands." DSA, 4 (1975), 1-35.

GADD, W. LAURENCE. "The Dickens Touch." Di, 36 (1939/40), 181-85.

HARDY, BARBARA. "Dickens and the Passions." NCF, 24 (1970), 449-66.

HERRING, PAUL D. "The Number Plans for Dombey and Son: Some Further Observations." MP, 68 (1970), 151-87.

HOWARTH, HERBERT. "Voices of the Past in Dickens and Others." UTQ, 41 (1972), 151-62.

KENNEDY, G. W. "Dickens's Endings." SNNTS, 6 (1974), 280-87.

KREUTZ, IRVING W. "Sly of Manner, Sharp of Tooth: A Study of Dickens's Villains." NCF, 22 (1968), 331-48.

LEAVIS, F. R. "Dombey and Son." SR, 70 (1962), 177-201.

LECKER, BARBARA. "Walter Gay and the Theme of Fancy in Dombey and Son." Di, 67 (1971), 21-30.

LEVINE, RICHARD A. "Dickens, the Two Nations, and Individual Possibility." SNNTS, 1 (1969), 157-80.

MacDONALD, ROBERT H. "The Dog Diogenes." N&Q, 210 (1965), 59.

MANHEIM, LEONARD F. "The Dickens Hero as Child." SNNTS, 1 (1969), 189-95.

McMASTER, R. D. "Dickens, the Dandy, and the Savage: A Victorian View of the Romantic." SNNTS, 1 (1969), 133-46.

_____. "Man into Beast in Dickensian Caricature." UTQ, 31 (1962), 354-61.

MECKIER, JEROME. "Dickens and King Lear: A Myth for Victorian England." SAQ, 71 (1972), 75-90.

MILNER, IAN. "The Dickens Drama: Mr. Dombey." NCF, 24 (1970), 477-87.

NELSON, HARLAND S. "Staggs's Gardens: The Railway Through Dickens' World." DSA, 3 (1974), 41-53.

PARTINGTON, WILFRED. "Should a Biographer Tell?" AM, 180 (Aug. 1947), 56-63.

PICKERING, SAMUEL F., JR. "Dombey and Son and Dickens's Unitarian Period." GaR, 26 (1972), 438-54.

REED, JOHN R. "Confinement and Character in Dickens' Novels." DSA, 1 (1970), 41-54.

ROBISON, ROSELEE. "Time, Death and the River in Dickens' Novels." ES, 53 (1972), 436-54.

ROLL-HANSEN, DIDERIK. "Characters and Contrasts in Great Expectations." Norwegian Studies in English, 9 (1963), 197-226.

ROOKE, ELEANOR. "Fathers and Sons in Dickens." E&S, N.S. 4 (1951), 53-69.

ROSENBERG, MARVIN. "The Dramatist in Dickens." JEGP, 59 (1960), 1-12.

SOBEL, MARGARET. "Balzac's Le Père Goriot and Dickens's Dombey and Son: A Comparison." RUS, 59 (Summer 1973), 71-81.

SPILKA, MARK. "Dickens and Kafka: 'The Technique of the Grotesque.'" MinnR, 1 (1961), 441-58.

STAPLES, L. C. "Shavings From Dickens's Workshop: Unpublished Fragments from the Novels." Di, 49 (1952/53), 37-43, 65-68.

STEIG, MICHAEL. "The Critic and the Illustrated Novel." HLQ, 36 (1972), 55-67.

_____. "Cruikshank's Peacock Feathers in Oliver Twist." Ariel, 4 (1973), 49-53.

_____. "Dombey and Son and the Railway Panic of 1845." Di, 67 (1971), 145-48.

_____. "Dombey and Son: Chapter XXXI, Plate 20." ELN, 7 (1969), 124-27.

_____. "Iconography of Sexual Conflict in Dombey and Son." DSA, 1 (1970), 161-67.

_____. "Structure and the Grotesque in Dickens: Dombey and Son; Bleak House." CentR, 14 (1970), 313-30.

STONE, HARRY. "Dickens and Leitmotif: Music-Staircase Imagery in Dombey and Son." CE, 25 (1963), 217-20.

_____. "The Novel as Fairy Tale: Dickens' Dombey and Son." ES, 47 (1966), 1-27.

TALON, HENRI. "Dombey and Son: A Closer Look at the Text." DSA, 1 (1970), 147-60.

Dombey and Son

TICK, STANLEY. "The Unfinished Business of Dombey and Son." MLQ, 36 (1975), 390–402.

TILLOTSON, KATHLEEN. "A Lost Sentence in Dombey and Son." Di, 47 (1950/51), 81–82.

TOMLINSON, T. B. "Dickens and Individualism: Dombey and Son, Bleak House." Critical Review, 15 (1972), 64–81.

WATT, IAN. "Oral Dickens." DSA, 3 (1974), 165–81.

WILSON, ARTHUR H. "The Great Theme in Charles Dickens." Susquehanna University Studies, 6 (Apr.–June 1959), 422–57.

ZAMBRANO, ANA LAURA. "Charles Dickens and Sergei Eisenstein: The Emergence of Cinema." Style, 9 (1975), 469–87.

David Copperfield

David Copperfield

CHARACTERIZATION

General: Bell, SEL, 8 (1968), 638-46; Collins, E&S, N.S. 23 (1970), 76-86; Hamilton, Di, 45 (1948/49), 141-43; Hornback, SEL, 8 (1968), 653-67; Hughes, ELH, 41 (1974), 91-105; Kincaid, DiS, 1 (1965), 66-75; NCF, 22 (1968), 317-29; SNNTS, 1 (1969), 196-204; Manheim, AI, 9 (1952), 22-43; McNulty, Di, 45 (1948/49), 153-55; Needham, NCF, 9 (1954), 87-107; Strong, Di, 46 (1949/50), 70-75; (prototypes): Bromhill, Di, 45 (1948/49), 161-62; Major, Di, 40 (1943/44), 15-18.

Caricature: Cox, BJRL, 52 (1970), 272-76; Hall, UTQ, 39 (1970), 245-50.

Comic: Kincaid, NCF, 22 (1968), 317-29.

Sexuality: Pearlman, AI, 28 (1971), 392-402.

Speech: Hurley, VN, 38 (Fall 1970), 1-5.

Through metaphor: Tick, NCF, 24 (1969), 142-53.

Women: Manning, Di, 71 (1975), 72-73.

CHARACTERS

Copperfield, David: Bell, SEL, 8 (1968), 638-47; Brown, DSA, 2 (1972), 197-207; Collins, E&S, N.S. 23 (1970), 71-86; Gilmour, Di, 71 (1975), 30-42; Grundy, L&P, 22 (1972), 100-105; Hamilton, Di, 45 (1948/49), 141-42; Hardy, VS, 5 (1961), 57-59; Herbert, VS, 17 (1974), 250; Hornback, SEL, 8 (1968), 662-67; Hughes, ELH, 41 (1974), 89-105; Hurley, VN, 38 (Fall 1970), 1-5; Kettle, REL, 2 (July 1961), 67-74; Kincaid, DiS, 1 (1965), 66-74; 2 (1966), 79-95; NCF, 22 (1968), 317-19; SNNTS, 1 (1969), 196-204; Manheim, AI, 9 (1952), 22-43; SNNTS, 1 (1969), 189-90; Marshall, TSL, 5 (1960), 57-65; Needham, NCF, 9 (1954), 81-107; Pearlman, AI, 28 (1971), 391-403; VN, 41 (Spring 1972), 18-20; Reed, DSA, 1 (1970), 51-54; Robison, ES, 53 (1972), 446-47; Spilka, CritQ, 1 (1959), 292-301; Thirkell, Di, 45 (1948/49), 120, 122; Tick, BuR, 16 (1968), 89-95.

David Copperfield

Creakle: D'Avanzo, Di, 64 (1968), 50–52; (prototype): Collins, N&Q, 206 (1961), 89–91.

Dartle, Rosa: Hall, UTQ, 39 (1970), 247–48; Manning, Di, 71 (1975), 73; Pearlman, AI, 28 (1971), 400–401; (prototype): Cardwell, Di, 56 (1960), 29–33.

Dick, Mr.: Colburn, Di, 54 (1958), 111–13; Franklin, DSA, 4 (1975), 17–18; Hurley, VN, 38 (Fall 1970), 2–3; Manheim, DSA, 2 (1972), 87–88; Tick, NCF, 24 (1969), 142–53.

Emily: Bell, SEL, 8 (1968), 640–41; Gilmour, Di, 71 (1975), 32.

Heep, Uriah: Cox, BJRL, 52 (1970), 275–76; Hall, UTQ, 39 (1970), 248–50; Hughes, ELH, 41 (1974), 97–98, 101–103; Hurley, VN, 38 (Fall 1970), 2; Lucas, RMS, 16 (1972), 97–98; Pearlman, AI, 28 (1971), 391–93, 395–99; (as Jew): Lane, PMLA, 73 (1958), 97; (prototype): Poston, Di, 71 (1975), 43–44.

Micawber, Mrs.: Kincaid, NCF, 22 (1968), 328.

Micawber, Wilkins: Colburn, Di, 54 (1958), 112–13; Ganz, DSA, 1 (1970), 32–33; Gibson, Di, 45 (1948/49), 158–59; Grundy, L&P, 22 (1972), 104; Hall, UTQ, 39 (1970), 245–47; Hurley, VN, 38 (Fall 1970), 1–2; Kincaid, NCF, 22 (1968), 315, 325–28; Oddie, Di, 63 (1967), 100–101, 103–10; Shuckburgh, Di, 45 (1948/49), 125–28; Tick, BuR, 16 (1968), 92–93; Wenger, PMLA, 62 (1947), 217–18; (prototype): Carlton, Di, 48 (1951/52), 101–104; Fielding, Listener, 46 (1951), 94.

Micawbers: Tomlin, EA, 23 (1970), 118–19.

Mills, Julia: Kincaid, NCF, 22 (1968), 321.

Mowcher, Miss: Kincaid, NCF, 22 (1968), 322–24; (prototype): Fielding, Listener, 46 (1951), 93–94.

Murdstone: Hughes, ELH, 41 (1974), 100–101, 102–103; Millhauser, NCF, 27 (1972), 342–44.

Murdstone, Miss: Cox, BJRL, 52 (1970), 272–73; Gard, EIC, 15 (1965), 314–16; Jump, BJRL, 54 (1972), 395.

Peggotty, Mr.: Pearlman, VN, 41 (Spring 1972), 20.

Spenlow, Dora: Bell, SEL, 8 (1968), 641–43; Collins, E&S, N.S. 23 (1970), 81–84; Darroll, ESA, 7 (1964), 82–85; Darwin, Di, 45 (1948/49), 139–40; Gilmour, Di, 71 (1975), 36–37; Kincaid, NCF, 22 (1968), 317–18; Pearlman, VN, 41 (Spring 1972), 18; Robison, ES, 53 (1972), 442–43; Stedman, Di, 59 (1963), 113–18; Strong, Di, 46 (1949/50), 71–73; Thirkell, Di, 45 (1948/49), 120.

David Copperfield

Steerforth, James: Gilmour, Di, 71 (1975), 38-39; Grundy, L&P, 22 (1972), 102; Harvey, NCF, 24 (1969), 307-309; Hughes, ELH, 41 (1974), 101-105; Marshall, TSL, 5 (1960), 57-65; Needham, NCF, 9 (1954), 89-91; Pearlman, AI, 28 (1971), 393-94, 399-402.

Strong, Annie: Hardy, VS, 5 (1961), 58-59; Millhauser, NCF, 27 (1972), 340-42; Needham, NCF, 9 (1954), 95, 97-101.

Strong, Dr.: Kincaid, NCF, 22 (1968), 323-24; (prototype): Cramp, Di, 48 (1951/52), 117-19; Skottowe, Di, 65 (1969), 30.

Traddles, Thomas: Kincaid, NCF, 22 (1968), 323-24; Needham, NCF, 9 (1954), 89-90; (prototype): Skottowe, Di, 65 (1969), 25-29.

Trotwood, Aunt Betsey: Gilmour, Di, 71 (1975), 35-36; Grundy, L&P, 22 (1972), 103-104; Kettle, REL, 2 (July 1961), 68-72; Kincaid, NCF, 22 (1968), 319-20; Stone, Criticism, 6 (1964), 324-27.

Wickfield, Agnes: Bell, SEL, 8 (1968), 643-44; Gilmour, Di, 71 (1975), 38; Pearlman, VN, 41 (Spring 1972), 18; Smith, RMS, 3 (1959), 136-38; Thirkell, Di, 45 (1948/49), 120-21.

COMPOSITION (See also TEXT)

General: Butt, RES, N.S. 1 (1950), 247-51.

Dr. Strong-Annie-Maldon relationship: Millhauser, NCF, 27 (1972), 340-42.

East Anglian scenes: Collins, Di, 61 (1965), 46-51.

Manuscript and proofs: Cowden, MQR, 9 (1970), 126-32.

Murdstone-Quinion-Passnidge relationship: Millhauser, NCF, 27 (1972), 342-44.

Serial parts: Butt, Di, 46 (1949/50), 90-94, 128-35, 176-80; 47 (1950/51), 33-38.

CRITICAL ASSESSMENT

General: Wilson, Susquehanna University Studies, 6 (Apr.-June 1959), 441-42.

Great Expectations and David Copperfield compared: Jones, SWR, 39 (1954), 328-30.

Historical survey of criticism: Adrian, MLQ, 11 (1950), 325-31.

Position in career: Hamilton, Di, 36 (1939/40), 242-44.

David Copperfield

EXPLANATORY NOTES, HISTORICAL BACKGROUND, and SOURCES

Brontë, <u>Jane Eyre</u>: Meckier, <u>Di</u>, 71 (1975), 5, 13.

Bruce Castle (prototype of Dr. Strong's school): Collins, <u>Di</u>, 51 (1954/55), 174-81.

Dialect: Fielding, <u>TLS</u>, 30 Apr. 1949, p. 288.

Miscellaneous annotations: Hill, <u>Di</u>, 39 (1942/43), 79-88, 123-31, 197-201; 40 (1943/44), 11-14.

"old mawther" (definition): Savage, <u>Di</u>, 37 (1940/41), 37-38.

Plate 1, "Our Pew at Church" (Hogarth): Steig, <u>DSN</u>, 2 (June 1971), 55-56.

Prison system: Collins, <u>N&Q</u>, 206 (1961), 86-91.

ILLUSTRATIONS

General: Bromhill, <u>Di</u>, 40 (1943/44), 47-50, 83-86; Steig, <u>HSL</u>, 2 (1970), 1-18.

Cover: Bromhill, <u>Di</u>, 40 (1943/44), 47.

Plate 1, "Our Pew at Church" (Hogarthian influence): Steig, <u>DSN</u>, 2 (June 1971), 55-56.

Plates 4 and 24 (peacock feathers indicate pride and misfortune): Steig, <u>Ariel</u>, 4 (1973), 50.

INFLUENCES (<u>See also</u> LITERARY PARALLELS)

(Dickens on) Dostoevsky (<u>The Possessed</u>): Katkov, <u>SEER</u>, 27 (1949), 473-88; Kafka: Spilka, <u>CritQ</u>, 1 (1959), 292-301; <u>CL</u>, 11 (1959), 298-305; <u>AI</u>, 16 (1959), 367-77; Kafka (<u>Amerika</u>): Tedlock, <u>CL</u>, 7 (1955), 52-62; Tolstoy: Cain, <u>CritQ</u>, 15 (1973), 237-45.

(on Dickens) psychopathological theory: Manheim, <u>DSA</u>, 2 (1972), 87-88.

LANGUAGE and STYLE (<u>See also</u> TECHNIQUES, VARIOUS)

General: Cox, <u>BJRL</u>, 52 (1970), 269-72.

Dialect, East Anglian: Fielding, <u>TLS</u>, 30 Apr. 1949, p. 288

Imagery: Hughes, <u>ELH</u>, 41 (1974), 96-98; (animals): Kincaid, <u>SNNTS</u>, 1 (1969), 200-201; (dreams): <u>ibid</u>., 203-204; (prison):

ibid., 202–203; (sea): ibid., 197–200; (water): Robison, ES, 53 (1972), 446–47.

Metaphor (characterization): Tick, NCF, 24 (1969), 142–53.

Monologue (interior): Kelty, Di, 57 (1961), 162–63.

Symbolism: Kincaid, SNNTS, 1 (1969), 196–204.

Tone (elegiac): Robison, ES, 53 (1972), 446–47.

LITERARY PARALLELS (See also INFLUENCES)

Brontë, Jane Eyre: Mason, Di, 43 (1946/47), 172–73.

Butler, Ernest Pontifex, or the Way of All Flesh: Schweitzer, Di, 63 (1967), 42–45.

DeQuincey (theme of memory): Herbert, VS, 17 (1974), 250.

Eliot, Middlemarch (marriages): Collins, TLS, 18 May 1974, pp. 556–57.

Kafka, The Metamorphosis: Spilka, CL, 11 (1959), 298–305.

Micawber (and Falstaff): Shuckburgh, Di, 45 (1948/49), 126–28; (and Skimpole): Dunn, DiS, 1 (1965), 122–23.

Scott, The Fortunes of Nigel (Heep prototype): Poston, Di, 71 (1975), 43–44.

Steerforth (and Bucket): Steig, PMASAL, 50 (1965), 581–83; (and Stavrogin): Katkov, SEER, 27 (1949), 473–88.

Tennyson, In Memoriam, Lyric 7, and Chapter 47: Sharrock, N&Q, 201 (1956), 502.

Tolstoy, War and Peace (and Aunt Betsey): Cain, CritQ, 15 (1973), 241–43, 245; (and David/Dora relationship): ibid., 237–41; (and seduction of Emily): ibid., 241, 243–45.

PLOT (See also STRUCTURE/UNITY)

General: Kincaid, DiS, 2 (1966), 77–95; Thirkell, Di, 45 (1948/49), 121–22.

Comic solution, subversion of: Kincaid, SNNTS, 1 (1969), 196–204.

Dora's marriage and death: Vann, VN, 22 (Fall 1962), 19–20.

End of novel: Kennedy, SNNTS, 6 (1974), 284.

David Copperfield

Fairy tale elements: Grob, TSLL, 5 (1964), 569-71; Stone, Criticism, 6 (1964), 324-30.

Fantasy (and realism): Cox, BJRL, 52 (1970), 268-83.

POINT OF VIEW

General: Hughes, ELH, 41 (1974), 89-105; Tick, BuR, 16 (1968), 89-95.

Memory: Cox, BJRL, 52 (1970), 277-81; Gilmour, Di, 71 (1975), 30-42.

Narrator vs. narration: Brown, DSA, 2 (1972), 198-207.

SETTING

World of novel: Bell, SEL, 8 (1968), 638-46; Gard, EIC, 15 (1965), 314-25; Hornback, SEL, 8 (1968), 653-67; Kincaid, DiS, 1 (1965), 66-75.

STRUCTURE/UNITY (See also PLOT)

General: Hughes, ELH, 41 (1974), 89-105; Kincaid, DiS, 1 (1965), 66-75; 2 (1966), 74-95; Marshall, TSL, 5 (1960), 57-65.

Montage (Chapter 31): Walker, Di, 51 (1954/55), 105-106.

Morality play: Pearlman, VN, 41 (Spring 1972), 18.

Old Testament/New Testament dichotomy: Pearlman, VN, 41 (Spring 1972), 19-20.

TECHNIQUES, VARIOUS

General: Brown, YR, 37 (1948), 661-66; Dunn, EJ, 54 (1965), 789-94; Gard, EIC, 15 (1965), 313-25; Hornback, SEL, 8 (1968), 653-67; Kettle, REL, 2 (July 1961), 67-74; Kincaid, DiS, 2 (1966), 74-95; Needham, NCF, 9 (1954), 81-107; Strong, Di, 46 (1949/50), 65-75.

Autobiography, use of: Collins, E&S, N.S. 23 (1970), 71-86; Major, Di, 40 (1943/44), 15-18; Manheim, AI, 9 (1952), 22-43; Oddie, Di, 63 (1967), 100-105, 108-10; Tick, NCF, 24 (1969), 142-53.

Comedy/humor: Kincaid, NCF, 22 (1968), 314-29; Oddie, Di, 63 (1967), 105-10.

David Copperfield

Dream (drowning): Pearlman, AI, 28 (1971), 391–402.

Food and drink (preparation or consumption): Watt, DSA, 3 (1974), 169–70.

Iconography: Steig, HSL, 2 (1970), 1–18.

Mesmerism, use of: Hughes, ELH, 41 (1974), 103–105.

Psychological projection: Spilka, CritQ, 1 (1959), 292–301.

Time, use of: Franklin, DSA, 4 (1975), 17–19; Harris, BuR, 16 (Mar. 1968), 115–18; Raleigh, NCF, 13 (1958), 135–37.

TEXT (See also COMPOSITION)

Cancelled passages of proofs: Staples, Di, 48 (1951/52), 158–61.

THEMES

General: Bell, SEL, 8 (1968), 638–46; Brown, YR, 37 (1948), 654–61; D'Avanzo, Di, 64 (1968), 51–52; Hornback, SEL, 8 (1968), 653–67.

Childhood/children: Brown, YR, 37 (1948), 654–56.

Family: Hornback, SEL, 8 (1968), 654–67.

Fathers and sons: Rooke, E&S, N.S. 4 (1951), 62–63.

Love: Hornback, SEL, 8 (1968), 653–67; (mistaken): Brown, YR, 37 (1948), 656–58.

Marriage: Gard, EIC, 15 (1965), 321–25.

Memory: Herbert, VS, 17 (1974), 250.

Past vs. present: Gilmour, Di, 71 (1975), 30–42.

Religion: Pearlman, VN, 41 (Spring 1972), 18–20.

Sexuality: Gard, EIC, 15 (1965), 313–25.

Time: Franklin, DSA, 4 (1975), 17–19; (and water imagery): Robison, ES, 53 (1972), 446–47.

Undisciplined heart: Needham, NCF, 9 (1954), 81–107.

Bibliography for
David Copperfield

ADRIAN, ARTHUR A. "David Copperfield: A Century of Critical and Popular Acclaim." MLQ, 11 (1950), 325-31.

BELL, VEREEN M. "The Emotional Matrix of David Copperfield." SEL, 8 (1968), 633-49.

BROMHILL, KENTLEY. "'The Originals.'" Di, 45 (1948/49), 161-62.

_____. "Phiz's Illustrations to David Copperfield." Di, 40 (1943/44), 47-50, 83-86.

BROWN, E. K. "David Copperfield." YR, 37 (1948), 651-66.

BROWN, JANET H. "The Narrator's Role in David Copperfield." DSA, 2 (1972), 197-207.

BUTT, JOHN E. "The Composition of David Copperfield." Di, 46 (1949/50), 90-94, 128-35, 176-80; 47 (1950/51), 33-38.

_____. "David Copperfield: From Manuscript to Print." RES, N.S. 1 (1950), 247-51.

CAIN, TOM. "Tolstoy's Use of David Copperfield." CritQ, 15 (1973), 237-46.

CARDWELL, MARGARET. "Rosa Dartle and Mrs. Brown." Di, 56 (1960), 29-33.

CARLTON, W. J. "'The Deed' in David Copperfield." Di, 48 (1951/52), 101-106.

COLBURN, WILLIAM E. "Dickens and the 'Life-Illusion.'" Di, 54 (1958), 110-18.

COLLINS, PHILIP. "Bruce Castle: A School Dickens Admired." Di, 51 (1954/55), 174-81.

_____. "David Copperfield: A Very Complicated Interweaving of Truth and Fiction." E&S, N.S. 23 (1970), 71-86.

_____. "David Copperfield and East Anglia." Di, 61 (1965), 46-51.

_____. "Dorothea's Husbands." TLS, 18 May 1974, pp. 556-57.

_____. "The Middlesex Magistrate in David Copperfield." N&Q, 206 (1961), 86-91.

David Copperfield

COWDEN, ROY W. "Dickens at Work." MQR, 9 (1970), 125-32.

COX, C. B. "Realism and Fantasy in David Copperfield." BJRL, 52 (1970), 267-83.

CRAMP, K. R. "Dr. Strong of Canterbury." Di, 48 (1951/52), 117-19.

DARROLL, G. M. H. "A Note on Dickens and Maria Beadnell, and Dickens's Comic Genius." ESA, 7 (1964), 82-87.

DARWIN, BERNARD. "In Defence of Dora." Di, 45 (1948/49), 139-40.

D'AVANZO, MARIO L. "Mr. Creakle and His Prison: A Note on Craft and Meaning." Di, 64 (1968), 50-52.

DUNN, RICHARD J. "David Copperfield: All Dickens is There." EJ, 54 (1965), 789-94.

_____. "Skimpole and Harthouse: The Dickens Character in Transition." DiS, 1 (1965), 121-28.

FIELDING, K. J. "David Copperfield and Dialect." TLS, 30 Apr. 1949, p. 288.

_____. "The Making of David Copperfield." Listener, 46 (1951), 93-95.

FRANKLIN, STEPHEN L. "Dickens and Time: The Clock Without Hands." DSA, 4 (1975), 1-35.

GANZ, MARGARET. "The Vulnerable Ego: Dickens' Humor in Decline." DSA, 1 (1970), 23-40.

GARD, ROGER. "David Copperfield." EIC, 15 (1965), 313-25.

GIBSON, FRANK A. "Was Dickens Tired? or the Poem of Memory." Di, 45 (1948/49), 157-59.

GILMOUR, ROBIN. "Memory in David Copperfield." Di, 71 (1975), 30-42.

GROB, SHIRLEY. "Dickens and Some Motifs of the Fairy Tale." TSLL, 5 (1964), 567-79.

GRUNDY, DOMINICK E. "Growing Up Dickensian." L&P, 22 (1972), 99-106.

HALL, WILLIAM F. "Caricature in Dickens and James." UTQ, 39 (1970), 242-57.

HAMILTON, ROBERT. "Dickens and Boz." Di, 36 (1939/40), 242-44.

_____. "Dickens's Favourite Child." Di, 45 (1948/49), 141-43.

HARDY, BARBARA. "The Change of Heart in Dickens' Novels." VS, 5 (1961), 49-67.

HARRIS, WENDELL V. "Of Time and the Novel." BuR, 16 (Mar. 1968), 114-29.

HARVEY, WILLIAM R. "Charles Dickens and the Byronic Hero." NCF, 24 (1969), 305-16.

HERBERT, CHRISTOPHER. "DeQuincey and Dickens." VS, 17 (1974), 247-63.

HILL, T. W. "Notes to David Copperfield." Di, 39 (1942/43), 79-88, 123-31, 197-201; 40 (1943/44), 11-14.

HORNBACK, BERT G. "Frustration and Resolution in David Copperfield." SEL, 8 (1968), 651-67.

HUGHES, FELICITY. "Narrative Complexity in David Copperfield." ELH, 41 (1974), 89-105.

HURLEY, EDWARD. "Dickens' Portrait of the Artist." VN, 38 (Fall 1970), 1-5.

JONES, HOWARD MUMFORD. "On Rereading Great Expectations." SWR, 39 (1954), 328-35.

JUMP, JOHN D. "Dickens and His Readers." BJRL, 54 (1972), 384-97.

KATKOV, G. "Steerforth and Stavrogin: On the Sources of The Possessed." SEER, 27 (1949), 469-88.

KELTY, JEAN McCLURE. "The Modern Tone of Charles Dickens." Di, 57 (1961), 160-65.

KENNEDY, G. W. "Dickens's Endings." SNNTS, 6 (1974), 280-87.

KETTLE, ARNOLD. "Thoughts on David Copperfield." REL, 2 (July 1961), 65-74.

KINCAID, JAMES R. "The Darkness of David Copperfield." DiS, 1 (1965), 65-75.

_____. "Dickens's Subversive Humor: David Copperfield." NCF, 22 (1968), 313-29.

_____. "The Structure of David Copperfield." DiS, 2 (1966), 74-95.

_____. "Symbol and Subversion in David Copperfield." SNNTS, 1 (1969), 196-206.

LANE, LAURIAT, JR. "Dickens' Archetypal Jew." PMLA, 73 (1958), 94-100.

LUCAS, JOHN. "Dickens and Arnold." RMS, 16 (1972), 86-111.

MAJOR, GWEN. "'Into the Shadowy World.'" Di, 40 (1943/44), 15-18.

MANHEIM, LEONARD F. "Dickens' Fools and Madmen." DSA, 2 (1972), 69-97.

_____. "The Dickens Hero as Child." SNNTS, 1 (1969), 189-95.

David Copperfield

_____. "The Personal History of David Copperfield: A Study in Psychoanalytic Criticism." AI, 9 (1952), 21-43.

MANNING, SYLVIA. "Dickens, January, and May." Di, 71 (1975), 67-75.

MARSHALL, WILLIAM H. "The Image of Steerforth and the Structure of David Copperfield." TSL, 5 (1960), 57-65.

MASON, LEO. "Jane Eyre and David Copperfield." Di, 43 (1946/47), 172-79.

McNULTY, J. H. "Copperfield, Fact or Fiction?" Di, 45 (1948/49), 153-55.

MECKIER, JEROME. "Some Household Words: Two New Accounts of Dickens's Conversation." Di, 71 (1975), 5-20.

MILLHAUSER, MILTON. "David Copperfield: Some Shifts of Plan." NCF, 27 (1972), 339-45.

NEEDHAM, GWENDOLYN B. "The Undisciplined Heart of David Copperfield." NCF, 9 (1954), 81-107.

ODDIE, WILLIAM. "Mr. Micawber and the Redefinition of Experience." Di, 63 (1967), 100-10.

PEARLMAN, E. "David Copperfield Dreams of Drowning." AI, 28 (1971), 391-403.

_____. "Two Notes on Religion in David Copperfield." VN, 41 (Spring 1972), 18-20.

POSTON, LAWRENCE. "Uriah Heep, Scott, and a Note on Puritanism." Di, 71 (1975), 43-44.

RALEIGH, JOHN HENRY. "Dickens and the Sense of Time." NCF, 13 (1958), 127-37.

REED, JOHN R. "Confinement and Character in Dickens' Novels." DSA, 1 (1970), 41-54.

ROBISON, ROSELEE. "Time, Death and the River in Dickens' Novels." ES, 53 (1972), 436-54.

ROOKE, ELEANOR. "Fathers and Sons in Dickens." E&S, N.S. 4 (1951), 53-69.

SAVAGE, OLIVER D. "Cheer Up, Old Mawther." Di, 37 (1940/41), 37-38.

SCHWEITZER, JOAN. "David Copperfield and Ernest Pontifex." Di, 63 (1967), 42-45.

SHARROCK, ROGER. "A Reminiscence of In Memoriam in David Copperfield." N&Q, 201 (1956), 502.

SHUCKBURGH, JOHN. "Wilkins Micawber." Di, 45 (1948/49), 125-28.

SKOTTOWE, P. F. "Thomas Talfourd and David Copperfield." Di, 65 (1969), 25-31.

SMITH, SHEILA M. "Anti-Mechanism and the Comic in the Writings of Charles Dickens." RMS, 3 (1959), 131-44.

SPILKA, MARK. "David Copperfield as Psychological Fiction." CritQ, 1 (1959), 292-301.

_____. "Kafka and Dickens: The Country Sweetheart." AI, 16 (1959), 367-78.

_____. "Kafka's Sources for The Metamorphosis." CL, 11 (1959), 289-307.

STAPLES, L. C. "Shavings from Dickens's Workshop. Unpublished Fragments from the Novels. Pt. 1. David Copperfield." Di, 48 (1951/52), 158-61.

STEDMAN, JANE W. "Child-Wives of Dickens." Di, 59 (1963), 112-18.

STEIG, MICHAEL. "Cruikshank's Peacock Feathers in Oliver Twist." Ariel, 4 (1973), 49-53.

_____. "David Copperfield, Plate 1: A Note on Phiz and Hogarth." DSN, 2 (June 1971), 55-56.

_____. "The Iconography of David Copperfield." HSL, 2 (1970), 1-18.

_____. "The Whitewashing of Inspector Bucket: Origins and Parallels." PMASAL, 50 (1965), 575-84.

STONE, HARRY. "Fairy Tales and Ogres: Dickens' Imagination and David Copperfield." Criticism, 6 (1964), 324-30.

STRONG, L. A. G. "David Copperfield." Di, 46 (1949/50), 65-75.

TEDLOCK, E. W., JR. "Kafka's Imitation of David Copperfield." CL, 7 (1955), 52-62.

THIRKELL, ANGELA. "David Copperfield Reconsidered." Di, 45 (1948/49), 119-22.

TICK, STANLEY. "The Memorializing of Mr. Dick." NCF, 24 (1969), 142-53.

_____. "On Not Being Charles Dickens." BuR, 16 (1968), 85-95.

TOMLIN, E. W. F. "The Englishness of Dickens." EA, 23 (1970), 113-24.

VANN, J. DON. "The Death of Dora Spenlow in David Copperfield." VN, 22 (Fall 1962), 19-20.

WALKER, SAXON. "The Artistry of Dickens as an English Novelist." Di, 51 (1954/55), 102-108.

David Copperfield

WATT, IAN. "Oral Dickens." DSA, 3 (1974), 165-81.

WENGER, JARED. "Character-Types of Scott, Balzac, Dickens, Zola." PMLA, 62 (1947), 213-32.

WILSON, ARTHUR H. "The Great Theme in Charles Dickens." Susquehanna University Studies, 6 (Apr.-June 1959), 422-57.

Bleak House

Bleak House

CHARACTERIZATION

General: Blount, MLQ, 25 (1964), 298-306; DiS, 1 (1965), 112-20;
EIC, 15 (1965), 414-26; Brogunier, Di, 61 (1965), 59-62;
Chartier, Di, 40 (1943/44), 121-25, 207-10; Cox, CritQ, 2
(1960), 58-60; Crompton, NCF, 12 (1958), 285-303; Deen,
Criticism, 3 (1961), 207-18; Delespinasse, NCF, 23 (1968),
254-64; Donovan, ELH, 29 (1962), 191-94; Farrow, Cithara, 13
(May 1974), 35-44; Franklin, DSA, 4 (1975), 21-26; Friedman,
Boston University Studies in English, 3 (1957), 148-66; Green,
Library Review, 22 (1970), 363-64; Jefferson, E&S, N.S. 27
(1974), 44-46; Johnson, NCF, 7 (1952), 76-89; Kenney, Di, 66
(1970), 36-41; Kettle, Zeitschrift für Anglistik und Americanistik, 9 (1961), 243-44; Roulet, Di, 60 (1964), 120-23;
Sadoff, VN, 46 (Fall 1974), 6-9; Tomlinson, Critical Review,
15 (1972), 73-81; Weinstein, DiS, 4 (1968), 5-18; Wilkinson,
ELH, 34 (1967), 238-46; (prototypes): Butt, CritQ, 1 (1959),
303-307.

Anal characters: Steig, VS, 13 (1970), 343-48.

Chancery litigants: Hirsch, DSA, 4 (1975), 140-46.

Fairy-tale influence: Flibbert, VN, 36 (Fall 1969), 1-5.

Grotesque: Steig, CentR, 14 (1970), 328-30.

Names: Bromhill, Di, 41 (1944/45), 93.

Relationship to external scene: Ousby, NCF, 29 (1975), 382-92.

Topicality: Butt, NCF, 10 (1955), 13-21.

Women: Moers, Di, 69 (1973), 13-24; Tomlinson, Critical Review,
15 (1972), 75-81.

CHARACTERS

Ada: Sadoff, VN, 46 (Fall 1974), 7-9.

Boythorn, Lawrence: Crompton, NCF, 12 (1958), 289-90; Fradin,
PMLA, 81 (1966), 105-106; Tomlinson, Critical Review, 15

Bleak House

   (1972), 77; (prototype): Cotterell, <u>Di</u>, 44 (1947/48), 209-16;
   Staples, <u>Di</u>, 41 (1944/45), 81.

Bucket, Inspector: Farrow, <u>Cithara</u>, 13 (May 1974), 37-38;
   Hirsch, <u>DSA</u>, 4 (1975), 150-52; Ousby, <u>NCF</u>, 29 (1975), 391-92;
   Parker, <u>ELN</u>, 12 (1974), 31-35; Steig, <u>PMASAL</u>, 50 (1965),
   575-84; <u>VS</u>, 13 (1970), 354; Steig and Wilson, <u>MLQ</u>, 33 (1972),
   289-98; Winner, <u>DSA</u>, 3 (1974), 106-108; (prototype): Butt,
   <u>NCF</u>, 10 (1955), 17-19; Collins, <u>Di</u>, 60 (1964), 88-89.

Carstone, Richard: Blount, <u>DiS</u>, 1 (1965), 117-18; Franklin, <u>DSA</u>,
   4 (1975), 26; Hirsch, <u>DSA</u>, 4 (1975), 143-46; Nadelhaft, <u>SNNTS</u>,
   1 (1969), 236-37.

Chadband: Blount, <u>MLQ</u>, 25 (1964), 295-307; Boo, <u>Cithara</u>, 5
   (1965), 19-20; Dunstan, <u>Di</u>, 56 (1960), 109-10; Smith, <u>RMS</u>, 3
   (1959), 134-36; Steig, <u>VS</u>, 13 (1970), 347.

Coavinses (prototype): de Suzannet, <u>Di</u>, 36 (1939/40), 180.

Dedlock, Lady: Cox, <u>CritQ</u>, 2 (1960), 58-60; Frank, <u>DSA</u>, 4
   (1975), 92, 95-99, 103, 109-10; Grundy, <u>L&P</u>, 22 (1972),
   102-103; Jefferson, <u>E&S</u>, N.S. 27 (1974), 37-44, 46-51; Johnson, <u>NCF</u>, 7 (1952), 76-77; Moers, <u>Di</u>, 69 (1973), 16; Ousby,
   <u>NCF</u>, 29 (1975), 383-84; Steig, <u>DiS</u>, 4 (1968), 21-22; Sucksmith, <u>RMS</u>, 9 (1965), 63-65; Wilson, <u>SAQ</u>, 73 (1974), 534;
   (prototype): Staples, <u>Di</u>, 41 (1944/45), 81.

Dedlock, Sir Leicester: Blount, <u>EIC</u>, 15 (1965), 414-26; <u>NCF</u>, 21
   (1966), 150-61, 164-65; Franklin, <u>DSA</u>, 4 (1975), 23; Johnson,
   <u>NCF</u>, 7 (1952), 82-83, 87-88; McCullen, <u>DSN</u>, 4 (1973), 18-19;
   Smith, <u>EIC</u>, 21 (1971), 160-62; Sucksmith, <u>DSA</u>, 4 (1975), 113,
   123-27, 130-31; (prototype): Staples, <u>Di</u>, 41 (1944/45),
   80-81.

Flite, Miss: Blount, <u>DiS</u>, 1 (1965), 112-14; Colburn, <u>Di</u>, 54
   (1958), 111-12; Hirsch, <u>DSA</u>, 4 (1975), 141-42; (prototype):
   Blount, <u>DiS</u>, 1 (1965), 112; Butt, <u>CritQ</u>, 1 (1959), 303-304;
   Carlton, <u>Di</u>, 48 (1951/52), 165; <u>N&Q</u>, 196 (1951), 521-22.

Gridley: Hirsch, <u>DSA</u>, 4 (1975), 141.

Guppy: Jump, <u>BJRL</u>, 54 (1972), 393-94.

Guster (prototype): Collins, <u>NCF</u>, 14 (1960), 346-48.

Hawdon, Captain (Nemo): Blount, <u>RES</u>, N.S. 14 (1963), 370-74.

Hortense: Frank, <u>DSA</u>, 4 (1975), 96-99; Moers, <u>Di</u>, 69 (1973),
   21-22; Steig and Wilson, <u>MLQ</u>, 33 (1972), 290-97.

Jarndyce, John: Axton, <u>UTQ</u>, 37 (1967), 33-34; Blount, <u>DiS</u>, 1
   (1965), 118-19; Grundy, <u>L&P</u>, 22 (1972), 105; Manheim, <u>AI</u>, 12
   (1955), 20-21; Nadelhaft, <u>SNNTS</u>, 1 (1969), 235-36; Sadoff, <u>VN</u>,
   46 (Fall 1974), 6-9.

Bleak House

Smallweed, Judy: Blount, DiS, 3 (1967), 66-67.

Smallweeds: Franklin, DSA, 4 (1975), 22-23; Luedtke, LWU, 3 (1970), 6; (prototype): Lovett, Di, 59 (1963), 124.

Snagsby (prototype): Blount, MLR, 60 (1965), 347.

Squod, Phil: Blount, EIC, 15 (1965), 422-23.

Summerson, Esther: Axton, MLQ, 26 (1965), 545-57; Di, 62 (1966), 158-63; Blount, DiS, 1 (1965), 119-20; Boo, Cithara, 5 (1965), 20-21; Broderick and Grant, MP, 55 (1958), 252-58; Burgan, MLQ, 36 (1975), 295-99; Crompton, NCF, 12 (1958), 288-89; Delespinasse, NCF, 23 (1968), 254-64; Dunn, Di, 62 (1966), 163-66; Farrow, Cithara, 13 (May 1974), 40-41; Fradin, PMLA, 81 (1966), 96-98, 107-109; Frank, DSA, 4 (1975), 91-112; Friedman, Boston University Studies in English, 3 (1957), 150, 153-54, 160-66; Grundy, L&P, 22 (1972), 100-105; Guerard, SoR, N.S. 5 (1969), 339-40; Hirsch, DSA, 4 (1975), 134-40; Jefferson, E&S, N.S. 27 (1974), 39-44, 46-51; Kilian, DR, 54 (1974), 318-27; Lucas, RMS, 16 (1972), 104-106; Manheim, TSLL, 7 (1965), 194-96; McCoy, Di, 63 (1967), 181-82; Middlebro', QQ, 77 (1970), 253-55; Moers, Di, 69 (1973), 14-16, 20; Ousby, NCF, 29 (1975), 388-92; Rosso, Di, 65 (1969), 90-94; Sadoff, VN, 46 (Fall 1974), 5-10; Steig, DiS, 4 (1968), 20-22; VS, 13 (1970), 351-53; Tomlinson, Critical Review, 15 (1972), 77-80; Wilson, SAQ, 73 (1974), 533-34; Zwerdling, PMLA, 88 (1973), 429-38; (as narrator): Axton, MLQ, 26 (1965), 550-57; Deen, Criticism, 3 (1961), 207, 211-16; Donovan, ELH, 29 (1962), 197-201; Monod, DiS, 5 (1969), 17-25; Smith, VN, 38 (Fall 1970), 10-14; (nicknames): Axton, Di, 62 (1966), 159-63; (prototype): Dunn, Di, 62 (1966), 164.

Tulkinghorn: Blount, EIC, 21 (1971), 435-36; Fradin, PMLA, 81 (1966), 102-105; Hirsch, DSA, 4 (1975), 146-50; Quirk, JEGP, 72 (1973), 526-35; Steig, VS, 13 (1970), 345-46; Steig and Wilson, MLQ, 33 (1972), 290-91, 297-98; Winner, DSA, 3 (1974), 107-108; (prototype): Carlton, Di, 48 (1951/52), 165.

Turveydrop: Blount, NCF, 21 (1966), 161-65; Colburn, Di, 54 (1958), 115; Jump, BJRL, 54 (1972), 392-93; McCullen, DSN, 4 (1973), 15-20; McMaster, SNNTS, 1 (1969), 137-38; (prototype): Stevenson, Di, 44 (1947/48), 39-41.

Vholes: Crompton, NCF, 12 (1958), 299-301; Galvin, Di, 64 (1968), 22-27; Lucas, RMS, 16 (1972), 108; Roulet, Di, 60 (1964), 121-22; Steele, Quadrant, 82 (1973), 21-22; Steig, VS, 13 (1970), 346; Van Ghent, SR, 58 (1950), 421-22.

Woodcourt, Allan: Fradin, PMLA, 81 (1966), 108-109.

COMPOSITION (See also TEXT)

    General: Ford, Di, 65 (1969), 84–89.

    Background: Stevenson, SR, 51 (1943), 399–403.

    Imagery (deletion in Chapter 1): Blount, N&Q, 207 (1962), 303–304.

    Memoranda and number plans: Sucksmith, RMS, 9 (1965), 47–85.

    Titles: Ford, Di, 65 (1969), 85–89.

CRITICAL ASSESSMENT

    General: Lucas, RMS, 16 (1972), 102–11; Stevenson, SR, 51 (1943), 403–405; Wilson, Susquehanna University Studies, 6 (Apr.–June 1959), 443–45; (survey of criticism): Staples, Di, 41 (1944/45), 135–37.

    Contemporary reaction: Stone, NCF, 12 (1957), 190–92; (spontaneous combustion): Haight, NCF, 10 (1955), 53–63.

EXPLANATORY NOTES, HISTORICAL BACKGROUND, and SOURCES

    Anality and excrement: Steig, VS, 13 (1970), 348–50.

    Bluebooks and statistics generally: Brantlinger, Criticism, 14 (1972), 328–44.

    Chancery: Blount, Di, 62 (1966), 49–52, 106–11, 167–71; Butt, NCF, 10 (1955), 3–7; Hamer, N&Q, 215 (1970), 341–47; Woolliams, Di, 41 (1944/45), 26–29.

    Chesney Wold: Staples, Di, 41 (1944/45), 80–81.

    East Wind: Schwarzbach, DSN, 6 (1975), 82–84.

    Gridley's case: Blount, Di, 62 (1966), 167–69.

    Growlery: Lovett, Di, 59 (1963), 124.

    Guster and Mrs. Jellyby: Collins, NCF, 14 (1960), 345–49.

    Jarndyce vs. Jarndyce: Blount, Di, 62 (1966), 170–71.

    Jo: Fielding and Brice, Di, 64 (1968), 135–40; 65 (1969), 35–40; Harris, Di, 64 (1968), 48–49; Worth, JEGP, 60 (1961), 44–47.

    Krook's shop (Mayhew): Dunn, NCF, 25 (1970), 348–53.

    Master/servant relationships: Blount, DiS, 3 (1967), 63–67.

    Military, the: Sullivan, Di, 46 (1949/50), 141–43.

Bleak House

Miscellaneous annotations: Hill, $\underline{Di}$, 40 (1943/44), 39-44, 65-70, 133-41.

Skimpole (name): Chaudhuri, $\underline{DSN}$, 6 (1975), 75-77.

Spontaneous combustion: Blount, $\underline{DSA}$, 1 (1970), 184-92; Perkins, $\underline{Di}$, 60 (1964), 62-63; Wallins, $\underline{DSN}$, 5 (1974), 68-70; Wiley, $\underline{Di}$, 58 (1962), 120-23; Wilkinson, $\underline{ELH}$, 34 (1967), 231-38; (contemporary scientific theories): Gaskell, $\underline{Di}$, 69 (1973), 25-35; Haight, $\underline{NCF}$, 10 (1955), 53-63.

Topicality: Butt, $\underline{NCF}$, 10 (1955), 1-21; (female emancipation): ibid., 13-17; (government): ibid., 7-9; (graveyards): Blount, $\underline{RES}$, N.S. 14 (1963), 370-78; (juvenile vagrancy and delinquency): Blount, $\underline{MP}$, 62 (1965), 328-39; (metropolitan police force): Butt, $\underline{NCF}$, 10 (1955), 17-19; (Puseyites): ibid., 1-2; (sanitation): ibid., 9-13; (slums): Blount, $\underline{MLR}$, 60 (1965), 341-51.

Wat Tyler, Dickens's conception of: Sucksmith, $\underline{DSA}$, 4 (1975), 114-27.

ILLUSTRATIONS

General: Bromhill, $\underline{Di}$, 40 (1943/44), 147-50, 192-95; Steig, $\underline{DiS}$, 4 (1968), 19-22; $\underline{CentR}$, 14 (1970), 326-27.

Chadband ("Mr. Chadband 'improving' a Tough Subject"): Steig, $\underline{HLQ}$, 36 (1972), 59-61, 65-67.

Esther: Steig, $\underline{DiS}$, 4 (1968), 20-22.

Frontispiece: Bromhill, $\underline{Di}$, 40 (1943/44), 146.

Lady Dedlock: Steig, $\underline{DiS}$, 4 (1968), 21-22.

Monthly wrapper: Bromhill, $\underline{Di}$, 40 (1943/44), 146; (analogous to Cruikshank's The Comic Blackstone): Gowans, $\underline{Di}$, 69 (1973), 78; Tye, $\underline{Di}$, 69 (1973), 39-41.

Title vignette: Bromhill, $\underline{Di}$, 40 (1943/44), 147.

Turveydrop ("A Model of Parental Deportment"): Steig, $\underline{HLQ}$, 36 (1972), 58-65, 66-67.

INFLUENCES (See also LITERARY PARALLELS)

(Dickens on) O. Henry ("Elsie in New York"): Marks, $\underline{ELN}$, 12 (1974), 35-37; Ortega y Gasset: Henley, Language Quarterly of the University of South Florida, 5 (1966), 2-3.

(on Dickens) General: Stevenson, SR, 51 (1943), 402; Carlyle, "Occasional Discourse on the Negro Question" and Latter-Day Pamphlets (and "foreign philanthropy question"): Tarr, SNNTS, 3 (1971), 275-80; Carlyle, Past and Present: Kenney, Di, 66 (1970), 36-41; Hawthorne, The Scarlet Letter: Stokes, AUMLA, 32 (1969), 177-89; Marryat (spontaneous combustion): Hawes, DSA, 2 (1972), 58-60; psychopathological theory: Manheim, DSA, 2 (1972), 80.

LANGUAGE and STYLE (See also TECHNIQUES, VARIOUS)

General: Lucas, RMS, 16 (1972), 109-11; Miller, NCF, 24 (1970), 475-76; Steele, Quadrant, 82 (1973), 20-23; Tomlinson, Critical Review, 15 (1972), 69-73.

Allusion (literary): Gill, NCF, 22 (1967), 146-54; Shatto, DSN, 6 (1975), 78-82, 108-15.

Grotesque exaggeration: Steig, CentR, 14 (1970), 313-14.

Imagery: Kettle, Zeitschrift für Anglistik und Americanistik, 9 (1961), 244-47; Passerini, DiS, 1 (1965), 27-28, 32-33; Pook, AWR, 19 (1970), 154-57; Wilkinson, ELH, 34 (1967), 238-47; (anality and excrement): Steig, VS, 13 (1970), 343-48, 350-54; (birds): Dettlebach, Di, 59 (1963), 177-81; (contrasting symbolic images): Friedman, Boston University Studies in English, 3 (1957), 147-66; (distortion and decay): Weinstein, DiS, 4 (1968), 4-14; (fire): Wilkinson, ELH, 34 (1967), 238-47; (fog): Schachterle, DSA, 1 (1970), 221-22; (Gothic castle): Ronald, DSN, 6 (1975), 71-75; (ironic): Deen, Criticism, 3 (1961), 208-18; (light/dark): Moth, DiS, 1 (1965), 76-85; (mechanization, systemization): Luedtke, LWU, 3 (1970), 1-9; (pastoral): Crompton, NCF, 12 (1958), 294-302; (religious): Axton, NCF, 22 (1968), 350-59; (river): Robison, ES, 53 (1972), 443; (scientific): Axton, NCF, 22 (1968), 350-59; (the spleen): Nadelhaft, SNNTS, 1 (1969), 230-38; (water): Wilkinson, ELH, 34 (1967), 238-41.

Irony: Sucksmith, RMS, 9 (1965), 57-65.

Jo's replies at inquest: Harris, Di, 64 (1968), 48-49.

Symbolism: Blount, NCF, 21 (1966), 150-65; Crompton, NCF, 12 (1958), 288-303; Johnson, NCF, 7 (1952), 79-89; Wilkinson, ELH, 34 (1967), 238-47; (Bleak House): Kelley, NCF, 25 (1970), 264-68; (Chancery): Blount, DiS, 1 (1965), 113-20; Fradin, PMLA, 81 (1966), 98-102; Wilkinson, ELH, 34 (1967), 239-47; (Chesney Wold): Kelley, NCF, 25 (1970), 254-57; (fog): Johnson, NCF, 7 (1952), 73-74, 80; (houses): Kelley, NCF, 25 (1970), 253-68; (Jarndyce vs. Jarndyce): Blount, DiS, 1

Bleak House

> (1965), 115-16; (Krook's shop): Kelley, NCF, 25 (1970),
> 263-64; (title): ibid., 253-68; (Tom-all-Alone's): Johnson,
> NCF, 7 (1952), 85, 88-89; Kelley, NCF, 25 (1970), 257-59.

LITERARY PARALLELS (See also INFLUENCES)

Bucket (and Artful Dodger): Steig, PMASAL, 50 (1965), 580; (and
    Jaggers): ibid., 583-84; (and Quilp): ibid., 580-81; (and
    Sam Weller): ibid., 579-80; (and Steerforth): ibid., 581-83.

Bulwer-Lytton, Lucretia: Eigner and Fradin, NCF, 24 (1969),
    98-102.

Bunyan, The Pilgrim's Progress (and Krook): Delaney, DSN, 3
    (1972), 101-105.

Detective fiction: Walton, NCF, 23 (1969), 456-61.

Eliot, Felix Holt: Dodds, N&Q, 190 (1945), 143-45.

Hard Times: Gibson, DiS, 1 (1965), 96-101.

Hood, Tylney Hall: Whitley, Di, 52 (1955/56), 183-84.

Little Dorrit: Pook, AWR, 19 (1970), 154-59.

Melville, "Bartleby the Scrivener" (and world of novel): Lane,
    DR, 51 (1971), 322-24.

O. Henry, "Elsie in New York" (and Jo): Marks, ELN, 12 (1974),
    35-37.

Punch (themes): Collins, DiS, 3 (1967), 7-13.

Shakespeare, Macbeth: McNulty, Di, 40 (1943/44), 188-90.

Skimpole and Micawber: Dunn, DiS, 1 (1965), 122-23.

Smith, Sydney ("Noodle's Oration"): McLean, VN, 38 (Fall 1970),
    24-25.

Spontaneous combustion (in C. B. Brown, Marryat, Melville):
    Perkins, Di, 60 (1964), 57-59; Wiley, Di, 58 (1962), 120-23;
    (in Zola): Perkins, Di, 60 (1964), 60-61; (The Terrific
    Register): McMaster, DR, 38 (1958), 21-23.

Tulkinghorn and Chillingworth (The Scarlet Letter): Stokes,
    AUMLA, 32 (1969), 182-89.

PLOT (See also STRUCTURE/UNITY)

General: Donovan, ELH, 29 (1962), 187-94; Jefferson, E&S,
    N.S. 27 (1974), 37-44, 46-51; Passerini, DiS, 1 (1965),
    30-31; Steig, CentR, 14 (1970), 327-29.

End of novel: Frank, <u>DSA</u>, 4 (1975), 106-12.

Fairy tale elements: Flibbert, <u>VN</u>, 36 (Fall 1969), 1-5; Grob, <u>TSLL</u>, 5 (1964), 571-72.

Foreshadowing: Gadd, <u>Di</u>, 36 (1939/40), 182.

Mystery, use of (sexual): Hirsch, <u>DSA</u>, 4 (1975), 132-52.

POINT OF VIEW

General: Deen, <u>Criticism</u>, 3 (1961), 206-17; Delespinasse, <u>NCF</u>, 23 (1968), 253-64; Donovan, <u>ELH</u>, 29 (1962), 194-201; Fradin, <u>PMLA</u>, 81 (1966), 95-98; Grenander, <u>NCF</u>, 10 (1956), 301-305; Guerard, <u>SoR</u>, N.S. 5 (1969), 339-49; Monod, <u>DiS</u>, 5 (1969), 5-25; Roulet, <u>Di</u>, 60 (1964), 119-20.

Authorial intrusion: Levine, <u>SNNTS</u>, 1 (1969), 168-69.

Dual narrative: Schachterle, <u>DSA</u>, 1 (1970), 219-20.

Narration (present tense): Carlisle, <u>JNT</u>, 1 (1971), 156-57; (subjective): Sorensen, <u>ES</u>, 40 (1959), 431-39.

Narrator: Guerard, <u>SoR</u>, N.S. 5 (1969), 341-49; Monod, <u>DiS</u>, 5 (1969), 6-17.

Popular realism: Kettle, <u>Zeitschrift für Anglistik und Americanistik</u>, 9 (1961), 241-47.

Relation to audience: Monod, <u>DiS</u>, 5 (1969), 5-25.

SETTING

Iron Country: Smith, <u>EIC</u>, 21 (1971), 163, 164, 167-68.

Pastoral, use of (Chesney Wold): Burgan, <u>MLQ</u>, 36 (1975), 297-99; (Esther's cottage): <u>ibid.</u>, 295-97.

Prototypes: Blount, <u>Di</u>, 61 (1965), 140-49.

World of novel: Deen, <u>Criticism</u>, 3 (1961), 206-18; Farrow, <u>Cithara</u>, 13 (May 1974), 34-44; Fradin, <u>PMLA</u>, 81 (1966), 95-109; Franklin, <u>DSA</u>, 4 (1975), 19-27; Kelley, <u>NCF</u>, 25 (1970), 253-68; Moth, <u>DiS</u>, 1 (1965), 76-85; Nadelhaft, <u>SNNTS</u>, 1 (1969), 232-38; Ousby, <u>NCF</u>, 29 (1975), 382-92; Steig, <u>VS</u>, 13 (1970), 343-48, 350-54; Weinstein, <u>DiS</u>, 4 (1968), 4-14; Wilkinson, <u>ELH</u>, 34 (1967), 225-31, 238-47; (urban environment): Burke, <u>SEL</u>, 9 (1969), 664-76.

Bleak House

STRUCTURE/UNITY (See also PLOT)

General: Deen, Criticism, 3 (1961), 206-18; Guerard, SoR, N.S. 5
(1969), 333-49; Roulet, Di, 60 (1964), 117-24; Wilkinson, ELH,
34 (1967), 225-31, 238-47.

Allegory: Delaney, DSN, 3 (1972), 100-105.

"keystone episode": Axton, UTQ, 37 (1967), 43-46.

Parallels: Blount, NCF, 21 (1966), 150-65; EIC, 21 (1971), 434,
435-36.

Psychological coherence: Hirsch, DSA, 4 (1975), 134-52.

Serial unity: Schachterle, DSA, 1 (1970), 212-24.

Single installment--Number 10, Chapters 30-32: Schachterle, DSA,
1 (1970), 215-17.

TECHNIQUES, VARIOUS

General: Blount, MLR, 60 (1965), 340-57; Boo, Cithara, 5 (1965),
15-22; Butt, CritQ, 1 (1959), 302-307; Crompton, NCF, 12
(1958), 284-303; Deen, Criticism, 3 (1961), 206-18; Donovan,
ELH, 29 (1962), 177-201; Fradin, PMLA, 81 (1966), 95-109;
Friedman, Boston University Studies in English, 3 (1957),
147-66; Green, Library Review, 22 (1970), 365-67; Johnson,
NCF, 7 (1952), 73-89; Nadelhaft, SNNTS, 1 (1969), 232-38;
Sucksmith, RMS, 9 (1965), 47-85; Wilkinson, ELH, 34 (1967),
225-47; Wilson, AM, 165 (1940), 684-86.

Aesthetic distance: Henley, Language Quarterly of the University
of South Florida, 5 (1966), 2.

Appearance vs. reality: Levine, SNNTS, 1 (1969), 161-63.

Arrest of Hortense: Steig and Wilson, MLQ, 33 (1972), 291-95.

Chancery, depiction of: Brogunier, Di, 61 (1965), 57-62.

Contrast: Boo, Cithara, 5 (1965), 16-22.

Death of Jo: Monod, DiS, 5 (1969), 12; Passerini, DiS, 1 (1965),
27-33.

Death of Krook: Blount, DSA, 1 (1970), 205-11; Monod, DiS, 5
(1969), 13-14; Nadelhaft, SNNTS, 1 (1969), 237-38; Wallins,
DSN, 5 (1974), 68-70.

Death of Nemo: Blount, RES, N.S. 14 (1963), 370-74.

Disease (the spleen), use of: Nadelhaft, SNNTS, 1 (1969),
230-38.

"East Wind," use of: Schwarzbach, DSN, 6 (1975), 82-84.

Grotesque, use of: Steele, Quadrant, 82 (1973), 15-23.

Observation: Burke, SEL, 9 (1969), 664-76.

Opening: Jump, BJRL, 54 (1972), 389-91; Tomlinson, Critical Review, 15 (1972), 69-72.

Spontaneous combustion: Blount, DSA, 1 (1970), 186-211; Perkins, Di, 60 (1964), 59-60; Wiley, Di, 58 (1962), 123-25; Wilkinson, ELH, 34 (1967), 241-47.

Tag gesture, use of (Bucket): Parker, ELN, 12 (1974), 31-35.

Time, use of: Franklin, DSA, 4 (1975), 19-27.

TEXT (See also COMPOSITION)

Cancelled passages from proofs: DeVries, Di, 66 (1970), 3-7; Staples, Di, 50 (1953/54), 188-91.

Compositors' errors: Monod, Di, 69 (1973), 3-12.

THEMES

General: Blount, RES, N.S. 14 (1963), 370-78; DiS, 1 (1965), 113-20; EIC, 15 (1965), 415-26; MP, 62 (1965), 327-39; Di, 62 (1966), 171-74; Chartier, Di, 40 (1943/44), 121-25, 207-10; Crompton, NCF, 12 (1958), 284-303; Friedman, Boston University Studies in English, 3 (1957), 149-66; Kenney, Di, 66 (1970), 36-41; Smith, VN, 38 (Fall 1970), 11-14; Wilkinson, ELH, 34 (1967), 238-47; Wilson, AM, 165 (1940), 684-86.

Art and life, severance between: Ericksen, JEGP, 72 (1973), 49, 52-59.

Change vs. changelessness: Sadoff, VN, 46 (Fall 1974), 5-10.

Childhood/children: Donovan, ELH, 29 (1962), 182-84.

Childhood vs. adulthood: Grundy, L&P, 22 (1972), 100-105.

Dandyism: McCullen, DSN, 4 (1973), 16-20.

Decency, generosity, disinterestedness: Brogunier, Di, 61 (1965), 58-62.

Disease: Middlebro', QQ, 77 (1970), 253-55.

Dissenters: Blount, MLQ, 25 (1964), 295-307.

Ecclesiastical institutions, depersonalization of: Luedtke, LWU, 3 (1970), 3-4.

Bleak House

Education: Blount, MP, 62 (1965), 332-36.

Evangelicalism: Boo, Cithara, 5 (1965), 17-20.

Evil, inherited: Axton, MLQ, 26 (1965), 546-57.

Fathers and sons: Rooke, E&S, N.S. 4 (1951), 63.

Financial institutions, depersonalization of: Luedtke, LWU, 3 (1970), 6-7.

Foreign missions, satire on: Tarr, SNNTS, 3 (1971), 276, 278-80.

Government institutions, depersonalization of: Luedtke, LWU, 3 (1970), 2-3.

Hidden relationships: Burke, SEL, 9 (1969), 664-76.

Identity: Frank, DSA, 4 (1975), 92-112.

Industrialism: Blount, EIC, 15 (1965), 419-26.

Juvenile vagrancy and delinquency: Blount, MP, 62 (1965), 328-39.

Law: Kettle, Zeitschrift für Anglistik und Americanistik, 9 (1961), 241-47; (and Chancery): Donovan, ELH, 29 (1962), 178-82; Gibson, Di, 59 (1963), 161-64.

Marriage: Donovan, ELH, 29 (1962), 184-86.

Moral order: Axton, NCF, 22 (1968), 350-59.

Parent/child relationships: Adrian, Di, 67 (1971), 6-7.

Philanthropic institutions, depersonalization of: Luedtke, LWU, 3 (1970), 4-6.

Political corruption: Johnson, NCF, 7 (1952), 83-84.

Religion: Franklin, DSA, 4 (1975), 19-27.

Responsibility: Donovan, ELH, 29 (1962), 177-86; Friedman, Boston University Studies in English, 3 (1957), 150-66.

Self-salvation: Wilson, SAQ, 73 (1974), 532-34.

Social criticism: Blount, MLR, 60 (1965), 340-51; NCF, 21 (1966), 149-65; Boo, Cithara, 5 (1965), 16-22; Butt, CritQ, 1 (1959), 302-307; Cooperman, CE, 22 (1960), 159-60; Crompton, NCF, 12 (1958), 284-303; Donovan, ELH, 29 (1962), 175-86; Johnson, NCF, 7 (1952), 73-89; Passerini, DiS, 1 (1965), 28-30; Pook, AWR, 19 (1970), 154-57; Steig, VS, 13 (1970), 353-54; Sucksmith, DSA, 4 (1975), 113-31; (aristocracy): Crompton, NCF, 12 (1958), 292-93; (Chancery): Blount, Di, 62 (1966), 48, 171-74; Jump, BJRL, 54 (1972), 396-97; (future inherent in Rouncewell's ironworks): Luedtke, LWU, 3 (1970), 7-9; (middle class): Crompton, NCF, 12 (1958), 285-87; (society and the

  individual): Fradin, PMLA, 81 (1966), 95-109; (the Two Nations): Levine, SNNTS, 1 (1969), 161-63, 168-69.

Systemization (vs. sympathy): Luedtke, LWU, 3 (1970), 1-13.

Time: Franklin, DSA, 4 (1975), 19-27.

Unity: Farrow, Cithara, 13 (May 1974), 42-44.

Urban observation: Burke, SEL, 9 (1969), 665-76.

Women, roles of: Moers, Di, 69 (1973), 13-24.

Bibliography for *Bleak House*

ADRIAN, ARTHUR A. "Dickens and Inverted Parenthood." <u>Di</u>, 67 (1971), 3-11.

AXTON, WILLIAM F. "Esther's Nicknames: A Study in Relevance." <u>Di</u>, 62 (1966), 158-63.

_____. "'Keystone' Structure in Dickens' Serial Novels." <u>UTQ</u>, 37 (1967), 31-50.

_____. "Religious and Scientific Imagery in <u>Bleak House</u>." <u>NCF</u>, 22 (1968), 349-59.

_____. "The Trouble with Esther." <u>MLQ</u>, 26 (1965), 545-57.

BLOUNT, TREVOR. "<u>Bleak House</u> and the Sloane Scandal of 1850 Again." <u>DiS</u>, 3 (1967), 63-67.

_____. "The Chadbands and Dickens' View of Dissenters." <u>MLQ</u>, 25 (1964), 295-307.

_____. "Chancery as Evil and Challenge in <u>Bleak House</u>." <u>DiS</u>, 1 (1965), 112-20.

_____. "Dickens and Mr. Krook's Spontaneous Combustion." <u>DSA</u>, 1 (1970), 183-211.

_____. "Dickens's Ironmaster Again." <u>EIC</u>, 21 (1971), 429-36.

_____. "Dickens's Slum Satire in <u>Bleak House</u>." <u>MLR</u>, 60 (1965), 340-51.

_____. "The Documentary Symbolism of Chancery in <u>Bleak House</u>." <u>Di</u>, 62 (1966), 47-52, 106-11, 167-74.

_____. "The Graveyard Satire of <u>Bleak House</u> in the Context of 1850." <u>RES</u>, N.S. 14 (1963), 370-78.

_____. "The Importance of Place in <u>Bleak House</u>." <u>Di</u>, 61 (1965), 140-49.

_____. "The Ironmaster and the New Acquisitiveness: Dickens's Views on the Rising Industrial Classes as Exemplified in <u>Bleak House</u>." <u>EIC</u>, 15 (1965), 414-27.

Bleak House

_____. "Poor Jo, Education, and the Problem of Juvenile Delinquency in Dickens' Bleak House." MP, 62 (1965), 325-39.

_____. "A Revised Image of the Opening Chapter of Dickens's Bleak House." N&Q, 207 (1962), 303-304.

_____. "Sir Leicester Dedlock and 'Deportment' Turveydrop: Some Aspects of Dickens's Use of Parallelism." NCF, 21 (1966), 149-65.

BOO, SISTER MARY RICHARD. "Jo's Journey Toward the Light in Bleak House." Cithara, 5 (1965), 15-22.

BRANTLINGER, PATRICK. "Bluebooks, the Social Organism, and the Victorian Novel." Criticism, 14 (1972), 328-44.

BRODERICK, JONAS H. and JOHN E. GRANT. "The Identity of Esther Summerson." MP, 55 (1958), 252-58.

BROGUNIER, JOSEPH. "The Funeral Pyre and Human Decency: The Fate of Chancery in Bleak House." Di, 61 (1965), 57-62.

BROMHILL, KENTLEY. "Names and Labels." Di, 41 (1944/45), 92-93.

_____. "Phiz's Illustrations to Bleak House." Di, 40 (1943/44), 146-50, 192-95.

BURGAN, WILLIAM. "Tokens of Winter in Dickens's Pastoral Settings." MLQ, 36 (1975), 293-315.

BURKE, ALAN R. "The Strategy and Theme of Urban Observation in Bleak House." SEL, 9 (1969), 659-76.

BUTT, JOHN E. "Bleak House in the Context of 1851." NCF, 10 (1955), 1-21.

_____. "Bleak House Once More." CritQ, 1 (1959), 302-307.

CARLISLE, JANICE. "Dombey and Son: The Reader and the Present Tense." JNT, 1 (1971), 146-57.

CARLTON, W. J. "Miss Fray and Miss Flite." N&Q, 196 (1951), 521-22.

_____. "Mr. Blackmore Engages an Office Boy." Di, 48 (1951/52), 162-67.

CHARTIER, EMILE. "Rambling about Bleak House with a French-Speaking Canadian." Di, 40 (1943/44), 121-25, 207-10.

CHAUDHURI, BRAHMA. "Leonard Skimpole in Bleak House." DSN, 6 (1975), 75-78.

COLBURN, WILLIAM E. "Dickens and the 'Life-Illusion.'" Di, 54 (1958), 110-18.

COLLINS, PHILIP. "Bleak House and Dickens's Household Narrative." NCF, 14 (1960), 345-49.

_____. "Dickens and Punch." DiS, 3 (1967), 4-21.

Bibliography

_____. "Inspector Bucket Visits the Princess Puffer." Di, 60 (1964), 88-90.

_____. "Mr. Pardiggle in Bleak House." N&Q, 207 (1962), 150-51.

COOPERMAN, STANLEY. "Dickens and the Secular Blasphemy: Social Criticism in Hard Times, Little Dorrit, and Bleak House." CE, 22 (1960), 156-60.

COTTERELL, T. STURGE. "The Real Boythorn--Walter Savage Landor." Di, 44 (1947/48), 209-16.

COX, C. B. "A Dickens Landscape." CritQ, 2 (1960), 58-60.

CROMPTON, LOUIS. "Satire and Symbolism in Bleak House." NCF, 12 (1958), 284-303.

DEEN, LEONARD W. "Style and Unity in Bleak House." Criticism, 3 (1961), 206-18.

DELANEY, PAUL. "Bleak House and Doubting Castle." DSN, 3 (1972), 100-106.

DELESPINASSE, DORIS STRINGHAM. "The Significance of Dual Point of View in Bleak House." NCF, 23 (1968), 253-64.

DETTLEBACH, CYNTHIA. "Bird Imagery in Bleak House." Di, 59 (1963), 177-81.

DeVRIES, DUANE. "The Bleak House Page-Proofs: More Shavings from Dickens's Workshop." Di, 66 (1970), 3-7.

DODDS, M. H. "George Eliot and Charles Dickens." N&Q, 190 (1945), 143-45.

DONOVAN, ROBERT A. "Structure and Idea in Bleak House." ELH, 29 (1962), 175-201.

DUNN, RICHARD J. "Dickens and Mayhew Once More." NCF, 25 (1970), 348-53.

_____. "Esther's Role in Bleak House." Di, 62 (1966), 163-66.

_____. "Skimpole and Harthouse: The Dickens Character in Transition." DiS, 1 (1965), 121-28.

DUNSTAN, J. LESLIE. "The Ministers in Dickens." Di, 56 (1960), 103-13.

EIGNER, EDWIN M. and JOSEPH I. FRADIN. "Bulwer-Lytton and Dickens' Jo." NCF, 24 (1969), 98-102.

ERICKSEN, DONALD H. "Harold Skimpole: Dickens and the Early 'Art for Art's Sake' Movement." JEGP, 72 (1973), 48-59.

Bleak House

FARROW, ANTHONY. "The Cosmic Point of View in Bleak House." Cithara, 13 (May 1974), 34-45.

FIELDING, K. J. "Leigh Hunt and Skimpole: Another Remonstrance." Di, 64 (1968), 5-9.

_____. "Skimpole and Leigh Hunt Again." N&Q, 200 (1955), 174-75.

_____ and ALEC W. BRICE. "Charles Dickens on 'The Exclusion of Evidence'-I." Di, 64 (1968), 131-40; II. 65 (1969), 35-41.

FLIBBERT, JOSEPH T. "Bleak House and the Brothers Grimm." VN, 36 (Fall 1969), 1-5.

FOGLE, STEPHEN F. "Skimpole Once More." NCF, 7 (1952), 1-18.

FORD, GEORGE H. "The Titles for Bleak House." Di, 65 (1969), 84-89.

FRADIN, JOSEPH I. "Will and Society in Bleak House." PMLA, 81 (1966), 95-109.

FRANK, LAWRENCE. "'Through a Glass Darkly': Esther Summerson and Bleak House." DSA, 4 (1975), 91-112.

FRANKLIN, STEPHEN L. "Dickens and Time: The Clock Without Hands." DSA, 4 (1975), 1-35.

FRIEDMAN, NORMAN. "The Shadow and the Sun: Notes Toward a Reading of Bleak House." Boston University Studies in English, 3 (1957), 147-66.

GADD, W. LAURENCE. "The Dickens Touch." Di, 36 (1939/40), 181-85.

GALVIN, THOMAS J. "Mr. Vholes of Symond's Inn." Di, 64 (1968), 22-27.

GASKELL, E. "More About Spontaneous Combustion." Di, 69 (1973), 25-35.

GIBSON, FRANK A. "Hard on the Lawyers?" Di, 59 (1963), 160-64.

GIBSON, JOHN W. "Hard Times, A Further Note." DiS, 1 (1965), 90-101.

GILL, STEPHEN C. "Allusion in Bleak House: A Narrative Device." NCF, 22 (1967), 145-54.

GOWANS, IAN. "Letter to the Editor." Di, 69 (1973), 78.

GREEN, MURIEL M. "The Variety of Dickens's Bleak House." Library Review, 22 (1970), 363-67.

GRENANDER, M. E. "The Mystery and the Moral: Point of View in Dickens's Bleak House." NCF, 10 (1956), 301-305.

GROB, SHIRLEY. "Dickens and Some Motifs of the Fairy Tale." TSLL, 5 (1964), 567-79.

Bibliography

GRUNDY, DOMINICK E. "Growing Up Dickensian." L&P, 22 (1972), 99-106.

GUERARD, ALBERT J. "Bleak House: Structure and Style." SoR, N.S. 5 (1969), 332-49.

HAIGHT, GORDON S. "Dickens and Lewes on Spontaneous Combustion." NCF, 10 (1955), 53-63.

HAMER, DOUGLAS. "Dickens: The Old Court of Chancery." N&Q, 215 (1970), 341-47.

HARRIS, WENDELL V. "Jo at the Inquest and the Reports of Parliamentary Commissions." Di, 64 (1968), 48-49.

HAWES, DONALD. "Marryat and Dickens: A Personal and Literary Relationship." DSA, 2 (1972), 39-68.

HENLEY, E. F. "Charles Dickens on Aesthetic Distance and a Possible Dickens Influence." Language Quarterly of the University of South Florida, 5 (1966), 2-4.

HILL, T. W. "Hunt-Skimpole." Di, 41 (1944/45), 180-84.

_____. "Notes on Bleak House." Di, 40 (1943/44), 39-44, 65-70, 133-41.

HIRSCH, GORDON D. "The Mysteries in Bleak House: A Psychoanalytic Study." DSA, 4 (1975), 132-52.

JEFFERSON, D. W. "The Artistry of Bleak House." E&S, N.S. 27 (1974), 37-51.

JOHNSON, EDGAR. "Bleak House: The Anatomy of Society." NCF, 7 (1952), 73-89.

JUMP, JOHN D. "Dickens and His Readers." BJRL, 54 (1972), 384-97.

KELLEY, ALICE van BUREN. "The Bleak Houses of Bleak House." NCF, 25 (1970), 253-68.

KENNEY, BLAIR G. "Carlyle and Bleak House." Di, 66 (1970), 36-41.

KETTLE, ARNOLD. "Dickens and the Popular Tradition." Zeitschrift für Anglistik und Americanistik, 9 (1961), 229-52.

KILIAN, CRAWFORD. "In Defence of Esther Summerson." DR, 54 (1974), 318-28.

LANE, LAURIAT, JR. "Dickens and Melville: Our Mutual Friends." DR, 51 (1971), 315-31.

LEVINE, RICHARD A. "Dickens, the Two Nations, and Individual Possibility." SNNTS, 1 (1969), 157-80.

LOVETT, ROBERT W. "Mr. Spectator in Bleak House." Di, 59 (1963), 124.

Bleak House

LUCAS, JOHN. "Dickens and Arnold." RMS, 16 (1972), 86-111.

LUEDTKE, LUTHER S. "System and Sympathy: The Structural Dialectic of Dickens's Bleak House." LWU, 3 (1970), 1-14.

MANHEIM, LEONARD F. "Dickens' Fools and Madmen." DSA, 2 (1972), 69-97.

_____. "Floras and Doras: The Women in Dickens' Novels." TSLL, 7 (1965), 181-200.

_____. "The Law as 'Father.'" AI, 12 (1955), 17-23.

MARKS, PATRICIA. "O. Henry and Dickens: Elsie in the Bleak House of Moral Decay." ELN, 12 (1974), 35-37.

McCOY, CONSTANCE. "Another Interpretation of Esther's Dream." Di, 63 (1967), 181-82.

McCULLEN, MAURICE L. "Turveydrop of Bleak House: Basis of Dickens' Redefinition of Dandyism." DSN, 4 (1973), 15-21.

McLEAN, ROBERT SIMPSON. "Tory Noodles in Sydney Smith and Charles Dickens: An Unnoticed Parallel." VN, 38 (Fall 1970), 24-25.

McMASTER, R. D. "Dickens and the Horrific." DR, 38 (1958), 18-28.

_____. "Dickens, the Dandy, and the Savage: A Victorian View of the Romantic." SNNTS, 1 (1969), 133-46.

McNULTY, J. H. "Bleak House and Macbeth." Di, 40 (1943/44), 188-91.

MIDDLEBRO', TOM. "Esther Summerson: A Plea for Justice." QQ, 77 (1970), 252-59.

MILLER, J. HILLIS. "The Sources of Dickens's Comic Art: From American Notes to Martin Chuzzlewit." NCF, 24 (1970), 467-76.

MOERS, ELLEN. "Bleak House: The Agitating Women." Di, 69 (1973), 13-24.

MONOD, SYLVÈRE. "Esther Summerson, Charles Dickens, and the Reader of Bleak House." DiS, 5 (1969), 5-25.

_____. "'When the Battle's Lost and Won...': Dickens vs. the Compositors of Bleak House." Di, 69 (1973), 3-12.

MOTH, SUSAN. "The Light/Darkness/Sight Imagery in Bleak House." DiS, 1 (1965), 76-85.

NADELHAFT, JANICE. "The English Malady, Corrupted Humors, and Krook's Death." SNNTS, 1 (1969), 230-39.

OUSBY, IAN. "The Broken Glass: Vision and Comprehension in Bleak House." NCF, 29 (1975), 381-92.

PARKER, DOROTHY. "Allegory and the Extension of Mr. Bucket's Forefinger." ELN, 12 (1974), 31-35.

Bibliography

PASSERINI, EDWARD M. "'Jo's Will,' Chapter XLVII of <u>Bleak House</u>." <u>DiS</u>, 1 (1965), 27-33.

PEDERSON, WINNIFRED J. "Jo in <u>Bleak House</u>." <u>Di</u>, 60 (1964), 162-67.

PERKINS, GEORGE. "Death by Spontaneous Combustion in Marryat, Melville, Dickens, Zola, and Others." <u>Di</u>, 60 (1964), 57-63.

POOK, JOHN. "<u>Bleak House</u> and <u>Little Dorrit</u>: A Comparison." <u>AWR</u>, 19 (1970), 154-59.

QUIRK, EUGENE F. "Tulkinghorn's Buried Life: A Study of Character in <u>Bleak House</u>." <u>JEGP</u>, 72 (1973), 526-35.

ROBISON, ROSELEE. "Time, Death and the River in Dickens' Novels." <u>ES</u>, 53 (1972), 436-54.

RONALD, ANN. "Dickens' Gloomiest Gothic Castle." <u>DSN</u>, 6 (1975), 71-75.

ROOKE, ELEANOR. "Fathers and Sons in Dickens." <u>E&S</u>, N.S. 4 (1951), 53-69.

ROSSO, MARTHA. "Dickens and Esther." <u>Di</u>, 65 (1969), 90-94.

ROULET, ANN. "A Comparative Study of <u>Nicholas Nickleby</u> and <u>Bleak House</u>." <u>Di</u>, 60 (1964), 117-24.

SADOFF, DIANNE F. "Change and Changelessness in <u>Bleak House</u>." <u>VN</u>, 46 (Fall 1974), 5-10.

SCHACHTERLE, LANCE. "<u>Bleak House</u> as a Serial Novel." <u>DSA</u>, 1 (1970), 212-24.

SCHROCK, R. T. and TREVOR BLOUNT. "Not So Curious as We Seem: A Note on Krook's Calligraphy." <u>DSN</u>, 2 (1971), 121-23.

SCHWARZBACH, F. S. "A Note on <u>Bleak House</u>: John Jarndyce and the East Wind." <u>DSN</u>, 6 (1975), 82-84.

SHATTO, SUSAN. "New Notes on <u>Bleak House</u>." <u>DSN</u>, 6 (1975), 78-82, 108-15.

SMITH, ANNE G. M. "Dickens's Ironmaster Again Again." <u>EIC</u>, 22 (1972), 218-20.

_____. "The Ironmaster in <u>Bleak House</u>." <u>EIC</u>, 21 (1971), 159-69.

SMITH, MARY DAEHLER. "'All Her Perfections Tarnished': The Thematic Function of Esther Summerson." <u>VN</u>, 38 (Fall 1970), 10-14.

SMITH, SHEILA M. "Anti-Mechanism and the Comic in the Writings of Charles Dickens." <u>RMS</u>, 3 (1959), 131-44.

SORENSEN, KNUD. "Subjective Narration in <u>Bleak House</u>." <u>ES</u>, 40 (1959), 431-39.

Bleak House

STAPLES, L. C. "Bleak House and the Critics." Di, 41 (1944/45), 135-37.

_____. "On Chesney Wold." Di, 41 (1944/45), 80-81.

_____. "Shavings from Dickens's Workshop: Unpublished Fragments from the Novels. Pt. 5, Bleak House." Di, 50 (1953/54), 188-91.

STEELE, PETER. "Dickens and the Grotesque." Quadrant, 82 (1973), 15-23.

STEIG, MICHAEL. "The Critic and the Illustrated Novel." HLQ, 36 (1972), 55-67.

_____. "Dickens' Excremental Vision." VS, 13 (1970), 339-54.

_____. "The Iconography of the Hidden Face in Bleak House." DiS, 4 (1968), 19-22.

_____. "Structure and the Grotesque in Dickens: Dombey and Son; Bleak House." CentR, 14 (1970), 313-30.

_____. "The Whitewashing of Inspector Bucket: Origins and Parallels." PMASAL, 50 (1965), 575-84.

_____ and F. A. C. Wilson. "Hortense Versus Bucket: The Ambiguity of Order in Bleak House." MLQ, 33 (1972), 289-98.

STEVENSON, LIONEL. "Dickens's Dark Novels, 1851-1857." SR, 51 (1943), 398-409.

_____. "Who Was Mr. Turveydrop?" Di, 44 (1947/48), 39-41.

STOKES, E. "Bleak House and The Scarlet Letter." AUMLA, 32 (1969), 177-89.

STONE, HARRY. "Charles Dickens and Harriet Beecher Stowe." NCF, 12 (1957), 188-202.

SUCKSMITH, HARVEY PETER. "Dickens at Work on Bleak House: A Critical Examination of His Memoranda and Number Plans." RMS, 9 (1965), 47-85.

_____. "Sir Leicester Dedlock, Wat Tyler, and the Chartists: The Role of the Ironmaster in Bleak House." DSA, 4 (1975), 113-31.

SULLIVAN, A. E. "Soldiers of the Queen--and of Charles Dickens." Di, 46 (1949/50), 138-43.

DE SUZANNET, A. "Slomans; Another Dickens Original." Di, 36 (1939/40), 180.

TARR, RODGER L. "The 'Foreign Philanthropy Question' in Bleak House: A Carlylean Influence." SNNTS, 3 (1971), 275-83.

TOMLINSON, T. B. "Dickens and Individualism: Dombey and Son, Bleak House." Critical Review, 15 (1972), 64-81.

TYE, J. R. "Legal Caricature: Cruikshank Analogues to the Bleak House Cover." Di, 69 (1973), 39–41.

VAN GHENT, DOROTHY. "The Dickens World: A View from Todgers's." SR, 58 (1950), 419–38.

WALLINS, ROGER P. "Dickens and Decomposition." DSN, 5 (1974), 68–70.

WALTON, JAMES. "Conrad, Dickens, and the Detective Novel." NCF, 23 (1969), 446–62.

WEINSTEIN, PHILIP M. "Structure and Collapse: A Study of Bleak House." DiS, 4 (1968), 4–18.

WHITLEY, ALVIN. "Two Hints for Bleak House." Di, 52 (1955/56), 183–84.

WILEY, ELIZABETH. "Four Strange Cases." Di, 58 (1962), 120–25.

WILKINSON, ANN Y. "Bleak House: From Faraday to Judgement Day." ELH, 34 (1967), 225–47.

WILSON, ARTHUR H. "The Great Theme in Charles Dickens." Susquehanna University Studies, 6 (Apr.–June 1959), 422–57.

WILSON, EDMUND. "Dickens and the Marshalsea Prison." AM, 165 (1940), 473–83, 681–91.

WILSON, JOHN R. "Dickens and Christian Mystery." SAQ, 73 (1974), 528–40.

WINNER, ANTHONY. "Character and Knowledge in Dickens: The Enigma of Jaggers." DSA, 3 (1974), 100–21.

WOOLLIAMS, W. P. "Of and Concerning 'Jarndyce vs. Jarndyce.'" Di, 41 (1944/45), 26–29.

WORTH, GEORGE J. "The Genesis of Jo the Crossing-Sweeper." JEGP, 60 (1961), 44–47.

ZWERDLING, ALEX. "Esther Summerson Rehabilitated." PMLA, 88 (1973), 429–39.

Hard Times

Hard Times

CHARACTERIZATION

General: Benn, DSA, 1 (1970), 169-82; Berman, NCF, 22 (1967),
289-93; Dyson, Di, 65 (1969), 71-79; Gibson, DiS, 1 (1965),
92-95; Green, TSLL, 11 (1970), 1389-92; Harrison, Di, 39
(1942/43), 187-91; Hirsch, Criticism, 6 (1964), 6-15; Leavis,
Scrutiny, 14 (1947), 201-203; Smith, Mosaic, 5 (Winter 1972),
109-11; Di, 69 (1973), 153-62; Sonstroem, PMLA, 84 (1969),
521-29; Sullivan, VN, 38 (Fall 1970), 6-10; Winters, DSA, 2
(1972), 218.

Black vs. white types: Sullivan, VN, 38 (Fall 1970), 5-10.

Childhood: Hurley, VN, 42 (Fall 1972), 11-16.

Children: Winters, DSA, 2 (1972), 234-35.

Parents: Winters, DSA, 2 (1972), 232-34.

Symbols: Gibson, DiS, 1 (1965), 91-101.

CHARACTERS

Bitzer: Benn, DSA, 1 (1970), 173; Palmer, DR, 52 (1972), 70;
Sadrin, YES, 3 (1973), 202; (prototype): Sloane, DSN, 5
(1974), 9-11.

Blackpool, Mrs.: Winters, DSA, 2 (1972), 226.

Blackpool, Stephen: Benn, DSA, 1 (1970), 178-82; Hurley, VN, 42
(Fall 1972), 12-16; Johnson, DiS, 5 (1969), 75-80; Leavis,
Scrutiny, 14 (1947), 201; Lougy, DSA, 2 (1972), 242-44; Sadock,
DSA, 2 (1972), 212-13; Smith, JNT, 2 (1972), 159-69; Di, 69
(1973), 155-58; Sullivan, VN, 38 (Fall 1970), 7-8; Winters,
DSA, 2 (1972), 226-27, 228-31.

Bounderby, Josiah: Benn, DSA, 1 (1970), 170, 172-73; Ganz, DSA,
1 (1970), 36-37; Green, TSLL, 11 (1970), 1378-79; Hurley, VN,
42 (Fall 1972), 12-13; Johnson, DiS, 5 (1969), 71-72; Jump,
BJRL, 54 (1972), 391-92; Lougy, DSA, 2 (1972), 245-48; Sadrin,

Hard Times

YES, 3 (1973), 198-99; Sedgley, Critical Review, 16 (1973),
126-27; Smith, Di, 69 (1973), 153-55; Winters, DSA, 2 (1972),
221-22.

Gradgrind, Louisa: Benn, DSA, 1 (1970), 176-78; Bornstein, NCF,
26 (1971), 165-66, 167-68; Deneau, Di, 60 (1964), 173-77;
Gibson, DiS, 1 (1965), 93; Hirsch, Criticism, 6 (1964), 9-10,
12-15; Hurley, VN, 42 (Fall 1972), 12; Johnson, DiS, 5 (1969),
64-69; Leavis, Scrutiny, 14 (1947), 193-96; Lougy, DSA, 2
(1972), 245-46, 248-49; Meckier, SAQ, 71 (1972), 88-90; Palmer,
DR, 52 (1972), 69-70, 72-74; Sedgley, Critical Review, 16
(1973), 118-21; Sullivan, VN, 38 (Fall 1970), 7; Winters, DSA,
2 (1972), 224-26.

Gradgrind, Mrs.: Sedgley, Critical Review, 16 (1973), 123-24.

Gradgrind, Thomas: Benn, DSA, 1 (1970), 169-70, 173-76; Bornstein, NCF, 26 (1971), 163-65, 168-70; Gibson, DiS, 1 (1965),
94; Green, TSLL, 11 (1970), 1376-78; Hardy, VS, 5 (1961),
59-60; Leavis, Scrutiny, 14 (1947), 193-200; Meckier, SAQ, 71
(1972), 88-90; Palmer, DR, 52 (1972), 69-70, 75-77; Sadock,
DSA, 2 (1972), 213-14; Sadrin, YES, 3 (1973), 196-97, 200-205;
Sedgley, Critical Review, 16 (1973), 116-21; (prototype):
Page, N&Q, 216 (1971), 413.

Gradgrind, Tom: Bornstein, NCF, 26 (1971), 166; Deneau, Di, 60
(1964), 173-77; Hirsch, Criticism, 6 (1964), 9-10; Johnson,
DiS, 5 (1969), 69-70; Leavis, Scrutiny, 14 (1947), 196-99;
Sadock, DSA, 2 (1972), 214; Sadrin, YES, 3 (1973), 199;
Winters, DSA, 2 (1972), 222-24.

Harthouse, James: Dunn, DiS, 1 (1965), 122, 125-28; Dyson, Di,
65 (1969), 72-73; Johnson, DiS, 5 (1969), 70; Leavis, Scrutiny, 14 (1947), 202; Palmer, DR, 52 (1972), 68-69, 70.

Jupe: Winters, DSA, 2 (1972), 233-34.

Jupe, Sissy: Hirsch, Criticism, 6 (1964), 3-6, 10-15; Hurley,
VN, 42 (Fall 1972), 12; Leavis, Scrutiny, 14 (1947), 186-88,
192; Lougy, DSA, 2 (1972), 250-51; Meckier, SAQ, 71 (1972),
78-79; Nelson, DSA, 3 (1974), 46-47; Palmer, DR, 52 (1972),
75-76; Sadock, DSA, 2 (1972), 210-12; Sullivan, VN, 38 (Fall
1970), 6-7; Winters, DSA, 2 (1972), 234.

Kidderminster, Master: Winters, DSA, 2 (1972), 235.

Rachel: Johnson, DiS, 5 (1969), 74-75; Winters, DSA, 2 (1972),
227-28.

Slackbridge: Johnson, DiS, 5 (1969), 73-74; Smith, Di, 69
(1973), 158-60.

Sleary: Winters, DSA, 2 (1972), 233.

Sparsit, Mrs.: Lougy, DSA, 2 (1972), 248; Sadock, DSA, 2 (1972), 215; Sedgley, Critical Review, 16 (1973), 126-31.

COMPOSITION (See also TEXT)

General: Shusterman, Di, 53 (1957), 30-31.

Background: Boulton, Di, 50 (1953/54), 57-63; Stevenson, SR, 51 (1943), 399-403.

CRITICAL ASSESSMENT

General: Stevenson, SR, 51 (1943), 405-406; Wilson, Susquehanna University Studies, 6 (Apr.-June 1959), 445-47; (Leavis): Hirsch, Criticism, 6 (1964), 1-16; Sadock, DSA, 2 (1972), 208-15.

Contemporary reaction (Ludwig): Thomas, Hermathena, 111 (1971), 38.

Criticism, survey of: Gilmour, VS, 11 (1967), 207-208; Winters, DSA, 2 (1972), 219-20.

EXPLANATORY NOTES, HISTORICAL BACKGROUND, and SOURCES

Coketown library: Gilmour, Di, 63 (1967), 21-24.

Department of Practical Art: Fielding, MLR, 48 (1953), 272-77.

Education: Fielding, NCF, 11 (1956), 148-51.

Factory masters: Smith, Di, 69 (1973), 153-55.

Miscellaneous annotations: Hill, Di, 48 (1951/52), 134-41, 177-85.

Preston strike: Carnall, VS, 8 (1964), 31-48; Fielding, Di, 50 (1953/54), 159-62.

The Times, reports in: Smith, Di, 69 (1973), 153-62.

Topicality: Gilmour, VS, 11 (1967), 208-24.

Workers: Smith, Di, 69 (1973), 155-62.

INFLUENCES (See also LITERARY PARALLELS)

(on Dickens) General: Stevenson, SR, 51 (1943), 402; Carlyle: Dunn, DSN, 2 (1971), 90-92; 3 (1972), 60-61; Tarr, DSN, 3 (1972), 25-27; Gaskell, Ruth (and Gradgrind): Page, N&Q, 216

Hard Times

(1971), 413; Shakespeare, <u>King Lear</u>: Meckier, <u>SAQ</u>, 71 (1972), 75-79, 84, 88-90.

LANGUAGE and STYLE (<u>See also</u> TECHNIQUES, VARIOUS)

General: Green, <u>TSLL</u>, 11 (1970), 1376-96.

Allusion (classical, from <u>Agamemnon</u>): Szirotny, <u>N&Q</u>, 213 (1968), 421-22; 217 (1972), 30; (religious): Bornstein, <u>NCF</u>, 26 (1971), 167-70.

Chapter 1: Tick, <u>VN</u>, 46 (Fall 1974), 20-22.

Imagery: Johnson, <u>DiS</u>, 5 (1969), 62-80; (black vs. white): Sullivan, <u>VN</u>, 38 (Fall 1970), 5-10; (Coketown): Bornstein, <u>NCF</u>, 26 (1971), 159-62; Sedgley, <u>Critical Review</u>, 16 (1973), 121-22; (dark cavern and yawning abyss): Palmer, <u>DR</u>, 52 (1972), 71; (field and garden): Bornstein, <u>NCF</u>, 26 (1971), 158-70; (fire): Johnson, <u>DiS</u>, 5 (1969), 64-80; Lougy, <u>DSA</u>, 2 (1972), 245-46; Palmer, <u>DR</u>, 52 (1972), 72-74; (life vs. life-lessness): Sonstroem, <u>PMLA</u>, 84 (1969), 521-26; (light): Palmer, <u>DR</u>, 52 (1972), 70-75; (shipwreck): <u>ibid</u>., 68-70.

Irony (opening scene): Leavis, <u>Scrutiny</u>, 14 (1947), 186-88.

Metaphor: Benn, <u>DSA</u>, 1 (1970), 169-82; Crockett, <u>Spectrum</u>, 6 (1962), 80-81.

Rhetoric, sermon: Green, <u>TSLL</u>, 11 (1970), 1390-96.

Speech: Roll-Hansen, <u>Norwegian Studies in English</u>, 9 (1963), 213-14.

Symbolism: Berman, <u>NCF</u>, 22 (1967), 288-93; Hirsch, <u>Criticism</u>, 6 (1964), 2-15; (circus): Leavis, <u>Scrutiny</u>, 14 (1947), 188-92; (circus ring): Sadock, <u>DSA</u>, 2 (1972), 213-14.

LITERARY PARALLELS (<u>See also</u> INFLUENCES)

<u>Bleak House</u>: Gibson, <u>DiS</u>, 1 (1965), 96-101.

Gaskell, <u>Mary Barton</u>: Smith, <u>Mosaic</u>, 5 (Winter 1972), 98-112; <u>North and South</u>: Carnall, <u>VS</u>, 8 (1964), 43-47.

Mill on utilitarianism: Alexander, <u>Di</u>, 65 (1969), 163-70.

<u>Piers Plowman</u> (and Blackpool): Jones, <u>VN</u>, 33 (Spring 1968), 53-56.

POINT OF VIEW

    Narrator: Sonstroem, PMLA, 84 (1969), 521–29.

SETTING

    Coketown: Nelson, DSA, 3 (1974), 45–46; Sadrin, YES, 3 (1973),
       197–98; Smith, RMS, 8 (1964), 88–91; Van Ghent, SR, 58 (1950),
       424–25.

    World of novel: Dyson, Di, 65 (1969), 68–79; Lougy, DSA, 2
       (1972), 239–54; Sedgley, Critical Review, 16 (1973), 121–25;
       Smith, Mosaic, 5 (Winter 1972), 106–11; Sonstroem, PMLA, 84
       (1969), 521–29.

STRUCTURE/UNITY (See also PLOT)

    General: Coolidge, Mississippi Quarterly, 14 (Fall 1961),
       193–94; Sadrin, YES, 3 (1973), 196–205.

    Allegory: Benn, DSA, 1 (1970), 169–82.

    Moral fable: Leavis, Scrutiny, 14 (1947), 185–203.

    Romance: Lougy, DSA, 2 (1972), 237–54.

TECHNIQUES, VARIOUS

    General: Benn, DSA, 1 (1970), 168–82; Dyson, Di, 65 (1969),
       69–79; Gibson, DiS, 1 (1965), 90–101; Hirsch, Criticism, 6
       (1964), 1–16; Leavis, Scrutiny, 14 (1947), 185–203; Lincks,
       EJ, 58 (1969), 214–18; Lougy, DSA, 2 (1972), 237–54; Monod,
       Di, 64 (1968), 94–99; Smith, Mosaic, 5 (Winter 1972), 106–12;
       Sonstroem, PMLA, 84 (1969), 521–29.

    Autobiography, use of: Winters, DSA, 2 (1972), 218–19, 221–36.

TEXT (See also COMPOSITION)

    Cancelled passages from proofs: Woodings, Di, 60 (1964), 42–43.

    Composition and revisions: Monod, Di, 64 (1968), 87–99.

Hard Times

THEMES

General: Benn, DSA, 1 (1970), 168-82; Berman, NCF, 22 (1967), 288-93; Dyson, Di, 65 (1969), 70-79.

Amusements for poor: Collins, Di, 61 (1965), 7, 16-18.

Childhood/children: Hurley, VN, 42 (Fall 1972), 12-16; Winters, DSA, 2 (1972), 218-36.

Education: Gilmour, VS, 11 (1967), 211-24.

Fact/fancy antithesis: Sonstroem, PMLA, 84 (1969), 520-29.

Fancy and imagination: Collins, ES, 42 (1961), 79-90.

Fathers and sons: Rooke, E&S, N.S. 4 (1951), 63-64.

Industrialism: Brantlinger, NCF, 26 (1971), 279-85; (attitudes toward): Fielding and Smith, NCF, 24 (1970), 404-27.

Love (vs. self-interest): Lamb, Paunch, 33 (Dec. 1968), 34-36.

Man, radical redefinition of (psychological): Lougy, DSA, 2 (1972), 238-54.

Nature vs. antinature: Bornstein, NCF, 26 (1971), 159-70; Sullivan, VN, 38 (Fall 1970), 5-10.

Salvation: Palmer, DR, 52 (1972), 67-68, 75-77.

Self-interest: Deneau, Di, 60 (1964), 173-77.

Social criticism: Bornstein, NCF, 26 (1971), 159-70; Cooperman, CE, 22 (1960), 157, 159-60; Gibson, DiS, 1 (1965), 95-101; Leavis, Scrutiny, 14 (1947), 186-202; Smith, Mosaic, 5 (Winter 1972), 105-12; (society as abstraction): McMaster, EA, 23 (1970), 128-30.

Trade unionism: Brantlinger, VS, 13 (1969), 43-44, 48-49, 50-52.

Utilitarianism: Alexander, Di, 65 (1969), 163-70; Crockett, Spectrum, 6 (1962), 80-81; Gilmour, VS, 11 (1967), 212-24; Winters, DSA, 2 (1972), 217-18.

Bibliography for *Hard Times*

ALEXANDER, EDWARD. "Disinterested Virtue: Dickens and Mill in Agreement." Di, 65 (1969), 163-70.

BENN, J. MIRIAM. "A Landscape with Figures: Characterization and Expression in Hard Times." DSA, 1 (1970), 168-82.

BERMAN, RONALD. "The Human Scale: A Note on Hard Times." NCF, 22 (1967), 288-93.

BORNSTEIN, GEORGE. "Miscultivated Field and Corrupted Garden: Imagery in Hard Times." NCF, 26 (1971), 158-70.

BOULTON, J. T. "Charles Knight and Charles Dickens: Knowledge is Power and Hard Times." Di, 50 (1953/54), 57-63.

BRANTLINGER, PATRICK. "The Case Against Trade Unions in Early Victorian Fiction." VS, 13 (1969), 37-52.

_____. "Dickens and the Factories." NCF, 26 (1971), 270-85.

CARNALL, GEOFFREY. "Dickens, Mrs. Gaskell, and the Preston Strike." VS, 8 (1964), 31-48.

COLLINS, PHILIP. "Dickens and Popular Amusements." Di, 61 (1965), 7-19.

_____. "Queen Mab's Chariot Among the Steam Engines: Dickens and 'Fancy.'" ES, 42 (1961), 78-90.

COOLIDGE, ARCHIBALD C., JR. "Great Expectations: The Culmination of a Developing Art." Mississippi Quarterly, 14 (Fall 1961), 190-96.

COOPERMAN, STANLEY. "Dickens and the Secular Blasphemy: Social Criticism in Hard Times, Little Dorrit, and Bleak House." CE, 22 (1960), 156-60.

CROCKETT, JUDITH. "Theme and Metaphor in Hard Times." Spectrum, 6 (1962), 80-81.

DENEAU, DANIEL P. "The Brother-Sister Relationship in Hard Times." Di, 60 (1964), 173-77.

DUNN, RICHARD J. "Carlyle and That Hard Times Dedication." DSN, 3 (1972), 60-61.

Hard Times

_____. "Dickens, Carlyle, and the Hard Times Dedication." DSN, 2 (1971), 90-92.

_____. "Skimpole and Harthouse: The Dickens Character in Transition." DiS, 1 (1965), 121-28.

DYSON, A. E. "Hard Times: The Robber Fancy." Di, 65 (1969), 67-79.

FIELDING, K. J. "The Battle for Preston." Di, 50 (1953/54), 159-62.

_____. "Charles Dickens and the Department of Practical Art." MLR, 48 (1953), 270-77.

_____. "Mill and Gradgrind." NCF, 11 (1956), 148-51.

_____ and ANNE SMITH. "Hard Times and the Factory Controversy: Dickens vs. Harriet Martineau." NCF, 24 (1970), 404-27.

GANZ, MARGARET. "The Vulnerable Ego: Dickens' Humor in Decline." DSA, 1 (1970), 23-40.

GIBSON, JOHN W. "Hard Times, A Further Note." DiS, 1 (1965), 90-101.

GILMOUR, ROBIN. "The Gradgrind School: Political Economy in the Classroom." VS, 11 (1967), 207-24.

_____. "Manchester Men and Their Books." Di, 63 (1967), 21-24.

GREEN, ROBERT. "Hard Times: The Style of a Sermon." TSLL, 11 (1970), 1375-96.

HARDY, BARBARA. "The Change of Heart in Dickens' Novels." VS, 5 (1961), 49-67.

HARRISON, LEWIS. "Dickens's Shadow Show." Di, 39 (1942/43), 187-91.

HILL, T. W. "Notes on Hard Times." Di, 48 (1951/52), 134-41, 177-85.

HIRSCH, DAVID M. "Hard Times and Dr. Leavis." Criticism, 6 (1964), 1-16.

HURLEY, EDWARD. "A Missing Childhood in Hard Times." VN, 42 (Fall 1972), 11-16.

JOHNSON, ALAN P. "Hard Times: 'Performance' or 'Poetry'?" DiS, 5 (1969), 62-80.

JONES, FLORENCE. "Dickens and Langland in Adjudication upon Meed." VN, 33 (Spring 1968), 53-56.

JUMP, JOHN D. "Dickens and His Readers." BJRL, 54 (1972), 384-97.

LAMB, CEDRIC. "Love and Self-Interest in Dickens' Novels." Paunch, 33 (Dec. 1968), 32-47.

LEAVIS, F. R. "The Novel as Dramatic Poem." Scrutiny, 14 (1947), 185-203.

Bibliography

LINCKS, JOHN F. "The Close Reading of Hard Times." EJ, 58 (1969), 212-18.

LOUGY, ROBERT E. "Dickens' Hard Times: The Romance as Radical Literature." DSA, 2 (1972), 237-54.

McMASTER, R. D. "'Society (whatever that was)': Dickens and Society as Abstraction." EA, 23 (1970), 125-35.

MECKIER, JEROME. "Dickens and King Lear: A Myth for Victorian England." SAQ, 71 (1972), 75-90.

MONOD, SYLVÈRE. "Dickens at Work on the Text of Hard Times." Di, 64 (1968), 86-99.

NELSON, HARLAND S. "Staggs's Gardens: The Railway Through Dickens' World." DSA, 3 (1974), 41-53.

PAGE, NORMAN. "Ruth and Hard Times: A Dickens Source." N&Q, 216 (1971), 413.

PALMER, WILLIAM J. "Hard Times: A Dickens Fable of Personal Salvation." DR, 52 (1972), 67-77.

ROLL-HANSEN, DIDERIK. "Characters and Contrasts in Great Expectations." Norwegian Studies in English, 9 (1963), 197-226.

ROOKE, ELEANOR. "Fathers and Sons in Dickens." E&S, N.S. 4 (1951), 53-69.

SADOCK, GEOFFREY JOHNSTON. "Dickens and Dr. Leavis: A Critical Commentary on Hard Times." DSA, 2 (1972), 208-16.

SADRIN, ANNY. "A Plea for Gradgrind." YES, 3 (1973), 196-205.

SEDGLEY, ANNE. "Hard Times: Facts or Fantasy?" Critical Review, 16 (1973), 116-32.

SHUSTERMAN, DAVID. "Peter Cunningham, Friend of Dickens?" Di, 53 (1957), 20-35.

SLOANE, DAVID E. E. "Phrenology in Hard Times: A Source for Bitzer." DSN, 5 (1974), 9-12.

SMITH, ANNE G. M. "Hard Times and The Times Newspaper." Di, 69 (1973), 153-62.

_____. "The Martyrdom of Stephen in Hard Times." JNT, 2 (1972), 159-70.

SMITH, DAVID. "Mary Barton and Hard Times: Their Social Insights." Mosaic, 5 (Winter 1972), 97-112.

SMITH, SHEILA M. "Truth and Propaganda in the Victorian Social Problem Novel." RMS, 8 (1964), 75-91.

SONSTROEM, DAVID. "Fettered Fancy in Hard Times." PMLA, 84 (1969), 520-29.

Hard Times

STEVENSON, LIONEL. "Dickens's Dark Novels, 1851-1857." SR, 51 (1943), 398-409.

SULLIVAN, MARY ROSE. "Black and White Characters in Hard Times." VN, 38 (Fall 1970), 5-10.

SZIROTNY, J. S. "A Classical Reference in Hard Times and in Middlemarch." N&Q, 213 (1968), 421-22.

_____. "A Classical Reference in Hard Times and in Middlemarch." N&Q, 217 (1972), 30.

TARR, RODGER L. "Carlyle and the Problem of the Hard Times Dedication." DSN, 3 (1972), 25-27.

THOMAS, L. H. C. "Otto Ludwig and Charles Dickens: A German Reading of Great Expectations and Other Novels." Hermathena, 111 (1971), 35-50.

TICK, STANLEY. "Hard Times, Page One: An Analysis." VN, 46 (Fall 1974), 20-22.

VAN GHENT, DOROTHY. "The Dickens World: A View from Todgers's." SR, 58 (1950), 419-38.

WILSON, ARTHUR H. "The Great Theme in Charles Dickens." Susquehanna University Studies, 6 (Apr.-June 1959), 422-57.

WINTERS, WARRINGTON. "Dickens' Hard Times: The Lost Childhood." DSA, 2 (1972), 217-36.

WOODINGS, R. B. "A Cancelled Passage in Hard Times." Di, 60 (1964), 42-43.

Little Dorrit

Little Dorrit

CHARACTERIZATION

General: Barnard, ES, 52 (1971), 522-32; Barrett, NCF, 25
   (1970), 205-15; Bell, NCF, 20 (1965), 181-84; Burgan, TSLL,
   15 (1973), 111-28; Carlisle, SNNTS, 7 (1975), 198-211; Feltes,
   VS, 17 (1974), 363-67; Gervais, CQ, 4 (1969), 47-50; McMaster,
   QQ, 67 (1961), 533-37; Meckier, DiS, 3 (1967), 52-62; Trilling, KR, 15 (1953), 580-90; Wilde, NCF, 19 (1964), 38-44.

Female ideal: Woodward, Di, 71 (1975), 140.

Master/servant relationships: Fleishman, SEL, 14 (1974), 575-86.

Natural vs. artificial: McMaster, SNNTS, 1 (1969), 140-45.

Passions, use of: Hardy, NCF, 24 (1970), 461-63.

Psychological: Bergler, AI, 14 (1957), 378-88.

Through confinement: Reed, DSA, 1 (1970), 45-48.

Types: Burgan, TSLL, 15 (1973), 112.

CHARACTERS

Affery: Fleishman, SEL, 14 (1974), 577-78.

Barnacle, Ferdinand: Heatley, DSA, 4 (1975), 158-59.

Barnacles: Jump, Critical Survey, 1 (1963), 103-105.

Casby: Roopnaraine, DSA, 3 (1974), 68.

Chivery, John: McMaster, SNNTS, 1 (1969), 143; Roopnaraine, DSA,
   3 (1974), 70-71.

Clennam, Arthur: Barrett, NCF, 25 (1970), 205-208, 212-13;
   Bergler, AI, 14 (1957), 385-87; Carlisle, SNNTS, 7 (1975),
   205-207; Feltes, VS, 17 (1974), 364-67; Fleishman, SEL, 14
   (1974), 582-86; Gervais, CQ, 4 (1969), 43-46; Goodheart, Di,
   54 (1958), 36-37; Grove, MLR, 68 (1973), 750-55; Hardy, NCF,
   24 (1970), 461-62; Heatley, DSA, 4 (1975), 159-63; McMaster,

Little Dorrit

Plornish, Mrs.: Burgan, MLQ, 36 (1975), 300-302; McMaster,
   SNNTS, 1 (1969), 143-44; Roopnaraine, DSA, 3 (1974), 70-71.

Prostitute: Burgan, TSLL, 15 (1973), 113-16.

Rigaud/Blandois: Barrett, NCF, 25 (1970), 210-11; Trilling, KR,
   15 (1953), 582-84; (prototype): Sucksmith, Di, 71 (1975),
   76-82.

Tattycoram: Fleishman, SEL, 14 (1974), 576-77; Hardy, VS, 5
   (1961), 60-61; Tick, DSA, 3 (1974), 94-95; Woodward, Di, 71
   (1975), 144-45.

Wade, Miss: Barrett, NCF, 25 (1970), 211-12; Bergler, AI, 14
   (1957), 378-80; Fleishman, SEL, 14 (1974), 578; Heatley, DSA,
   4 (1975), 157-58; Thomas, DSA, 3 (1974), 135-36; Trilling,
   KR, 15 (1953), 584-85; Woodward, Di, 71 (1975), 143-48.

COMPOSITION (See also TEXT)

   Background: Stevenson, SR, 51 (1943), 399-403.

   Monthly number plans: Herring, MP, 64 (1966), 22-63.

CRITICAL ASSESSMENT

   General: Stevenson, SR, 51 (1943), 406-408; Wilson, Susquehanna
      University Studies, 6 (Apr.-June 1959), 447-48.

   Contemporary reaction (Ludwig): Thomas, Hermathena, 111 (1971),
      39.

   Dickens's theory of fiction: Carlisle, SNNTS, 7 (1975), 195-212.

EXPLANATORY NOTES, HISTORICAL BACKGROUND, and SOURCES

   Circumlocution Office: Stuart-Bunning, Di, 42 (1945/46), 35-38;
      (patronage): Burn, Nineteenth Century, 143 (1948), 98-101.

   "going down to...Dun Cow--to claim the flitch of bacon," Bk. II,
      Ch. XVI (identification): Magoun, Neuphilologische Mitteil-
      ungen, 72 (1971), 302.

   Marshalsea, life in (case of Giles Hemens): Easson, DSA, 3
      (1974), 77-80, 86.

   Miscellaneous annotations: Hill, Di, 41 (1944/45), 196-203; 42
      (1945/46), 38-44, 82-91.

Little Dorrit

Railway mania (in fact and in fiction): Smith and Smith, <u>Di</u>, 67
(1971), 131-44.

Topicality: Butt, <u>UTQ</u>, 29 (1959), 1-9.

ILLUSTRATIONS

"The pensioner entertainment" (peacock feathers indicate pride or
misfortune): Steig, <u>Ariel</u>, 4 (1973), 50.

INFLUENCES (<u>See also</u> LITERARY PARALLELS)

(Dickens on) Eliot and James: Leavis, <u>HudR</u>, 8 (1955), 423-38;
Wilde (Miss Prism and Mrs. General): Nethercot, <u>MD</u>, 6 (1963),
112-16; Zola: Atkins, <u>MLQ</u>, 8 (1947), 302-308.

(on Dickens) General: Stevenson, <u>SR</u>, 51 (1943), 402; <u>Black-</u>
<u>wood's</u>, Tale of Terror (and Merdle): Sucksmith, <u>NCF</u>, 26
(1971), 150; DeQuincey, <u>Confessions of an English Opium Eater</u>:
Woodhead, <u>N&Q</u>, 217 (1972), 409; psychopathological theory:
Manheim, <u>DSA</u>, 2 (1972), 89.

LANGUAGE and STYLE (<u>See also</u> TECHNIQUES, VARIOUS)

Allusion (Dr. Johnson): Savage, <u>Di</u>, 48 (1951/52), 42.

Euphemism and circumlocution: Meckier, <u>DiS</u>, 3 (1967), 59-62.

Imagery: Alter, <u>GaR</u>, 29 (1975), 51-53; Jump, <u>Critical Survey</u>, 1
(1963), 104-105; (infection and disease): Barrett, <u>NCF</u>, 25
(1970), 200-15; (labyrinth): Barnard, <u>ES</u>, 52 (1971), 523;
(masculine/feminine, conflict between): Heatley, <u>DSA</u>, 4
(1975), 156-64; (mechanization): Barnard, <u>ES</u>, 52 (1971),
525-27; ("pilgrimage of life"): <u>ibid</u>., 521-23; (prison):
<u>ibid</u>., 524-25, 530-32; Bergler, <u>AI</u>, 14 (1957), 371-73; (ship):
Meckier, <u>DiS</u>, 3 (1967), 56-58; (water): Robison, <u>ES</u>, 53
(1972), 447.

Metaphor (circle): Roopnaraine, <u>DSA</u>, 3 (1974), 54-76.

Monologue (interior): Kaplan, <u>NCF</u>, 23 (1968), 344-46.

Opening: Gervais, <u>CQ</u>, 4 (1969), 39-41.

Symbolism (Circumlocution Office): Meckier, <u>DiS</u>, 3 (1967),
59-62; (prison): Trilling, <u>KR</u>, 15 (1953), 578-81; (psychological imprisonment, Chapter 28): Grove, <u>MLR</u>, 68 (1973),
750-55.

LITERARY PARALLELS (See also INFLUENCES)

Bleak House: Pook, AWR, 19 (1970), 154-59.

Flora and Molly Bloom: Kaplan, NCF, 23 (1968), 344-46.

MacDonald, George, Phantastes: Crago, DiS, 5 (1969), 89-90.

Mayhew, The Great World of London: Sucksmith, NCF, 24 (1969), 347-49.

Shaw, Widowers' Houses: Rockman, Shaw Bulletin, 2 (1957), 8-10.

Smith, Sydney ("Noodle's Oration"): McLean, VN, 38 (Fall 1970), 24-25.

Zola, Thérèse Raquin: Atkins, MLQ, 8 (1947), 304-308.

PLOT (See also STRUCTURE/UNITY)

General: Carlisle, SNNTS, 7 (1975), 204-11.

End of novel: Levine, SNNTS, 1 (1969), 169-70.

Foreshadowing: Gadd, Di, 36 (1939/40), 181-82.

Moral growth: Wall, REL, 6 (Jan. 1965), 60-63.

Mystery, use of: Gibson, Di, 56 (1960), 178.

SETTING

Characters, use in: Burgan, TSLL, 15 (1973), 111-28.

Gothic elements (prison): Kirkpatrick, VN, 31 (Spring 1967), 21-22.

Italian scenes: Burgan, NCF, 29 (1975), 393-411.

Pastoral, use of (Plornishes' shop): Burgan, MLQ, 36 (1975), 300-302.

World of novel: Barrett, NCF, 25 (1970), 201-15; Gervais, CQ, 4 (1969), 39-53; Heatley, DSA, 4 (1975), 154-64; McNulty, Di, 45 (1948/49), 36-38; Reed, DSA, 1 (1970), 45-48; Roopnaraine, DSA, 3 (1974), 55-76; (savage): Barnard, ES, 52 (1971), 527-30.

STRUCTURE/UNITY (See also PLOT)

General: Gervais, CQ, 4 (1969), 50-51.

Analogical: Wilde, NCF, 19 (1964), 37-44.

Little Dorrit

Circularity: Roopnaraine, DSA, 3 (1974), 56-76.

Romance (myth and imagery): McMaster, QQ, 67 (1961), 532-38.

Variation (contrast): Meckier, DiS, 3 (1967), 51-62.

TECHNIQUES, VARIOUS

General: Gervais, CQ, 4 (1969), 39-53; Wilde, NCF, 19 (1964), 33-44; Wilson, AM, 165 (1940), 687-91.

Appearance vs. reality: Levine, SNNTS, 1 (1969), 163-65.

Chance encounters: Burgan, TSLL, 15 (1973), 113-22.

Growth and diffusion of rumor: Briggs, JFI, 7 (1970), 6-8.

January-May motif: Manning, Di, 71 (1975), 69-70.

Psychic masochism, use of: Bergler, AI, 14 (1957), 372-88.

TEXT (See also COMPOSITION and PUBLICATION)

Unpublished material (from corrected proofs): Staples, Di, 49 (1952/53), 169-74.

THEMES

General: Bell, NCF, 20 (1965), 177-84; Meckier, DiS, 3 (1967), 51-62; Stevenson, SR, 51 (1943), 406-407; Wilson, AM, 165 (1940), 687-91.

Community: Burgan, TSLL, 15 (1973), 112-28.

Confinement: Reed, DSA, 1 (1970), 45-48.

Disease and infection: Barrett, NCF, 25 (1970), 200-15.

Futility: Roopnaraine, DSA, 3 (1974), 59-61.

Imprisonment: Kirkpatrick, VN, 31 (Spring 1967), 22-23; Meckier, DiS, 3 (1967), 51-53; Trilling, KR, 15 (1953), 578-81.

Individual possibility: Levine, SNNTS, 1 (1969), 169-70.

Industrialism: Brantlinger, NCF, 26 (1971), 272-73, 278-79.

Liability: Feltes, VS, 17 (1974), 364-67.

Parent/child relationships: Adrian, Di, 67 (1971), 7-8.

Parenthood (delinquent): Trilling, KR, 15 (1953), 585-86.

Personal liberation: Fleishman, SEL, 14 (1974), 576-86.

Little Dorrit

Religion: Heatley, <u>DSA</u>, 4 (1975), 153-64.

Responsibility: Meckier, <u>DiS</u>, 3 (1967), 54-56.

Sexuality: Woodward, <u>Di</u>, 71 (1975), 140-48.

Social criticism: Cooperman, <u>CE</u>, 22 (1960), 158-60; Pook, <u>AWR</u>, 19 (1970), 157-59; (Circumlocution Office): Jump, <u>Critical Survey</u>, 1 (1963), 103-106; (society as abstraction): McMaster, <u>EA</u>, 23 (1970), 131-33; (society vs. the human will): Trilling, <u>KR</u>, 15 (1953), 578-90; (the Two Nations): Levine, <u>SNNTS</u>, 1 (1969), 163-65.

Tenant-landlord relations: Fielding, <u>Di</u>, 61 (1965), 157-58.

Time: Roopnaraine, <u>DSA</u>, 3 (1974), 61-75.

Bibliography for *Little Dorrit*

ADRIAN, ARTHUR A. "Dickens and Inverted Parenthood." Di, 67 (1971), 3-11.

ALTER, ROBERT. "History and Imagination in the Nineteenth Century Novel." GaR, 29 (1975), 42-60.

ATKINS, STUART. "A Possible Dickens Influence in Zola." MLQ, 8 (1947), 302-308.

BARNARD, ROBERT. "The Imagery of Little Dorrit." ES, 52 (1971), 520-32.

BARRETT, EDWIN B. "Little Dorrit and the Disease of Modern Life." NCF, 25 (1970), 199-215.

BELL, VEREEN M. "Mrs. General as Victorian England: Dickens's Image of His Times." NCF, 20 (1965), 177-84.

BERGLER, EDMUND. "Little Dorrit and Dickens' Intuitive Knowledge of Psychic Masochism." AI, 14 (1957), 371-88.

BRANTLINGER, PATRICK. "Dickens and the Factories." NCF, 26 (1971), 270-85.

BRIGGS, KATHARINE M. "The Folklore of Charles Dickens." JFI, 7 (1970), 3-20.

BURGAN, WILLIAM. "Little Dorrit in Italy." NCF, 29 (1975), 393-411.

_____. "People in the Setting of Little Dorrit." TSLL, 15 (1973), 111-28.

_____. "Tokens of Winter in Dickens's Pastoral Settings." MLQ, 36 (1975), 293-315.

BURN, W. L. "The Neo-Barnacles." Nineteenth Century, 143 (1948), 98-103.

BUTT, JOHN E. "The Topicality of Little Dorrit." UTQ, 29 (1959), 1-10.

CARLISLE, JANICE. "Little Dorrit: Necessary Fictions." SNNTS, 7 (1975), 195-214.

Little Dorrit

COLBURN, WILLIAM E. "Dickens and the 'Life-Illusion.'" Di, 54 (1958), 110-18.

COLLINS, PHILIP. "Dickens on the Education of Girls." Di, 57 (1961), 86-96.

COOPERMAN, STANLEY. "Dickens and the Secular Blasphemy: Social Criticism in Hard Times, Little Dorrit, and Bleak House." CE, 22 (1960), 156-60.

CRAGO, H. "Charles Dickens and George MacDonald: A Note." DiS, 5 (1969), 86-90.

DARROLL, G. M. H. "A Note on Dickens and Maria Beadnell, and Dickens's Comic Genius." ESA, 7 (1964), 82-87.

EASSON, ANGUS. "Marshalsea Prisoners." DSA, 3 (1974), 77-86.

FELTES, N. N. "Community and the Limits of Liability in Two Mid-Victorian Novels." VS, 17 (1974), 355-69.

FIELDING, K. J. "Dickens's Work with Miss Coutts: I. Nova Scotia Gardens and What Grew There." Di, 61 (1965), 112-19; "II. Casby and the Westminster Landlords," 155-60.

FLEISHMAN, AVROM. "Master and Servant in Little Dorrit." SEL, 14 (1974), 575-86.

GADD, W. LAURENCE. "The Dickens Touch." Di, 36 (1939/40), 181-85.

GANZ, MARGARET. "The Vulnerable Ego: Dickens' Humor in Decline." DSA, 1 (1970), 23-40.

GERVAIS, DAVID. "The Poetry of Little Dorrit." CQ, 4 (1969), 38-53.

GIBSON, FRANK A. "Mysteries in Dickens." Di, 56 (1960), 176-78.

GOODHEART, EUGENE. "Dickens's Method of Characterization." Di, 54 (1958), 35-37.

GROVE, T. N. "The Psychological Prison of Arthur Clennam in Dickens's Little Dorrit." MLR, 68 (1973), 750-55.

HARDY, BARBARA. "The Change of Heart in Dickens' Novels." VS, 5 (1961), 49-67.

_____. "Dickens and the Passions." NCF, 24 (1970), 449-66.

_____. "Dickens's Storytellers." Di, 69 (1973), 71-78.

HEATLEY, EDWARD. "The Redeemed Feminine of Little Dorrit." DSA, 4 (1975), 153-64.

HERRING, PAUL D. "Dickens' Monthly Number Plans for Little Dorrit." MP, 64 (1966), 22-63.

HILL, T. W. "Notes on Little Dorrit." Di, 41 (1944/45), 196-203; 42 (1945/46), 38-44, 82-91.

Bibliography

JUMP, JOHN D. "Clennam at the Circumlocution Office: An Analysis." Critical Survey, 1 (1963), 103-106.

KAPLAN, FRED. "Dickens' Flora Finching and Joyce's Molly Bloom." NCF, 23 (1968), 343-46.

KIRKPATRICK, LARRY. "The Gothic Flame of Charles Dickens." VN, 31 (Spring 1967), 20-24.

LEAVIS, Q. D. "A Note on Literary Indebtedness: Dickens, George Eliot, Henry James--." HudR, 8 (1955), 423-28.

LEVINE, RICHARD A. "Dickens, the Two Nations, and Individual Possibility." SNNTS, 1 (1969), 157-80.

MAGOUN, F. P., JR. "Charles Dickens: Two Analogues." Neuphilologische Mitteilungen, 72 (1971), 302-303.

MANHEIM, LEONARD F. "Dickens' Fools and Madmen." DSA, 2 (1972), 69-97.

MANNING, SYLVIA. "Dickens, January, and May." Di, 71 (1975), 67-75.

McLEAN, ROBERT SIMPSON. "Tory Noodles in Sydney Smith and Charles Dickens: An Unnoticed Parallel." VN, 38 (Fall 1970), 24-25.

McMASTER, R. D. "Dickens, the Dandy, and the Savage: A Victorian View of the Romantic." SNNTS, 1 (1969), 133-46.

_____. "Little Dorrit: Experience and Design." QQ, 67 (1961), 530-38.

_____. "'Society (whatever that was)': Dickens and Society as Abstraction." EA, 23 (1970), 125-35.

McNULTY, J. H. "On the Alleged Gloominess of Little Dorrit." Di, 45 (1948/49), 36-38.

MECKIER, JEROME. "Dickens's Little Dorrit: 'Sundry Curious Variations on the Same Tune.'" DiS, 3 (1967), 51-62.

NETHERCOT, ARTHUR H. "Prunes and Miss Prism." MD, 6 (1963), 112-16.

POOK, JOHN. "Bleak House and Little Dorrit: A Comparison." AWR, 19 (1970), 154-59.

REED, JOHN R. "Confinement and Character in Dickens' Novels." DSA, 1 (1970), 41-54.

ROBISON, ROSELEE. "Time, Death and the River in Dickens' Novels." ES, 53 (1972), 436-54.

ROCKMAN, ROBERT E. "Dickens and Shaw: Another Parallel." Shaw Bulletin, 2 (1957), 8-10.

ROLL-HANSEN, DIDERIK. "Characters and Contrasts in Great Expectations." Norwegian Studies in English, 9 (1963), 197-226.

Little Dorrit

ROOPNARAINE, R. RUPERT. "Time and the Circle in Little Dorrit."
    DSA, 3 (1974), 54-76.

SAVAGE, OLIVER D. "Johnson and Dickens: A Comparison." Di, 48
    (1951/52), 42-44.

SIPE, SAMUEL M. "The Intentional World of Dickens's Fiction." NCF,
    30 (1975), 1-19.

SMITH, GRAHAME and ANGELA SMITH. "Dickens as a Popular Artist." Di,
    67 (1971), 131-44.

STAPLES, L. C. "Shavings from Dickens's Workshop: Unpublished Frag-
    ments from the Novels. III. Little Dorrit." Di, 49 (1952/53),
    169-74.

STEIG, MICHAEL. "Cruikshank's Peacock Feathers in Oliver Twist."
    Ariel, 4 (1973), 49-53.

STEVENSON, LIONEL. "Dickens's Dark Novels, 1851-1857." SR, 51
    (1943), 398-409.

STUART-BUNNING, G. H. "The Circumlocution Office." Di, 42 (1945/46),
    35-38.

SUCKSMITH, HARVEY PETER. "Dickens and Mayhew: A Further Note."
    NCF, 24 (1969), 345-49.

_____. "The Melodramatic Villain in Little Dorrit." Di, 71 (1975),
    76-83.

_____. "The Secret of Immediacy: Dickens' Debt to the Tale of Ter-
    ror in Blackwood's." NCF, 26 (1971), 145-57.

THOMAS, DEBORAH A. "The Equivocal Explanation of Dickens' George
    Silverman." DSA, 3 (1974), 134-43.

THOMAS, L. H. C. "Otto Ludwig and Charles Dickens: A German Reading
    of Great Expectations and Other Novels." Hermathena, 111 (1971),
    35-50.

TICK, STANLEY. "The Sad End of Mr. Meagles." DSA, 3 (1974), 87-99.

TRILLING, LIONEL. "Little Dorrit." KR, 15 (1953), 577-90.

WALL, STEPHEN. "Dickens's Plot of Fortune." REL, 6 (Jan. 1965),
    56-67.

WILDE, ALAN. "Mr. F.'s Aunt and the Analogical Structure of Little
    Dorrit." NCF, 19 (1964), 33-44.

WILSON, ARTHUR H. "The Great Theme in Charles Dickens." Susquehanna
    University Studies, 6 (Apr.-June 1959), 422-57.

WILSON, EDMUND. "Dickens and the Marshalsea Prison." AM, 165
    (1940), 473-83, 681-91.

WINNER, ANTHONY. "Character and Knowledge in Dickens: The Enigma of Jaggers." <u>DSA</u>, 3 (1974), 100-21.

WOODHEAD, M. R. "DeQuincey and <u>Little Dorrit</u>." <u>N&Q</u>, 217 (1972), 409.

WOODWARD, KATHLEEN. "Passivity and Passion in <u>Little Dorrit</u>." <u>Di</u>, 71 (1975), 140-48.

A Tale of Two Cities

A Tale of Two Cities

CHARACTERIZATION

General: Manheim, DSA, 1 (1970), 230-35; Monod, NCF, 24 (1970), 497-501.

Doubling: Hardy, VS, 5 (1961), 52-53.

Father-figures: Manheim, DSA, 1 (1970), 233-35.

CHARACTERS

Carton, Sydney: Collins, DSA, 2 (1972), 345-49; Hardy, VS, 5 (1961), 52-53; Harvey, NCF, 24 (1969), 310-12; Manheim, DSA, 1 (1970), 230-31; Monod, NCF, 24 (1970), 498-500; Robison, ES, 53 (1972), 444; (prototype): Ryan, DiS, 2 (1966), 147-51.

Darnay, Charles: Manheim, DSA, 1 (1970), 230-31; Monod, NCF, 24 (1970), 498-99.

Manette, Dr.: Manheim, DSA, 1 (1970), 234-35.

Manette, Lucie: Manheim, DSA, 1 (1970), 231-33.

Stryver: Monod, NCF, 24 (1970), 500-501; (prototype): Ryan, DiS, 2 (1966), 148-49.

COMPOSITION

Background: Manheim, DSA, 1 (1970), 226-35.

CRITICAL ASSESSMENT

General: Wilson, Susquehanna University Studies, 6 (Apr.-June 1959), 448-51.

Contemporary reaction: Collins, DSA, 2 (1972), 336-37.

Position in career: Collins, DSA, 2 (1972), 336-47, 349.

A Tale of Two Cities

EXPLANATORY NOTES, HISTORICAL BACKGROUND, and SOURCES

Carlyle, French Revolution: Stange, EJ, 46 (1957), 383-85.

Miscellaneous annotations: Hill, Di, 41 (1944/45), 68-74, 129-35.

Mob violence, attitude toward: Oddie, Di, 68 (1972), 3-15.

Plot: Dolmetsch, Di, 55 (1959), 179-87.

Wine drinking (Chapter 5): McCelvey, N&Q, 206 (1961), 96-97.

INFLUENCES (See also LITERARY PARALLELS)

(Dickens on) Griffith, D. W.: Zambrano, Lang&S, 7 (1974), 53-61.

LANGUAGE and STYLE (See also TECHNIQUES, VARIOUS)

Imagery (river): Robison, ES, 53 (1972), 443-44.

Symbolism: Alter, Novel, 2 (1969), 136-42; Marshall, Di, 57 (1961), 185-89.

LITERARY PARALLELS (See also INFLUENCES)

Disraeli, Sybil (characters): Arnold, Di, 63 (1967), 26-31.

Eisenstein (structure and characterization): Zambrano, Style, 9 (1975), 481-87.

Phillips, The Dead Heart: Dolmetsch, Di, 55 (1959), 179-87.

The Terrific Register: McMaster, DR, 38 (1958), 20-21.

Twain, Huckleberry Finn: Blair, MP, 55 (1957), 22-26, 32-33.

PLOT (See also STRUCTURE/UNITY)

End of novel: Alter, Novel, 2 (1969), 141-42.

Foreshadowing: Gadd, Di, 36 (1939/40), 183-84.

POINT OF VIEW

Authorial intrusion: Monod, NCF, 24 (1970), 501-505.

Three narrators: Monod, NCF, 24 (1970), 491-97.

Subject Index

SETTING

    World of novel: Alter, <u>Novel</u>, 2 (1969), 136-42; Gibson, <u>Di</u>, 60
    (1964), 30-32.

STRUCTURE/UNITY (<u>See also</u> PLOT)

    General: Marshall, <u>Di</u>, 57 (1961), 183-89.

    Allegory: Alter, <u>Novel</u>, 2 (1969), 138-39, 140-41.

    Montage: Zambrano, <u>Style</u>, 9 (1975), 473-76.

TECHNIQUES, VARIOUS

    General: Alter, <u>Novel</u>, 2 (1969), 135-42; Manheim, <u>DSA</u>, 1 (1970),
    230-31; Stange, <u>EJ</u>, 46 (1957), 385-90; Zambrano, <u>Lang&S</u>, 7
    (1974), 54-55, 57, 59-60.

    Life/death antithesis: Marshall, <u>Di</u>, 57 (1961), 184-89.

    Speech (Old Bailey speech): Gregory, <u>REL</u>, 6 (Apr. 1965), 43-55.

THEMES

    Fear for England: Arnold, <u>Di</u>, 63 (1967), 30-31.

    Violence: Alter, <u>Novel</u>, 2 (1969), 137-38, 140-42.

Bibliography for
A Tale of Two Cities

ALTER, ROBERT. "The Demons of History in Dickens' Tale." Novel, 2 (1969), 135-42.

ARNOLD, BETH R. "Disraeli and Dickens on Young England." Di, 63 (1967), 26-31.

BLAIR, WALTER. "The French Revolution and Huckleberry Finn." MP, 55 (1957), 21-35.

COLLINS, PHILIP. "A Tale of Two Novels: A Tale of Two Cities and Great Expectations in Dickens' Career." DSA, 2 (1972), 336-51.

DOLMETSCH, CARL R. "Dickens and The Dead Heart." Di, 55 (1959), 179-87.

GADD, W. LAURENCE. "The Dickens Touch." Di, 36 (1939/40), 181-85.

GIBSON, FRANK A. "The Saddest Book." Di, 60 (1964), 30-32.

GREGORY, MICHAEL. "Old Bailey Speech in A Tale of Two Cities." REL, 6 (Apr. 1965), 42-55.

HARDY, BARBARA. "The Change of Heart in Dickens' Novels." VS, 5 (1961), 49-67.

HARVEY, WILLIAM R. "Charles Dickens and the Byronic Hero." NCF, 24 (1969), 305-16.

HILL, T. W. "Notes on A Tale of Two Cities." Di, 41 (1944/45), 68-74, 129-35.

MANHEIM, LEONARD F. "A Tale of Two Characters: A Study in Multiple Projection." DSA, 1 (1970), 225-37.

MARSHALL, WILLIAM H. "The Method of A Tale of Two Cities." Di, 57 (1961), 183-89.

McCELVEY, GEORGE. "A Tale of Two Cities and Gin Drinking." N&Q, 206 (1961), 96-97.

McMASTER, R. D. "Dickens and the Horrific." DR, 38 (1958), 18-28.

MONOD, SYLVÈRE. "Dickens's Attitudes in A Tale of Two Cities." NCF, 24 (1970), 488-505.

A Tale of Two Cities

ODDIE, WILLIAM. "Dickens and the Indian Mutiny." <u>Di</u>, 68 (1972), 3-15.

ROBISON, ROSELEE. "Time, Death and the River in Dickens' Novels." <u>ES</u>, 53 (1972), 436-54.

RYAN, J. S. "<u>A Tale of Two Cities</u>: London and Wellington." <u>DiS</u>, 2 (1966), 147-51.

STANGE, G. ROBERT. "Dickens and the Fiery Past: <u>A Tale of Two Cities</u> Reconsidered." <u>EJ</u>, 46 (1957), 381-90.

WILSON, ARTHUR H. "The Great Theme in Charles Dickens." <u>Susquehanna University Studies</u>, 6 (Apr.-June 1959), 422-57.

ZAMBRANO, ANA LAURA. "Charles Dickens and Sergei Eisenstein: The Emergence of Cinema." <u>Style</u>, 9 (1975), 469-87.

_____. "The Styles of Dickens and Griffith: <u>A Tale of Two Cities</u> and <u>Orphans of the Storm</u>." <u>Lang&S</u>, 7 (1974), 53-61.

Great Expectations

Great Expectations

CHARACTERIZATION

General: Barry, Di, 64 (1968), 44-46; Bell, VN, 27 (Spring 1965), 21-24; Connolly, PQ, 34 (1955), 53-55; French, EIC, 24 (1974), 147-49, 160-61, 165-68; Goldfarb, VN, 21 (Spring 1962), 18-19; Hagan, NCF, 9 (1954), 170-74; ELH, 21 (1954), 60-65; Hallam, DiS, 2 (1966), 26-33; Hardy, EIC, 13 (1963), 351-63; Hynes, ELH, 30 (1963), 259-92; Jones, SWR, 39 (1954), 331-35; Levine, NCF, 18 (1963), 177-81; Marcus, VN, 26 (Fall 1964), 9-12; DiS, 2 (1966), 57-73; Marshall, Personalist, 44 (1963), 338-47; McWilliams, DSA, 2 (1972), 257-65; Millhauser, DSA, 2 (1972), 268-76; Moynahan, EIC, 10 (1960), 64-77; New, DiS, 3 (1967), 113-21; Stange, CE, 16 (1954), 10-17; Stone, KR, 24 (1962), 669-90; Wentersdorf, NCF, 21 (1966), 203-24; Wolfe, SAQ, 73 (1974), 340-42.

Contrasts: Stone, KR, 24 (1962), 668-90.

Doubling: Dunn, Di, 63 (1967), 125-27; Wentersdorf, NCF, 21 (1966), 203-24.

Fathers: Barnard, DSA, 1 (1970), 247-50; Lelchuk, SR, 78 (1970), 412-16.

Hands, use of: Forker, TSLL, 3 (1961), 280-93.

Passions, use of: Hardy, NCF, 24 (1970), 463-66.

Self-alienation: Marcus, VN, 26 (Fall 1964), 9-12.

Through imagery: New, DiS, 3 (1967), 113-21.

Through language: Vande Kieft, NCF, 15 (1961), 325-32.

Women (and eating): Watt, DSA, 3 (1974), 172-73.

CHARACTERS

Avenger (Pepper): Wentersdorf, NCF, 21 (1966), 214-16.

Coiler, Mrs.: Rosenberg, Di, 69 (1973), 90-100.

Great Expectations

Compeyson: Axton, DSA, 2 (1972), 287-89; Marcus, VN, 26 (Fall 1964), 11.

Drummle, Bentley: Dunn, Di, 63 (1967), 125-27; French, EIC, 24 (1974), 165-66; Marcus, VN, 26 (Fall 1964), 11; Moynahan, EIC, 10 (1960), 73-74; Wentersdorf, NCF, 21 (1966), 211-13, 217-18.

Estella: Emmett, North Dakota Quarterly, 41 (Autumn 1973), 6-7; French, EIC, 24 (1974), 151-58, 160; Marcus, VN, 26 (Fall 1964), 10; Millhauser, DSA, 2 (1972), 269, 273-74; Shores, MSE, 3 (1972), 91-99; Smith, Thoth, 12 (Fall 1971), 13-17; Stange, CE, 16 (1954), 13.

Gargery, Joe: Barnard, DSA, 1 (1970), 247-48; Franklin, DSA, 4 (1975), 30-31; French, EIC, 24 (1974), 150-51; Marshall, Personalist, 44 (1963), 339-40; New, DiS, 3 (1967), 113; Stange, CE, 16 (1954), 13-14; Talon, VN, 42 (Fall 1972), 8-9; Vande Kieft, NCF, 15 (1961), 326-30; Wolfe, SAQ, 73 (1974), 341-42.

Gargery, Mrs. Joe: Axton, DSA, 2 (1972), 280-82; Carolan, DR, 52 (1972), 375-77; French, EIC, 24 (1974), 161, 166-67; Lindberg, CE, 23 (1961), 118-22; New, DiS, 3 (1967), 113.

Havisham, Miss: Axton, DSA, 2 (1972), 289-91; Colburn, Di, 54 (1958), 116-17; Connolly, PQ, 34 (1955), 53-54; Drew, Di, 52 (1955/56), 124-27; French, EIC, 24 (1974), 154-59, 160, 163; Hardy, VS, 5 (1961), 62-63; House, Di, 44 (1947/48), 69-70; Jones, SWR, 39 (1954), 333-35; Lelchuk, SR, 78 (1970), 423-25; Marcus, VN, 26 (Fall 1964), 10; New, DiS, 3 (1967), 116-18; Stange, CE, 16 (1954), 13; Talon, DSA, 3 (1974), 131-32; Tate, SoRA, 7 (1974), 161-63; Van Ghent, SR, 58 (1950), 422-23; (genesis): Meisel, PMLA, 81 (1966), 278-85; (prototype): Fraser, NCF, 9 (1955), 301-307; Friedman, VN, 39 (Spring 1971), 24-25; Hutchings, Di, 61 (1965), 97-100; Ryan, Australian Literary Studies, 1 (1963), 134-36; Stone, NCF, 10 (1955), 85-86; VN, 33 (Spring 1968), 5-8.

Jaggers: Dessner, Ariel, 6 (Apr. 1975), 68-71, 72; Dilnot, EIC, 25 (1975), 437-42; Gordon, Di, 65 (1969), 3-11; Grundy, L&P, 22 (1972), 104; Hagan, NCF, 9 (1954), 178; Hardy, NCF, 24 (1970), 465-66; Di, 69 (1973), 75; Lane, DR, 51 (1971), 321; Lelchuk, SR, 78 (1970), 414-16, 420-21; Lucas, RMS, 16 (1972), 98-99, 100; Marcus, VN, 26 (Fall 1964), 11; Marshall, Personalist, 44 (1963), 340; Stange, CE, 16 (1954), 15-16; Tate, SoRA, 7 (1974), 159; Winner, DSA, 3 (1974), 100-102, 110-18, 120-21.

Magwitch, Abel: Axton, DSA, 2 (1972), 288-89, 292; Barnard, DSA, 1 (1970), 249-50; Drew, Di, 52 (1955/56), 125-27; Emmett, North Dakota Quarterly, 41 (Autumn 1973), 7-9; French, EIC, 24 (1974), 164-65; Goldfarb, VN, 21 (Spring 1962), 18-19; Grundy, L&P, 22 (1972), 103; Hagan, NCF, 9 (1954), 170-71; Lelchuk,

Great Expectations

   Pocket, Herbert: Wentersdorf, NCF, 21 (1966), 207-10, 222-24.

   Pocket, Mrs.: Axton, DSA, 2 (1972), 289; Rosenberg, Di, 69
      (1973), 90-100.

   Skiffins, Miss: Dessner, Ariel, 6 (Apr. 1975), 76-77.

   Startop: Dunn, Di, 63 (1967), 126-27; Wentersdorf, NCF, 21
      (1966), 212-13.

   Trabb's Boy: Bort, VN, 29 (Spring 1966), 27-28; Flamm, Di, 66
      (1970), 17-18; Wentersdorf, NCF, 21 (1966), 214-17.

   Wemmick, John: Dessner, Ariel, 6 (Apr. 1975), 65-79; Grundy,
      L&P, 22 (1972), 104; Marcus, VN, 26 (Fall 1964), 11; Peyrouton,
      DiS, 1 (1965), 39-47; Tate, SoRA, 7 (1974), 159-60, 161-63;
      Winner, DSA, 3 (1974), 108-10; (prototype): Carlton, Di, 56
      (1960), 151-52.

   Wopsle: Barry, Di, 64 (1968), 43-47; Clinton-Baddeley, Di, 57
      (1961), 150-59.

COMPOSITION (See also TEXT)

   General: House, Di, 44 (1947/48), 183-84.

   Magwitch: Rosenberg, DSA, 2 (1972), 309-13.

   Manuscript vs. print (Chapters 22 and 23): Rosenberg, Di, 69
      (1973), 90-101.

   Plans for conclusion: Butt, Di, 45 (1948/49), 78-80.

CRITICAL ASSESSMENT

   General: Fielding, REL, 2 (July 1961), 76-88; Moynahan, EIC, 11
      (1961), 239-41; Rodriques, Literary Criterion, 7 (1966), 51-53;
      Wilson, Susquehanna University Studies, 6 (Apr.-June 1959),
      451-53.

   Contemporary reaction: Collins, DSA, 2 (1972), 337-38; (Ludwig):
      Thomas, Hermathena, 111 (1971), 41-48.

   David Copperfield and Great Expectations compared: Jones, SWR,
      39 (1954), 328-30.

   Position in career: Collins, DSA, 2 (1972), 336-38, 348-51.

Great Expectations

EXPLANATORY NOTES, HISTORICAL BACKGROUND, and SOURCES

"brought up by hand" (definition): Parish, NCF, 17 (1962),
286-88.

"The Finches of the Grove" (name): Murray, N&Q, 216 (1971), 414.

Miscellaneous annotations: Hill, Di, 53 (1957), 119-26, 184-86;
54 (1958), 53-60, 123-25, 185; 55 (1959), 57-59; 56 (1960),
121-26; (chronology): Deneau, Di, 60 (1964), 27-29.

Theater: Clinton-Baddeley, Di, 57 (1961), 150-59.

INFLUENCES (See also LITERARY PARALLELS)

(Dickens on) W. S. Gilbert: Stedman, Di, 58 (1962), 171-78.

LANGUAGE and STYLE (See also TECHNIQUES, VARIOUS)

General: Vande Kieft, NCF, 15 (1961), 325-32.

Animism: Dobie, NCF, 25 (1971), 414-15.

Communication, modes of: Sossaman, DSN, 5 (1974), 66-68; Vande
Kieft, NCF, 15 (1961), 325-34.

Imagery: Hynes, ELH, 30 (1963), 258-92; (animal): Barnard, DSA,
1 (1970), 242-47; (Barnard's Inn): Ericksen, Illinois Quarterly, 33 (Sept. 1970), 7-8; (demonic): ibid., 4-11; (the four
elements): New, DiS, 3 (1967), 111-21; (garden): Crawford,
RS, 39 (1971), 63-67; (hearts and hands): Moore, Di, 61
(1965), 52-56; (Jaggers' office): Ericksen, Illinois Quarterly, 33 (Sept. 1970), 5-6; (prison): Barnard, DSA, 1 (1970),
241-42; (river): Robison, ES, 53 (1972), 444-46, 447-49.

Irony (contrast): Roll-Hansen, Norwegian Studies in English, 9
(1963), 207-208.

Monologue (interior): Kelty, Di, 57 (1961), 161, 163-65.

Repetition in Chapter I: Cappel, Style, 4 (1970), 241-44.

Speech: Roll-Hansen, Norwegian Studies in English, 9 (1963),
209-16.

Symbolism: Barnard, DSA, 1 (1970), 241-47; Dobie, NCF, 25
(1971), 415-16; Hynes, ELH, 30 (1963), 258-92; Marshall, Personalist, 44 (1963), 342-44; (beacon and gibbet): McWilliams,
DSA, 2 (1972), 256-66; (birds): Hynes, ELH, 30 (1963), 264-65;
(castle): Tate, SoRA, 7 (1974), 161-67; (contrasts): Hynes,
ELH, 30 (1963), 275-78; (eating): Goldfarb, VN, 21 (Spring

Great Expectations

1962), 18-19; Hardy, EIC, 13 (1963), 351-63; (grave): Hagan,
NCF, 9 (1954), 176-78; Hynes, ELH, 30 (1963), 259-60; (hands):
Forker, TSLL, 3 (1961), 280-93; Levine, Ball State University
Forum, 6 (Spring 1965), 22-24; (light): Hynes, ELH, 30 (1963),
281-92; (marshes): Hagan, NCF, 9 (1954), 175-76; (pipe smoking): Reeves, Di, 62 (1966), 174-78; (prison, chains, etc.):
Hynes, ELH, 30 (1963), 260-92; (setting): ibid., 268-70;
(ship): ibid., 278-79; McWilliams, DSA, 2 (1972), 260-66;
(things paired): Hynes, ELH, 30 (1963), 273-75.

LITERARY PARALLELS (See also INFLUENCES)

Balzac (Illusions Perdues): Schilling, Adam, 331-33 (1969),
119-22.

A Christmas Carol (Christmas celebrations): Carolan, DR, 52
(1972), 375-77.

Faulkner, Miss Emily ("A Rose for Emily") and Miss Havisham:
Stewart, FurmS, 6 (1958), 21-23.

Fitzgerald, The Great Gatsby: Friedman, Accent, 14 (1954),
250-63; Vasta, Di, 60 (1964), 167-72.

"George Silverman's Explanation": Flamm, Di, 66 (1970), 16-19.

Glasgow, The Romance of a Plain Man: Wagenknecht, Boston University Studies in English, 3 (1957), 57-60.

Household Words (Magwitch): Carolan, DSN, 3 (1972), 27-28.

Jaggers and Bucket: Steig, PMASAL, 50 (1965), 583-84.

Kafka, The Castle: Tate, SoRA, 7 (1974), 157-68.

MacDonald, George: Crago, DiS, 5 (1969), 86-89.

Melville, Pierre (as disguised autobiography): Lane, DR, 51
(1971), 320-22.

Shakespeare, Hamlet (past influences present): French, EIC, 24
(1974), 147-48.

Sydney, Astrophil and Stella: Endicott, Di, 63 (1967), 158-62.

Telemachus story: Warner, Di, 60 (1964), 52-54.

Twain, Huckleberry Finn: Mills, JAmS, 4 (1970), 62-72; Ridland,
NCF, 20 (1965), 287-90.

West, Nathanael, Miss Lonelyhearts: Pinsker, Topic, 18 (1969),
44-46.

Great Expectations

PLOT (See also STRUCTURE/UNITY)

General: Drew, Di, 52 (1955/56), 123-27; Marcus, DiS, 2 (1966), 57-73; Monod, Di, 56 (1960), 134-36; Stange, CE, 16 (1954), 10-15.

End of novel: Butt, Di, 45 (1948/49), 78-80; Eigner, NCF, 25 (1970), 104-108; Emmett, North Dakota Quarterly, 41 (Autumn 1973), 5-11; Greenberg, PLL, 6 (1970), 152-62; Gregory, EIC, 19 (1969), 405-409; Kennedy, SNNTS, 6 (1974), 282-83; Levine, SNNTS, 1 (1969), 170-71; Meisel, EIC, 15 (1965), 326-31; Millhauser, DSA, 2 (1972), 267-77; Reed, Di, 55 (1959), 12-18; Shores, MSE, 3 (1972), 97-99; Smith, Thoth, 12 (Fall 1971), 11-17.

Fairy tale elements: Grob, TSLL, 5 (1964), 572-74; Stone, KR, 24 (1962), 668-91.

Fantasy, use of: Moynahan, EIC, 10 (1960), 67-69, 75-77.

Foreshadowing: Gadd, Di, 36 (1939/40), 184.

Moral growth: Wall, REL, 6 (Jan. 1965), 63-65.

Myth: Marshall, Personalist, 44 (1963), 337-47; (City of Destruction archetype): Ericksen, Illinois Quarterly, 33 (Sept. 1970), 4-11.

Suspense: Marcus, DiS, 2 (1966), 60-73.

POINT OF VIEW

General: Partlow, CE, 23 (1961), 123-31; Roll-Hansen, Norwegian Studies in English, 9 (1963), 216-19.

Stream-of-consciousness: Dobie, NCF, 25 (1971), 405-16.

SETTING

General: Hallam, DiS, 2 (1966), 26-32.

Date of action: Edminson, NCF, 13 (1958), 23-35.

Walworth, description of: Lelchuk, SR, 78 (1970), 417-18.

World of novel: Robison, QQ, 78 (1971), 54-59; Van Ghent, SR, 58 (1950), 430-31, 435-38; (society): Winner, DSA, 3 (1974), 108-21.

Great Expectations

STRUCTURE/UNITY (See also PLOT)

General: Coolidge, Mississippi Quarterly, 14 (Fall 1961),
194-96; Friedman, Accent, 14 (1954), 250-63; Hallam, DiS, 2
(1966), 26-33; McWilliams, DSA, 2 (1972), 255-66; Roll-Hansen,
Norwegian Studies in English, 9 (1963), 219-26; Stone, KR, 24
(1962), 662-91; Wolfe, SAQ, 73 (1974), 335-47.

"keystone episode": Axton, UTQ, 37 (1967), 46-49.

Montage: Dobie, NCF, 25 (1971), 413-14.

Repetition: Hagan, ELH, 21 (1954), 60-65.

Three stages: Hagan, ELH, 21 (1954), 54-60.

TECHNIQUES, VARIOUS

General: Connolly, PQ, 34 (1955), 48-55; Fielding, REL, 2 (July
1961), 81-86; House, Di, 44 (1947/48), 64-70; Jones, SWR, 39
(1954), 328-35; Marshall, Personalist, 44 (1963), 337-47;
Monod, Di, 56 (1960), 134-40; Moynahan, EIC, 10 (1960), 60-79;
Rodriques, Literary Criterion, 7 (1966), 45-51; Stange, CE, 16
(1954), 9-17.

Autobiography, use of: Nisbet, VN, 15 (Spring 1959), 10-13;
Stone, KR, 24 (1962), 663-66.

Christmas, use of: Carolan, DR, 52 (1972), 374-78.

Comedy/humor: Monod, Di, 56 (1960), 136-37; Talon, VN, 42 (Fall
1972), 6-11.

Food and drink (preparation or consumption): Watt, DSA, 3 (1974),
170-71.

Motifs, use of: Coolidge, Mississippi Quarterly, 14 (Fall 1961),
190-92.

Opening: French, EIC, 24 (1974), 160-61.

Space, use of: Talon, DSA, 3 (1974), 125-26.

Time, use of: Franklin, DSA, 4 (1975), 27-31; Hynes, ELH, 30
(1963), 279-81; Roll-Hansen, Norwegian Studies in English, 9
(1963), 200-205; Talon, DSA, 3 (1974), 123-33.

TEXT (See also COMPOSITION)

Preparing a critical edition: Rosenberg, DSA, 2 (1972), 294-335;
(conceived for monthly publication): ibid., 321-26; (Dickens
in 1861): ibid., 318-20; (Dickens's notebook): ibid.,

Great Expectations

307-308; (letters): ibid., 313-18; (memoranda notes): ibid., 326-34; (running headlines): ibid., 308-13; (vocabulary annotation): ibid., 296-300, 302-304.

THEMES

General: Barnard, DSA, 1 (1970), 238-51; Connolly, PQ, 34 (1955), 48-49; Drew, Di, 52 (1955/56), 124-27; Gregory, EIC, 19 (1969), 403-409; Hardy, EIC, 13 (1963), 351-63; House, Di, 44 (1947/48), 64-69; Lindberg, CE, 23 (1961), 118-22; Millhauser, DSA, 2 (1972), 267-77; Monod, Di, 56 (1960), 138-40; Moore, Di, 61 (1965), 52-56; Moynahan, EIC, 10 (1960), 60-79; Robison, QQ, 78 (1971), 54-59; Roll-Hansen, Norwegian Studies in English, 9 (1963), 223-25; Rosenberg, DSA, 2 (1972), 333; Stange, CE, 16 (1954), 9-17; Vasta, Di, 60 (1964), 167-72; Wentersdorf, NCF, 21 (1966), 223-24; Wolfe, SAQ, 73 (1974), 339-47.

Ambition: Moynahan, EIC, 10 (1960), 69-79.

Childhood/children: Bell, VN, 27 (Spring 1965), 21-24.

Childhood vs. adulthood: Grundy, L&P, 22 (1972), 100-105.

Christmas, attitude toward: Carolan, DR, 52 (1972), 374-78.

Class consciousness: Roll-Hansen, Norwegian Studies in English, 9 (1963), 205-10.

Communication: Levine, NCF, 18 (1963), 175-81.

Expectations: Barry, Di, 64 (1968), 43-47; Pinsker, Topic, 18 (1969), 44-45.

Family: Lelchuk, SR, 78 (1970), 410-26.

Forgiveness: Axton, DSA, 2 (1972), 291-93.

"Fortunate Fall": DeHaven, DSN, 6 (1975), 42-46.

Free Will: French, EIC, 24 (1974), 160-65.

Guilt: Barnard, DSA, 1 (1970), 238-44, 250-51; Gordon, Di, 65 (1969), 6-11; Hallam, DiS, 2 (1966), 32-33; Moynahan, EIC, 10 (1960), 60-79; Stange, CE, 16 (1954), 10-17; Van Ghent, SR, 58 (1950), 435-38.

Human relationships: Levine, NCF, 18 (1963), 175-81; Vande Kieft, NCF, 15 (1961), 330-34.

Identity: Cappel, Style, 4 (1970), 241-44, Lelchuk, SR, 78 (1970), 407-16, 421-26.

Individual possibility: Levine, SNNTS, 1 (1969), 170-71.

Great Expectations

Influence of past on present: French, EIC, 24 (1974), 147-60.

Injustice: Axton, DSA, 2 (1972), 278-91.

Love: Axton, DSA, 2 (1972), 292-93; Hardy, EIC, 13 (1963), 351-63; (Christian): Barnard, DSA, 1 (1970), 247-51.

Moral maturity, growth to: Rodriques, Literary Criterion, 7 (1966), 46-51.

Parasitism: Barnard, DSA, 1 (1970), 246-47.

Personal responsibility: Axton, DSA, 2 (1972), 278-93; Gordon, Di, 65 (1969), 6-11.

Redemption: Meisel, EIC, 15 (1965), 327-31.

Revenge: Axton, DSA, 2 (1972), 278-91.

Self-alienation: Marcus, VN, 26 (Fall 1964), 9-12.

Self-salvation: Wilson, SAQ, 73 (1974), 534-36.

Selfhood: Winner, DSA, 3 (1974), 101-102, 108-21.

Social criticism: Hagan, NCF, 9 (1954), 170-78; Lelchuk, SR, 78 (1970), 408-11, 416-26; Mills, JAmS, 4 (1970), 62-72.

Time: Franklin, DSA, 4 (1975), 27-31; Talon, DSA, 3 (1974), 123-33; (and water imagery): Robison, ES, 53 (1972), 444-46.

"True Fatherhood": Barnard, DSA, 1 (1970), 247-50.

Bibliography for
Great Expectations

AUERBACH, NINA. "Incarnation of the Orphan." <u>ELH</u>, 42 (1975), 395–419.

AXTON, WILLIAM F. "<u>Great Expectations</u> Yet Again." <u>DSA</u>, 2 (1972), 278–93.

_____. "'Keystone' Structure in Dickens' Serial Novels." <u>UTQ</u>, 37 (1967), 31–50.

BARNARD, ROBERT. "Imagery and Theme in <u>Great Expectations</u>." <u>DSA</u>, 1 (1970), 238–51.

BARRY, JAMES D. "Wopsle Once More." <u>Di</u>, 64 (1968), 43–47.

BELL, VEREEN M. "Parents and Children in <u>Great Expectations</u>." <u>VN</u>, 27 (Spring 1965), 21–24.

BORT, BARRY D. "Trabb's Boy and Orlick." <u>VN</u>, 29 (Spring 1966), 27–28.

BUTT, JOHN E. "Dickens's Plan for the Conclusion of <u>Great Expectations</u>." <u>Di</u>, 45 (1948/49), 76–80.

CAPPEL, WILLIAM. "Repetition in the Language of Fiction." <u>Style</u>, 4 (1970), 239–44.

CARLTON, W. J. "The Strange Story of Thomas Mitton." <u>Di</u>, 56 (1960), 141–52.

CAROLAN, KATHERINE. "Dickens' Last Christmases." <u>DR</u>, 52 (1972), 373–83.

_____. "<u>Great Expectations</u> and a <u>Household Words</u> Sketch." <u>DSN</u>, 3 (1972), 27–28.

CLINTON-BADDELEY, V. C. "Wopsle." <u>Di</u>, 57 (1961), 150–59.

COLBURN, WILLIAM E. "Dickens and the 'Life-Illusion.'" <u>Di</u>, 54 (1958), 110–18.

COLLINS, PHILIP. "A Tale of Two Novels: <u>A Tale of Two Cities</u> and <u>Great Expectations</u> in Dickens' Career." <u>DSA</u>, 2 (1972), 336–51.

CONNOLLY, THOMAS E. "Technique in <u>Great Expectations</u>." <u>PQ</u>, 34 (1955), 48–55.

Great Expectations

COOLIDGE, ARCHIBALD C., JR. "Great Expectations: The Culmination of a Developing Art." Mississippi Quarterly, 14 (Fall 1961), 190-96.

CRAGO, H. "Charles Dickens and George MacDonald: A Note." DiS, 5 (1969), 86-90.

CRAWFORD, JOHN W. "The Garden Imagery in Great Expectations." RS, 39 (1971), 63-67.

DeHAVEN, MARY ALICE. "Pip and the Fortunate Fall." DSN, 6 (1975), 42-46.

DENEAU, DANIEL P. "Pip's Age and Other Notes on Great Expectations." Di, 60 (1964), 27-29.

DESSNER, LAWRENCE JAY. "Great Expectations: The Tragic Comedy of John Wemmick." Ariel, 6 (Apr. 1975), 65-80.

DILNOT, A. F. "The Case of Mr. Jaggers." EIC, 25 (1975), 437-43.

DOBIE, ANN B. "Early Stream-of-Consciousness Writing: Great Expectations." NCF, 25 (1971), 405-16.

DREW, ARNOLD P. "Structure in Great Expectations." Di, 52 (1955/56), 123-27.

DUNN, RICHARD J. "Drummle and Startop: Doubling in Great Expectations." Di, 63 (1967), 125-27.

EDMINSON, MARY. "The Date of the Action in Great Expectations." NCF, 13 (1958), 22-35.

EIGNER, EDWIN M. "Bulwer-Lytton and the Changed Ending of Great Expectations." NCF, 25 (1970), 104-108.

EMMETT, V. J., JR. "The Endings of Great Expectations." North Dakota Quarterly, 41 (Autumn 1973), 5-11.

ENDICOTT, ANNABEL. "Pip, Philip and Astrophil: Dickens's Debt to Sidney?" Di, 63 (1967), 158-62.

ERICKSEN, DONALD H. "Demonic Imagery and the Quest for Identity in Great Expectations." Illinois Quarterly, 33 (Sept. 1970), 4-11.

FIELDING, K. J. "The Critical Autonomy of Great Expectations." REL, 2 (July 1961), 75-88.

FLAMM, DUDLEY. "The Prosecutor Within: Dickens's Final Explanation." Di, 66 (1970), 16-23.

FORKER, CHARLES R. "The Language of Hands in Great Expectations." TSLL, 3 (1961), 280-93.

FRANKLIN, STEPHEN L. "Dickens and Time: The Clock Without Hands." DSA, 4 (1975), 1-35.

Bibliography

FRASER, RUSSELL. "A Charles Dickens Original." NCF, 9 (1955), 301-307.

FRENCH, A. L. "Beating and Cringing: Great Expectations." EIC, 24 (1974), 147-68.

FRIEDMAN, NORMAN. "Versions of Form in Fiction--Great Expectations and The Great Gatsby." Accent, 14 (1954), 246-64.

FRIEDMAN, STANLEY. "Another Possible Source for Dickens' Miss Havisham." VN, 39 (Spring 1971), 24-25.

GADD, W. LAURENCE. "The Dickens Touch." Di, 36 (1939/40), 181-85.

GOLDFARB, RUSSELL M. "The Menu of Great Expectations." VN, 21 (Spring 1962), 18-19.

GORDON, ANDREW. "Jaggers and the Moral Scheme of Great Expectations." Di, 65 (1969), 3-11.

GREENBERG, ROBERT A. "On Ending Great Expectations." PLL, 6 (1970), 152-62.

GREGORY, MARSHALL W. "Values and Meaning in Great Expectations: The Two Endings Revisited." EIC, 19 (1969), 402-409.

GROB, SHIRLEY. "Dickens and Some Motifs of the Fairy Tale." TSLL, 5 (1964), 567-79.

GRUNDY, DOMINICK E. "Growing Up Dickensian." L&P, 22 (1972), 99-106.

HAGAN, JOHN H., JR. "The Poor Labyrinth: The Theme of Social Injustice in Dickens's Great Expectations." NCF, 9 (1954), 169-78.

_____. "Structural Patterns in Dickens's Great Expectations." ELH, 21 (1954), 54-66.

HALLAM, CLIFFORD B. "The Structure of Great Expectations in Respect to Style and Artistry." DiS, 2 (1966), 26-33.

HARDY, BARBARA. "The Change of Heart in Dickens' Novels." VS, 5 (1961), 49-67.

_____. "Dickens and the Passions." NCF, 24 (1970), 449-66.

_____. "Dickens's Storytellers." Di, 69 (1973), 71-78.

_____. "Work in Progress IV: Food and Ceremony in Great Expectations." EIC, 13 (1963), 351-63.

HILL, T. W. "Notes on Great Expectations." Di, 53 (1957), 119-26, 184-86; 54 (1958), 53-60, 123-25, 185; 55 (1959), 57-59; 56 (1960), 121-26.

HOUSE, HUMPHRY. "G. B. S. on Great Expectations." Di, 44 (1947/48), 63-70, 183-86.

Great Expectations

HUTCHINGS, RICHARD J. "Dickens at Bonchurch." Di, 61 (1965), 79-100.

HYNES, JOSEPH A. "Image and Symbol in Great Expectations." ELH, 30 (1963), 258-92.

JONES, HOWARD MUMFORD. "On Rereading Great Expectations." SWR, 39 (1954), 328-35.

KELTY, JEAN McCLURE. "The Modern Tone of Charles Dickens." Di, 57 (1961), 160-65.

KENNEDY, G. W. "Dickens's Endings." SNNTS, 6 (1974), 280-87.

LANE, LAURIAT, JR. "Dickens and Melville: Our Mutual Friends." DR, 51 (1971), 315-31.

LELCHUK, ALAN. "Self, Family, and Society in Great Expectations." SR, 78 (1970), 407-26.

LEVINE, GEORGE. "Communication in Great Expectations." NCF, 18 (1963), 175-81.

LEVINE, M. H. "Hand and Hearts in Great Expectations." Ball State University Forum, 6 (Spring 1965), 22-24.

LEVINE, RICHARD A. "Dickens, the Two Nations, and Individual Possibility." SNNTS, 1 (1969), 157-80.

LINDBERG, JOHN. "Individual Conscience and Social Injustice in Great Expectations." CE, 23 (1961), 118-22.

LUCAS, JOHN. "Dickens and Arnold." RMS, 16 (1972), 86-111.

MARCUS, MORDECAI. "The Pattern of Self-Alienation in Great Expectations." VN, 26 (Fall 1964), 9-12.

MARCUS, PHILLIP L. "Theme and Suspense in the Plot of Great Expectations." DiS, 2 (1966), 57-73.

MARSHALL, WILLIAM H. "The Conclusion of Great Expectations as the Fulfillment of Myth." Personalist, 44 (1963), 337-47.

McWILLIAMS, JOHN P., JR. "Great Expectations: The Beacon, the Gibbet, and the Ship." DSA, 2 (1972), 255-66.

MEISEL, MARTIN. "The Ending of Great Expectations." EIC, 15 (1965), 326-31.

_____. "Miss Havisham Brought to Book." PMLA, 81 (1966), 278-85.

MILLHAUSER, MILTON. "Great Expectations: Three Endings." DSA, 2 (1972), 267-77.

MILLS, NICOLAUS C. "Social and Moral Vision in Great Expectations and Huckleberry Finn." JAmS, 4 (1970), 61-72.

MILNER, IAN. "The Nature of the Hero in Dickens and the Eighteenth Century Tradition." Philologica, 9 (1957), 57-67.

MONOD, SYLVÈRE. "Great Expectations: A Hundred Years After." Di, 56 (1960), 133-40.

MOORE, JACK B. "Hearts and Hands in Great Expectations." Di, 61 (1965), 52-56.

MOYNAHAN, JULIAN. "Dickens Criticism." EIC, 11 (1961), 239-41.

_____. "The Hero's Guilt: The Case of Great Expectations." EIC, 10 (1960), 60-79.

MURRAY, ISOBEL. "Great Expectations and The Critic." N&Q, 216 (1971), 414.

NEW, WILLIAM H. "The Four Elements in Great Expectations." DiS, 3 (1967), 111-21.

NISBET, ADA. "The Autobiographical Matrix of Great Expectations." VN, 15 (Spring 1959), 10-13.

PARISH, CHARLES. "A Boy Brought Up 'By Hand.'" NCF, 17 (1962), 286-88.

PARTLOW, ROBERT B., JR. "The Moving I: A Study of the Point of View in Great Expectations." CE, 23 (1961), 122-31.

PEYROUTON, N. C. "John Wemmick: Enigma?" DiS, 1 (1965), 39-47.

PINSKER, SANFORD. "Charles Dickens and Nathanael West: Great Expectations Unfulfilled." Topic, 18 (1969), 40-52.

REED, JAMES. "The Fulfillment of Pip's Expectations." Di, 55 (1959), 12-18.

REED, JOHN R. "Confinement and Character in Dickens' Novels." DSA, 1 (1970), 41-54.

REEVES, BRUCE. "Pipes and Pipe Smoking in Great Expectations." Di, 62 (1966), 174-78.

RIDLAND, J. M. "Huck, Pip, and Plot." NCF, 20 (1965), 286-90.

ROBISON, ROSELEE. "The Several Worlds of Great Expectations." QQ, 78 (1971), 54-59.

_____. "Time, Death and the River in Dickens' Novels." ES, 53 (1972), 436-54.

RODRIQUES, EUSEBIO L. "The Dickens of Great Expectations." Literary Criterion, 7 (1966), 41-53.

ROLL-HANSEN, DIDERIK. "Characters and Contrasts in Great Expectations." Norwegian Studies in English, 9 (1963), 197-226.

215

Great Expectations

ROSENBERG, EDGAR. "A Preface to Great Expectations: The Pale Usher Dusts His Lexicons." DSA, 2 (1972), 294-335.

_____. "Small Talk in Hammersmith: Chapter 23 of Great Expectations." Di, 69 (1973), 90-101.

RYAN, J. S. "A Possible Australian Source for Miss Havisham." Australian Literary Studies, 1 (1963), 134-36.

SCHILLING, BERNARD N. "Balzac, Dickens and 'This Harsh World.'" Adam, 331-33 (1969), 109-22.

SHORES, LUCILLE P. "The Character of Estella." MSE, 3 (1972), 91-99.

SMITH, JOHN T. "The Two Endings of Great Expectations: A Re-Evaluation." Thoth, 12 (Fall 1971), 11-17.

SMITH, SHEILA M. "Anti-Mechanism and the Comic in the Writings of Charles Dickens." RMS, 3 (1959), 131-44.

SOSSAMAN, STEPHEN. "Language and Communication in Great Expectations." DSN, 5 (1974), 66-68.

STANGE, G. ROBERT. "Expectations Well Lost: Dickens' Fable for His Time." CE, 16 (1954), 9-17.

STEDMAN, JANE W. "Boz and Bab." Di, 58 (1962), 171-78.

STEIG, MICHAEL. "The Whitewashing of Inspector Bucket: Origins and Parallels." PMASAL, 50 (1965), 575-84.

STEWART, JAMES T. "Miss Havisham and Miss Grierson." FurmS, 6 (1958), 21-23.

STONE, HARRY. "An Added Note on Dickens and Miss Havisham." NCF, 10 (1955), 85-86.

_____. "Dickens' Woman in White." VN, 33 (Spring 1968), 5-8.

_____. "Fire, Hand, and Gate: Dickens' Great Expectations." KR, 24 (1962), 662-91.

SWEENEY, PATRICIA R. "Mr. House, Mr. Thackeray, and Mr. Pirrip: The Question of Snobbery in Great Expectations." Di, 64 (1968), 55-63.

TALON, HENRI. "On Some Aspects of the Comic in Great Expectations." VN, 42 (Fall 1972), 6-11.

_____. "Space, Time, and Memory in Great Expectations." DSA, 3 (1974), 122-33.

TATE, ELEANOR. "Kafka's The Castle: Another Dickens Novel?" SoRA, 7 (1974), 157-68.

THOMAS, L. H. C. "Otto Ludwig and Charles Dickens: A German Reading of Great Expectations and Other Novels." Hermathena, 111 (1971), 35–50.

VAN GHENT, DOROTHY. "The Dickens World: A View from Todgers's." SR, 58 (1950), 419–38.

VANDE KIEFT, RUTH M. "Patterns of Communication in Great Expectations." NCF, 15 (1961), 325–34.

VASTA, EDWARD. "Great Expectations and The Great Gatsby." Di, 60 (1964), 167–72.

WAGENKNECHT, EDWARD. "Great Expectations and Ellen Glasgow." Boston University Studies in English, 3 (1957), 57–60.

WALL, STEPHEN. "Dickens's Plot of Fortune." REL, 6 (Jan. 1965), 56–67.

WARNER, JOHN R. "Dickens Looks at Homer." Di, 60 (1964), 52–54.

WATT, IAN. "Oral Dickens." DSA, 3 (1974), 165–81.

WENTERSDORF, KARL P. "Mirror Images in Great Expectations." NCF, 21 (1966), 203–24.

WILSON, ARTHUR H. "The Great Theme in Charles Dickens." Susquehanna University Studies, 6 (Apr.–June 1959), 422–57.

WILSON, JOHN R. "Dickens and Christian Mystery." SAQ, 73 (1974), 528–40.

WINNER, ANTHONY. "Character and Knowledge in Dickens: The Enigma of Jaggers." DSA, 3 (1974), 100–21.

WOLFE, PETER. "The Fictional Crux and the Double Structure of Great Expectations." SAQ, 73 (1974), 335–47.

Our Mutual Friend

Our Mutual Friend

CHARACTERIZATION

General: Barnard, REL, 2 (July 1961), 89-99; Collins, Di, 65
(1969), 32-34; Gribble, EIC, 25 (1975), 206-13; Hobsbaum, EIC,
13 (1963), 231-35; Lanham, VN, 24 (Fall 1963), 7-11; Miyoshi,
VN, 26 (Fall 1964), 6-9; Muir, E&S, N.S. 19 (1966), 93-105;
Palmer, PMLA, 89 (1974), 487-94; Robison, ES, 53 (1972),
449-52; Robson, DSA, 3 (1974), 199-213; Sharp, University of
Kansas City Review, 27 (Summer 1961), 308-11; 28 (Autumn
1961), 75-80; Sherer, TSLL, 13 (1971), 511-21; Stewart, ELH,
40 (1973), 110-30; Wilson, New Republic, 102 (4 Mar. 1940),
340-42; SAQ, 73 (1974), 536-38.

Devil, use of: Lane, DR, 51 (1971), 326-27.

Grotesque: Dunn, SNNTS, 1 (1969), 150-55.

Melodramatic: Purton, EA, 28 (1975), 24-26.

Moral exemplars: Collins, Di, 65 (1969), 32-34.

Names: Kennedy, NCF, 28 (1973), 167-78; Robson, DSA, 3 (1974),
210-12.

Predators: McMaster, DR, 40 (1960), 373-80.

Reading or literacy, use of: Friedman, NCF, 28 (1973), 40-61.

CHARACTERS

Boffin, Mrs.: Shea, Di, 63 (1967), 38-40.

Boffin, Noddy: Friedman, NCF, 28 (1973), 40-47, 49-53; Hobsbaum,
EIC, 13 (1963), 234-35; Marlow, DSN, 5 (1974), 7-8; McMaster,
DR, 40 (1960), 374; Palmer, PMLA, 89 (1974), 487-88; Shea, Di,
63 (1967), 37-40.

Dolls, Mr.: Stewart, ELH, 40 (1973), 120-21.

Fledgeby, Fascination: Sherer, TSLL, 13 (1971), 514-15; Stewart,
ELH, 40 (1973), 121-22.

Our Mutual Friend

Harmon, John: Friedman, NCF, 28 (1973), 57; Kennedy, NCF, 28
(1973), 167-68, 176-77; Lamb, Paunch, 33 (Dec. 1968), 40-42;
McMaster, DR, 40 (1960), 377-78; Miyoshi, VN, 26 (Fall 1964),
7-9; Palmer, PMLA, 89 (1974), 491-92.

Headstone, Bradley: Barnard, REL, 2 (July 1961), 96-97; Collins,
The University of Leeds Institute of Education Researches and
Studies, 22 (1961), 43-55; Dunn, SNNTS, 1 (1969), 150-51;
Gribble, EIC, 25 (1975), 201-206; Lamb, Paunch, 33 (Dec. 1968),
45; Lane, Di, 55 (1959), 50-52; Purton, EA, 28 (1975), 25;
Wilson, New Republic, 102 (4 Mar. 1940), 341-42.

Hexam, Charley: Collins, The University of Leeds Institute of
Education Researches and Studies, 22 (1961), 44-55; Friedman,
NCF, 28 (1973), 55; Robson, DSA, 3 (1974), 208.

Hexam, Gaffer: Friedman, NCF, 28 (1973), 54; Lanham, VN, 24
(Fall 1963), 7; Passerini, DiS, 2 (1966), 22-25; (prototype):
Nelson, NCF, 20 (1965), 217-22.

Hexam, Lizzie: Hobsbaum, EIC, 13 (1963), 234; Page, Di, 65
(1969), 101-107; Palmer, PMLA, 89 (1974), 489-90, 493-94;
Robson, DSA, 3 (1974), 208.

Higden, Betty: Hill, Di, 43 (1946/47), 41-42; Robison, ES, 53
(1972), 442; Stewart, ELH, 40 (1973), 129; (prototype):
Nelson, NCF, 20 (1965), 207-17.

Lammles: Gribble, EIC, 25 (1975), 208-12.

Podsnap, John: Barnard, REL, 2 (July 1961), 97-98; Friedman,
NCF, 28 (1973), 57; Sherer, TSLL, 13 (1971), 511-12; (prototype): Davies, Di, 70 (1974), 152-57.

Riah: Gibson, Di, 62 (1966), 118-19; Stone, VS, 2 (1959),
246-49; (as Jew): Lane, PMLA, 73 (1958), 98-99.

Riderhood, Rogue: Friedman, NCF, 28 (1973), 54-55; Kennedy, NCF,
28 (1973), 171-72; Lane, Di, 55 (1959), 51-52; Passerini, DiS,
2 (1966), 22-25.

Sloppy, Mr.: Stewart, ELH, 40 (1973), 128-29.

Tippins, Lady: McMaster, SNNTS, 1 (1969), 136-37.

Twemlow: Palmer, PMLA, 89 (1974), 494.

Veneering: Friedman, NCF, 28 (1973), 57; McMaster, DR, 40
(1960), 377-78; Sherer, TSLL, 13 (1971), 513-14.

Venus: Dunn, SNNTS, 1 (1969), 152-53; McMaster, DR, 40 (1960),
375-76; Stewart, ELH, 40 (1973), 111.

Wegg, Silas: Dunn, SNNTS, 1 (1969), 151-52; Friedman, NCF, 28
(1973), 51-52; Kennedy, NCF, 28 (1973), 166; McMaster, DR, 40

Our Mutual Friend

(1960), 374, 375-76; Sherer, TSLL, 13 (1971), 520-21; Van
Ghent, SR, 58 (1950), 420-21.

Wilfer: Sherer, TSLL, 13 (1971), 516.

Wilfer, Bella: Andersen, Discourse, 12 (1969), 428-29; Friedman,
NCF, 28 (1973), 56-57; Hardy, VS, 5 (1961), 63-64; Kennedy,
NCF, 28 (1973), 175-77; Lamb, Paunch, 33 (Dec. 1968), 38-42;
Marlow, DSN, 5 (1974), 7-8; Miyoshi, VN, 26 (Fall 1964), 7-9;
Newman, Di, 38 (1941/42), 181-82; Sherer, TSLL, 13 (1971),
516-17; Stedman, Di, 59 (1963), 113-18; Winters, North Dakota
Quarterly, 34 (1966), 96.

Wrayburn, Eugene: Andersen, Discourse, 12 (1969), 430-32;
Burgan, MLQ, 36 (1975), 307-10; Collins, The University of
Leeds Institute of Education Researches and Studies, 22
(1961), 49-55; Goodheart, Di, 54 (1958), 36; Gribble, EIC, 25
(1975), 197-206; Harvey, NCF, 24 (1969), 312-14; Hobsbaum,
EIC, 13 (1963), 231-33; Kennedy, NCF, 28 (1973), 172-73; Lamb,
Paunch, 33 (Dec. 1968), 42-45; McMaster, DR, 40 (1960),
379-80; Palmer, PMLA, 89 (1974), 492-94; Sherer, TSLL, 13
(1971), 518-19; Stewart, ELH, 40 (1973), 126-28; Wilson, SAQ,
73 (1974), 537-38.

Wren, Jenny: Burgan, MLQ, 36 (1975), 306; Dunn, SNNTS, 1 (1969),
153-55; Kennedy, NCF, 28 (1973), 167, 168, 173-75; Palmer,
PMLA, 89 (1974), 490-91; Stewart, ELH, 40 (1973), 105-107,
110-30; Winters, North Dakota Quarterly, 34 (1966), 96-99.

COMPOSITION (See also TEXT)

Monthly number plans: Boll, MP, 42 (1944), 96-122.

CRITICAL ASSESSMENT

General: Hobsbaum, EIC, 13 (1963), 231-39; Wilson, Susquehanna
University Studies, 6 (Apr.-June 1959), 454-55; Wright, Carnegie Magazine, 39 (Jan. 1965), 29-31.

EXPLANATORY NOTES, HISTORICAL BACKGROUND, and SOURCES

Boffin's misers (identification): Young, Di, 43 (1946/47),
13-17.

Dust mounds: Sucksmith, EIC, 23 (1973), 206-11.

Education (trained teachers): Collins, The University of Leeds
Institute of Education Researches and Studies, 22 (1961),
45-55.

Our Mutual Friend

Jews, attitude toward: Lane, PMLA, 73 (1958), 94-100; Stone, VS, 2 (1959), 223-53.

Mayhew, London Labour and London Poor: Nelson, NCF, 20 (1965), 207-22.

Miscellaneous annotations: Hill, Di, 43 (1946/47), 85-90.

Railway signals: Bomans, TLS, 1 Jan. 1960, p. 7; (Book 3, Chapter 9): Fellows, N&Q, 191 (1946), 21, 152, 218; Mabbott, N&Q, 191 (1946), 129; Wulcko, N&Q, 191 (1946), 64-65.

Retrieval of corpses from Thames: Collins, Di, 70 (1974), 29.

INFLUENCES (See also LITERARY PARALLELS)

(Dickens on) Twain, Huckleberry Finn: Gardner, MP, 66 (1968), 155-56.

(on Dickens) Melodrama: Purton, EA, 28 (1975), 24-26; Walton, The Compleat Angler: Patterson, DSA, 1 (1970), 254-64.

LANGUAGE and STYLE (See also TECHNIQUES, VARIOUS)

General: Gribble, EIC, 25 (1975), 207-11; Kennedy, NCF, 28 (1973), 165-78.

Allusion (Gibbon): Page, Di, 68 (1972), 115; (nursery rhymes, ballads, romances, etc.): Robson, DSA, 3 (1974), 205-206; (Priam): R., N&Q, 188 (1945), 232-33.

Imagery (fire): Andersen, Discourse, 12 (1969), 428; (predators): McMaster, DR, 40 (1960), 373-80; (river): Robison, ES, 53 (1972), 444-46, 449-52; (water): Andersen, Discourse, 12 (1969), 423-25; (wind): ibid., 426-27.

Solecism (last installment): Marlow, DSN, 5 (1974), 7.

Speech: Barnard, REL, 2 (July 1961), 89-91; Page, Di, 65 (1969), 101-107.

Symbolism: Muir, E&S, N.S. 19 (1966), 94-105; (bower motif): Stewart, ELH, 40 (1973), 106-30; (dust/mounds): Andersen, Discourse, 12 (1969), 427; Fielding, Di, 61 (1965), 117-19; Hobsbaum, EIC, 13 (1963), 235-38; Muir, E&S, N.S. 19 (1966), 98-102; Sucksmith, EIC, 23 (1973), 206-11; (fire): Palmer, PMLA, 89 (1974), 489-90; (river): Hobsbaum, EIC, 13 (1963), 238-39; Lane, DR, 51 (1971), 325; Muir, E&S, N.S. 19 (1966), 96-98; Patterson, DSA, 1 (1970), 252-64; Sharp, University of Kansas City Review, 27 (Summer 1961), 307-11; 28 (Autumn 1961), 74-80; (use of double): Lane, Di, 55 (1959), 50-52; Morse, PR, 16 (1949), 284-86.

LITERARY PARALLELS (See also INFLUENCES)

Austen, Emma: Collins, Di, 65 (1969), 32–34.

Fitzgerald, The Great Gatsby: LeVot, FitzN, 20 (1963), 1–4.

Hawthorne (themes and technique): Passerini, DiS, 2 (1966), 18–25.

Melville, The Confidence Man (as prose satires): Lane, DR, 51 (1971), 324–27.

Shaw and Ibsen: Weintraub, NCF, 13 (1958), 67–69.

Twain, Huckleberry Finn (Pap and Hexam): Gardner, MP, 66 (1968), 155–56.

PLOT (See also STRUCTURE/UNITY)

General: Marlow, DSN, 5 (1974), 7–9; Muir, E&S, N.S. 19 (1966), 93–94.

Alteration: Shea, PLL, 4 (1968), 170–81.

End of novel: Kennedy, SNNTS, 6 (1974), 288.

Fairy tale elements: Grob, TSLL, 5 (1964), 574–79; Kennedy, NCF, 28 (1973), 173–77.

Foreshadowing: Gadd, Di, 36 (1939/40), 184–85.

Moral growth: Wall, REL, 6 (Jan. 1965), 65–67.

SETTING

Gothic elements: Kirkpatrick, VN, 31 (Spring 1967), 23–24.

Pastoral elements: Patterson, DSA, 1 (1970), 254–64; (papermill and vicinity): Burgan, MLQ, 36 (1975), 306–11.

World of novel: Gribble, EIC, 25 (1975), 198; McMaster, DR, 40 (1960), 373–80; Robson, DSA, 3 (1974), 202–13.

STRUCTURE/UNITY (See also PLOT)

Comic: Sherer, TSLL, 13 (1971), 509–21.

Rhetorical (first number): Robson, DSA, 3 (1974), 199–213.

Scene and dialogue, fusion of (Chapter 10): Walker, Di, 51 (1954/55), 106–108.

Our Mutual Friend

TECHNIQUES, VARIOUS

General: Barnard, REL, 2 (July 1961), 89-99; Lanham, VN, 24 (Fall 1963), 6-11; Morse, PR, 16 (1949), 284-86; Shea, PLL, 4 (1968), 170-81.

Comedy/humor: Barnard, REL, 2 (July 1961), 93-96; Sherer, TSLL, 13 (1971), 509-21.

Food and drink (preparation or consumption): Watt, DSA, 3 (1974), 170.

Melodrama: Purton, EA, 28 (1975), 24-26.

Murder of Radfoot: Friedman, DSN, 1 (Sept. 1970), 18-20.

Reading, motif of: Friedman, NCF, 28 (1973), 38-61.

TEXT (See also COMPOSITION)

Revisions: Shea, Di, 63 (1967), 37-40.

THEMES

General: Barnard, REL, 2 (July 1961), 91-93; Hobsbaum, EIC, 13 (1963), 235-39; Lanham, VN, 24 (Fall 1963), 6-11; Morse, PR, 16 (1949), 283-86.

Death (and regeneration): Sharp, University of Kansas City Review, 28 (Autumn 1961), 74-80; (and river imagery): Robison, ES, 53 (1972), 449-52.

Doubleness: Morse, PR, 16 (1949), 284-86.

Education (trained teachers): Collins, The University of Leeds Institute of Education Researches and Studies, 22 (1961), 44-55.

Fathers and sons: Rooke, E&S, N.S. 4 (1951), 65-68.

Fishing (for men): Patterson, DSA, 1 (1970), 256-64.

History, dead past forms vs. potential forms for future: Palmer, PMLA, 89 (1974), 487-94.

Identity: Gribble, EIC, 25 (1975), 197-213; Miyoshi, VN, 26 (Fall 1964), 6-9.

Language (degeneration of): Kennedy, NCF, 28 (1973), 169-73; (names): ibid., 165-78.

Love (father-daughter): Winters, North Dakota Quarterly, 34 (1966), 96-99; (vs. self-interest): Lamb, Paunch, 33 (Dec. 1968), 37-45.

Our Mutual Friend

Bibliography for
Our Mutual Friend

ADRIAN, ARTHUR A. "Dickens and Inverted Parenthood." Di, 67 (1971), 3-11.

ANDERSEN, SALLY S. "The De-Spiritualization of the Elements in Our Mutual Friend." Discourse, 12 (1969), 423-33.

BARNARD, ROBERT. "The Choral Symphony: Our Mutual Friend." REL, 2 (July 1961), 89-99.

BOLL, ERNEST. "The Plotting of Our Mutual Friend." MP, 42 (1944), 96-122.

BOMANS, GODFRIED. "Dickens and the Railway." TLS, 1 Jan. 1960, p. 7.

BURGAN, WILLIAM. "Tokens of Winter in Dickens's Pastoral Settings." MLQ, 36 (1975), 293-315.

COLLINS, PHILIP. "Dickens and the Trained Schoolmaster." The University of Leeds Institute of Education Researches and Studies, 22 (1961), 43-55.

_____. "Letter to the Editor." Di, 70 (1974), 29.

COLLINS, THOMAS J. "Some Mutual Sets of Friends: Moral Monitors in Emma and Our Mutual Friend." Di, 65 (1969), 32-34.

DAVIES, JAMES A. "Forster and Dickens: The Making of Podsnap." Di, 70 (1974), 145-58.

DUNN, RICHARD J. "Dickens and the Tragi-Comic Grotesque." SNNTS, 1 (1969), 147-56.

FELLOWS, REGINALD B. "Railway Signals." N&Q, 191 (1946); 21, 152, 218.

FIELDING, K. J. "Dickens's Work with Miss Coutts: I. Nova Scotia Gardens and What Grew There." Di, 61 (1965), 112-19; "II. Casby and the Westminster Landlords," 155-60.

FRIEDMAN, STANLEY. "A Loose Thread in Our Mutual Friend." DSN, 1 (Sept. 1970), 18-20.

_____. "The Motif of Reading in Our Mutual Friend." NCF, 28 (1973), 38-61.

Our Mutual Friend

GADD, W. LAURENCE. "The Dickens Touch." Di, 36 (1939/40), 181-85.

GARDNER, JOSEPH H. "Gaffer Hexam and Pap Finn." MP, 66 (1968), 155-56.

GIBSON, FRANK A. "The Impossible Riah." Di, 62 (1966), 118-19.

GOODHEART, EUGENE. "Dickens's Method of Characterization." Di, 54 (1958), 35-37.

GRIBBLE, JENNIFER. "Depth and Surface in Our Mutual Friend." EIC, 25 (1975), 197-214.

GROB, SHIRLEY. "Dickens and Some Motifs of the Fairy Tale." TSLL, 5 (1964), 567-79.

HARDY, BARBARA. "The Change of Heart in Dickens' Novels." VS, 5 (1961), 49-67.

HARVEY, WILLIAM R. "Charles Dickens and the Byronic Hero." NCF, 24 (1969), 305-16.

HILL, T. W. "Betty." Di, 43 (1946/47), 41-42.

_____. "Notes to Our Mutual Friend." Di, 43 (1946/47), 85-90.

HOBSBAUM, PHILIP. "The Critics and Our Mutual Friend." EIC, 13 (1963), 231-40.

KENNEDY, G. W. "Dickens's Endings." SNNTS, 6 (1974), 280-87.

_____. "Naming and Language in Our Mutual Friend." NCF, 28 (1973), 165-78.

KIRKPATRICK, LARRY. "The Gothic Flame of Charles Dickens." VN, 31 (Spring 1967), 20-24.

LAMB, CEDRIC. "Love and Self-Interest in Dickens' Novels." Paunch, 33 (Dec. 1968), 32-47.

LANE, LAURIAT, JR. "Dickens and Melville: Our Mutual Friends." DR, 51 (1971), 315-31.

_____. "Dickens and the Double." Di, 55 (1959), 47-55.

_____. "Dickens' Archetypal Jew." PMLA, 73 (1958), 94-100.

LANHAM, RICHARD A. "Our Mutual Friend: The Birds of Prey." VN, 24 (Fall 1963), 6-12.

LeVOT, A. E. "Our Mutual Friend and The Great Gatsby." FitzN, 20 (1963), 1-4.

MABBOTT, THOMAS O. "Railway Signals." N&Q, 191 (1946), 129.

MARLOW, JAMES E. "The Solecism in Our Mutual Friend." DSN, 5 (1974), 7-9.

Bibliography

McMASTER, R. D. "Birds of Prey: A Study of Our Mutual Friend." DR, 40 (1960), 372-81.

_____. "Dickens, the Dandy, and the Savage: A Victorian View of the Romantic." SNNTS, 1 (1969), 133-46.

_____. "'Society (whatever that was)': Dickens and Society as Abstraction." EA, 23 (1970), 125-35.

MIYOSHI, MASAO. "Resolution of Identity in Our Mutual Friend." VN, 26 (Fall 1964), 5-9.

MORSE, ROBERT. "Our Mutual Friend." PR, 16 (1949), 277-89.

MUIR, KENNETH. "Image and Structure in Our Mutual Friend." E&S, N.S. 19 (1966), 92-105.

NELSON, HARLAND S. "Dickens's Our Mutual Friend and Henry Mayhew's London Labour and the London Poor." NCF, 20 (1965), 207-22.

NEWMAN, V. M. "The Most Human Heroine." Di, 38 (1941/42), 181-82.

PAGE, NORMAN. "'A Language Fit for Heroes': Speech in Oliver Twist and Our Mutual Friend." Di, 65 (1969), 100-107.

_____. "Silas Wegg Reads Gibbon." Di, 68 (1972), 115.

PALMER, WILLIAM J. "The Movement of History in Our Mutual Friend." PMLA, 89 (1974), 487-95.

PASSERINI, EDWARD M. "Hawthornesque Dickens." DiS, 2 (1966), 18-25.

PATTERSON, ANNABEL M. "Our Mutual Friend: Dickens as the Compleat Angler." DSA, 1 (1970), 252-64.

PURTON, VALERIE. "Dickens and 'Cheap Melodrama.'" EA, 28 (1975), 22-26.

R., V. "Dickens and a Classical Reference." N&Q, 188 (1945), 232-33.

ROBISON, ROSELEE. "Time, Death and the River in Dickens' Novels." ES, 53 (1972), 436-54.

ROBSON, JOHN M. "Our Mutual Friend: A Rhetorical Approach to the First Number." DSA, 3 (1974), 198-213.

ROOKE, ELEANOR. "Fathers and Sons in Dickens." E&S, N.S. 4 (1951), 53-69.

SHARP, SISTER M. CORONA. "The Archetypal Feminine: Our Mutual Friend." University of Kansas City Review, 27 (Summer 1961), 307-11.

_____. "A Study of the Archetypal Feminine." University of Kansas City Review, 28 (Autumn 1961), 74-80.

Our Mutual Friend

SHEA, FRANCIS X., S.J. "Mr. Venus Observed: The Plot Change in Our Mutual Friend." PLL, 4 (1968), 170-81.

_____. "No Change of Intention in Our Mutual Friend." Di, 63 (1967), 37-40.

SHERER, RAY J. "Laughter in Our Mutual Friend." TSLL, 13 (1971), 509-21.

STEDMAN, JANE W. "Child-Wives of Dickens." Di, 59 (1963), 112-18.

STEWART, GARRET. "The 'Golden Bower' of Our Mutual Friend." ELH, 40 (1973), 105-30.

STONE, HARRY. "Dickens and the Jews." VS, 2 (1959), 223-53.

SUCKSMITH, HARVEY PETER. "The Dust-Heaps in Our Mutual Friend." EIC, 23 (1973), 206-12.

THOMPSON, LESLIE M. "The Masks of Pride in Our Mutual Friend." Di, 60 (1964), 124-28.

VAN GHENT, DOROTHY. "The Dickens World: A View from Todgers's." SR, 58 (1950), 419-38.

WALKER, SAXON. "The Artistry of Dickens as an English Novelist." Di, 51 (1954/55), 102-108.

WALL, STEPHEN. "Dickens's Plot of Fortune." REL, 6 (Jan. 1965), 56-67.

WATT, IAN. "Oral Dickens." DSA, 3 (1974), 165-81.

WEINTRAUB, STANLEY. "Ibsen's 'Doll's House' Metaphor Foreshadowed in Victorian Fiction." NCF, 13 (1958), 67-69.

WILSON, ARTHUR H. "The Great Theme in Charles Dickens." Susquehanna University Studies, 6 (Apr.-June 1959), 422-57.

WILSON, EDMUND. "Dickens: The Two Scrooges." New Republic, 102 (4 Mar. 1940), 297-300, 339-42.

WILSON, JOHN R. "Dickens and Christian Mystery." SAQ, 73 (1974), 528-40.

WINTERS, WARRINGTON. "Charles Dickens: Our Mutual Friend." North Dakota Quarterly, 34 (1966), 96-99.

WRIGHT, AUSTIN. "Our Mutual Friend a Century Later." Carnegie Magazine, 39 (Jan. 1965), 29-31.

WULCKO, LAWRANCE M. "Railway Signals." N&Q, 191 (1946), 64-65.

YOUNG, G. F. "Noddy Boffin's Misers." Di, 43 (1946/47), 14-17.

The Mystery of Edwin Drood

The Mystery of Edwin Drood

CHARACTERIZATION

General: Aylmer, Di, 47 (1950/51), 133-39; Baker, NCF, 4 (1949),
111-28; Bilham, Di, 62 (1966), 182-83; Blakeney, Di, 51
(1954/55), 182-85; Bleifuss, Di, 50 (1953/54), 111-14; Cohen,
DiS, 3 (1967), 126-45; Cox, Di, 58 (1962), 33-42; DiS, 3
(1967), 22-37; Lane, DR, 51 (1971), 327-31; Mitchell, ELH, 33
(1966), 230-46; Pakenham, Di, 51 (1954/55), 120-21; Robison,
ES, 53 (1972), 453-54.

Interior and exterior selves: Mitchell, ELH, 33 (1966), 230-46.

Minor characters: Baker, NCF, 4 (1950), 285-97; 5 (1950), 47-52.

CHARACTERS

Bazzard: Baker, NCF, 2 (1948), 220-21; 5 (1950), 50; Cohen, DiS,
3 (1967), 139-41, 144.

Crisparkle, Rev. Septimus: Cohen, DiS, 3 (1967), 136-37; Dunstan,
Di, 56 (1960), 111; Mitchell, ELH, 33 (1966), 240-41.

Datchery, Dick: Baker, NCF, 4 (1949), 77-81; Bleifuss, Di, 51
(1954/55), 24-29; Cohen, DiS, 3 (1967), 143-44; MacVicar, NCF,
4 (1949), 75-77; (identification): Baker, NCF, 2 (1948),
201-22; 3 (1948), 35-53.

Deputy: Baker, NCF, 5 (1950), 47-50.

Drood, Edwin: Baker, NCF, 2 (1948), 207-208; 4 (1949), 111-28,
221-36; Bleifuss, Di, 50 (1953/54), 176-86; Brend, Di, 52
(1955/56), 20-24; Cohen, DiS, 3 (1967), 128-29; Mitchell,
ELH, 33 (1966), 234-35.

Durdles: Mitchell, ELH, 33 (1966), 232-33.

Grewgious, Hiram: Baker, NCF, 3 (1948), 35-53; 4 (1949), 77-81;
Cohen, DiS, 3 (1967), 137-38; MacVicar, NCF, 4 (1949), 75-77;
Mitchell, ELH, 33 (1966), 237-39.

The Mystery of Edwin Drood

Honeythunder, Luke: Baker, NCF, 5 (1950), 51-52; Fielding, Listener, 48 (1952), 1083-84.

Jasper, John: Baker, Trollopian, 3 (1948), 99-118, 197-99; Bleifuss, Di, 50 (1953/54), 111-14; Cohen, DiS, 3 (1967), 126-28, 144-45; Cox, Di, 58 (1962), 32-38; DiS, 3 (1967), 22-36; Dyson, CritQ, 11 (1969), 147-48, 151-57; Franklin, DSA, 4 (1975), 33-34; Gottschalk, DSA, 1 (1970), 266-71; Lane, Di, 55 (1959), 52-55; DR, 51 (1971), 328-29; Mitchell, ELH, 33 (1966), 230-45; Wing, SEL, 13 (1973), 678-80, 681-82, 684-86.

Landless, Helena: Baker, NCF, 2 (1948), 209-17; (prototype): Winstedt, N&Q, 195 (1950), 325.

Landless, Neville: Baker, NCF, 2 (1948), 208-209; Cox, Di, 58 (1962), 39-42; DiS, 3 (1967), 29-37; Mitchell, ELH, 33 (1966), 239-40.

Princess Puffer: Baker, NCF, 4 (1950), 286-97; (prototype): Collins, Di, 60 (1964), 89-90.

Rosa: Cohen, DiS, 3 (1967), 129-30.

Sapsea, Thomas: Cohen, DiS, 3 (1967), 134-36; Mitchell, ELH, 33 (1966), 232-34.

Tartar, Lieutenant: Baker, NCF, 2 (1948), 217-19; Mitchell, ELH, 33 (1966), 242-44.

Twinkleton, Miss: Cohen, DiS, 3 (1967), 130-32; Collins, Di, 57 (1961), 94-96.

COMPOSITION

General: Cox, DiS, 2 (1966), 33-44.

Dickens's notebook: Ford, NCF, 6 (1952), 277-80.

CRITICAL ASSESSMENT

General: Bleifuss, Di, 50 (1953/54), 110-11; Pritchett, NSN, N.S. 27 (1944), 143; Wilson, Susquehanna University Studies, 6 (Apr.-June 1959), 455-56; (as detective fiction): Wing, SEL, 13 (1973), 677-87.

EXPLANATORY NOTES, HISTORICAL BACKGROUND, and SOURCES

"A Confession" (Master Humphrey's Clock): Baker, NCF, 3 (1949), 281-85.

The Mystery of Edwin Drood

Miscellaneous annotations: Hill, Di, 40 (1943/44), 198-204; 41 (1944/45), 30-37.

Plot: Bilham, Di, 62 (1966), 181; C., N&Q, 186 (1944), 131-33, 184.

Setting (date of action): Hill, Di, 40 (1943/44), 113-17.

ILLUSTRATIONS

Cathedral scene (newly-discovered Collins sketch): Cardwell, Di, 70 (1974), 31-34; 71 (1975), 45-46.

Cover: Baker, NCF, 4 (1950), 279-85; Pakenham, Di, 51 (1954/55), 120.

INFLUENCES (See also LITERARY PARALLELS)

(on Dickens) "An Experience" (Emily Jolly): Baker, NCF, 3 (1949), 285-95; The Disappearance of Jack Ackland (Robert Lytton): ibid., 4 (1949), 37-46.

LANGUAGE and STYLE (See also TECHNIQUES, VARIOUS)

Allusion to Governor Eyre (Chapter 17): Fielding, Listener, 48 (1952), 1083-84.

Imagery (river): Robison, ES, 53 (1972), 444-46, 452-54.

Symbolism (use of double): Lane, Di, 55 (1959), 52-55.

LITERARY PARALLELS (See also INFLUENCES)

Hardy, Desperate Remedies (and Jasper): Wing, SEL, 13 (1973), 682, 684.

Melville, Billy Budd, Sailor (as moral fable): Lane, DR, 51 (1971), 327.

PLOT

General: Aylmer, Di, 47 (1950/51), 133-39; Bilham, Di, 62 (1966), 181-83; Blakeney, Di, 51 (1954/55), 182-85; Bleifuss, Di, 50 (1953/54), 110-15, 176-86; 51 (1954/55), 24-29; Cox, DiS, 3 (1967), 22-37; Dyson, CritQ, 11 (1969), 148-51; Pakenham, Di, 51 (1954/55), 119-21; Wing, SEL, 13 (1973), 678-80.

The Mystery of Edwin Drood

Foreshadowing: Gadd, <u>Di</u>, 36 (1939/40), 185.

Genesis: Baker, <u>NCF</u>, 3 (1949), 281-95; 4 (1949), 37-50.

Inconsistencies: Gibson, <u>Di</u>, 50 (1953/54), 88.

Murder of Drood: Baker, <u>NCF</u>, 4 (1949), 111-28, 221-36.

SETTING

Pastoral, use of (Cloisterham Cathedral): Burgan, <u>MLQ</u>, 36 (1975), 311-13.

TECHNIQUES, VARIOUS

General: Baker, <u>Trollopian</u>, 3 (1948), 99-118, 177-99; <u>NCF</u>, 4 (1950), 275-97; 5 (1950), 47-65; Bleifuss, <u>Di</u>, 50 (1953/54), 110-15, 176-86; 51 (1954/55), 24-29; Brend, <u>Di</u>, 51 (1954/55), 87-88; Cox, <u>Di</u>, 58 (1962), 33-42; Dyson, <u>CritQ</u>, 11 (1969), 141-55; Greenhalgh, <u>Di</u>, 55 (1959), 68-75; Mitchell, <u>ELH</u>, 33 (1966), 228-46; Pritchett, <u>NSN</u>, N.S. 27 (1944), 143.

Animal magnetism: Baker, <u>NCF</u>, 5 (1950), 52-61; Cox, <u>DiS</u>, 3 (1967), 22-36.

Christmas, use of: Carolan, <u>DR</u>, 52 (1972), 378-82.

Fathers and sons, use of: Winters, <u>L&P</u>, 6 (1966), 114-15.

Sapsea fragment: Baker, <u>NCF</u>, 4 (1950), 277-79.

Time, use of: Franklin, <u>DSA</u>, 4 (1975), 31-34; Gottschalk, <u>DSA</u>, 1 (1970), 265-72.

THEMES

General: Bleifuss, <u>Di</u>, 50 (1953/54), 111-14.

Christmas, attitude toward: Brown, <u>Di</u>, 60 (1964), 19; Carolan, <u>DR</u>, 52 (1972), 378-82.

Death (and river imagery): Robison, <u>ES</u>, 53 (1972), 452-54.

Fathers and sons: Rooke, <u>E&S</u>, N.S. 4 (1951), 68-69.

Psychology of murder: Cox, <u>Di</u>, 58 (1962), 33-42.

Time: Franklin, <u>DSA</u>, 4 (1975), 31-34; Gottschalk, <u>DSA</u>, 1 (1970), 265-72; (and water imagery): Robison, <u>ES</u>, 53 (1972), 444-46.

Bibliography for
The Mystery of Edwin Drood

AYLMER, FELIX. "First Aid for the Drood Audience." Di, 47
(1950/51), 133-39.

BAKER, RICHARD M. "The Datchery Assumption: Reply." NCF, 4 (1949),
77-81.

_____. "The Genesis of Edwin Drood." NCF, 3 (1949), 281-95; 4
(1949), 37-50.

_____. "John Jasper--Murderer." Trollopian, 3 (1948), 99-118,
177-99.

_____. "Was Edwin Drood Murdered?" NCF, 4 (1949), 111-28, 221-36.

_____. "What Might Have Been: A Study for Droodians." NCF, 4
(1950), 275-97; 5 (1950), 47-65.

_____. "Who Was Dick Datchery? A Study for Droodians." NCF, 2
(1948), 201-22; 3 (1948), 35-53.

BILHAM, D. M. "Edwin Drood--To Resolve a Mystery?" Di, 62 (1966),
181-83.

BLAKENEY, T. S. "Problems of Edwin Drood." Di, 51 (1954/55),
182-85.

BLEIFUSS, WILLIAM W. "A Re-Examination of Edwin Drood." Di, 50
(1953/54), 110-15, 176-86; 51 (1954/55), 24-29.

BREND, GAVIN. "Edwin Drood and the Four Witnesses." Di, 52
(1955/56), 20-24.

_____. "A Re-Examination of Edwin Drood." Di, 51 (1954/55), 87-88.

BROWN, F. J. "Those Dickens Christmases." Di, 60 (1964), 17-20.

BURGAN, WILLIAM. "Tokens of Winter in Dickens's Pastoral Settings."
MLQ, 36 (1975), 293-315.

C., D. "A Mystery of Edwin Drood." N&Q, 186 (1944), 131-33, 184.

CARDWELL, MARGARET. "Collins's Sketches for Edwin Drood: A Post-
script." Di, 71 (1975), 45-46.

_____. "A Newly Discovered Version of a Collins Sketch for Edwin
Drood." Di, 70 (1974), 31-34.

The Mystery of Edwin Drood

CAROLAN, KATHERINE. "Dickens' Last Christmases." DR, 52 (1972), 373-83.

COHEN, JANE RABB. "Dickens's Artists and Artistry in The Mystery of Edwin Drood." DiS, 3 (1967), 126-45.

COLLINS, PHILIP. "Dickens on the Education of Girls." Di, 57 (1961), 86-96.

_____. "Inspector Bucket Visits the Princess Puffer." Di, 60 (1964), 88-90.

COX, ARTHUR J. "The Drood Remains." DiS, 2 (1966), 33-44.

_____. "'If I hide my watch--.'" DiS, 3 (1967), 22-37.

_____. "The Morals of Edwin Drood." Di, 58 (1962), 32-42.

DUNSTAN, J. LESLIE. "The Ministers in Dickens." Di, 56 (1960), 103-13.

DYSON, A. E. "Edwin Drood: A Horrible Wonder Apart." CritQ, 11 (1969), 138-57.

FIELDING, K. J. "Edwin Drood and Governor Eyre." Listener, 48 (1952), 1083-84.

FORD, GEORGE H. "Dickens's Notebook and Edwin Drood." NCF, 6 (1952), 275-80.

FRANKLIN, STEPHEN L. "Dickens and Time: The Clock Without Hands." DSA, 4 (1975), 1-35.

GADD, W. LAURENCE. "The Dickens Touch." Di, 36 (1939/40), 181-85.

GIBSON, FRANK A. "Discomforts in Dickens." Di, 50 (1953/54), 86-89.

GOTTSCHALK, PAUL. "Time in Edwin Drood." DSA, 1 (1970), 265-72.

GREENHALGH, MOLLIE. "Edwin Drood: The Twilight of a God." Di, 55 (1959), 68-75.

HILL, T. W. "Drood Time in Cloisterham." Di, 40 (1943/44), 113-17.

_____. "Notes on The Mystery of Edwin Drood." Di, 40 (1943/44), 198-204; 41 (1944/45), 30-37.

LANE, LAURIAT, JR. "Dickens and Melville: Our Mutual Friends." DR, 51 (1971), 315-31.

_____. "Dickens and the Double." Di, 55 (1959), 47-55.

MacVICAR, H. M. "The Datchery Assumption: Expostulation." NCF, 4 (1949), 75-77.

MITCHELL, CHARLES. "The Mystery of Edwin Drood: The Interior and Exterior of Self." ELH, 33 (1966), 228-46.

PAKENHAM, PANSY. "The Memorandum Book, Forster and Edwin Drood."
  Di, 51 (1954/55), 117-21.

PRITCHETT, V. S. "Books in General." NSN, N.S. 27 (1944), 143.

ROBISON, ROSELEE. "Time, Death and the River in Dickens' Novels."
  ES, 53 (1972), 436-54.

ROOKE, ELEANOR. "Fathers and Sons in Dickens." E&S, N.S. 4 (1951),
  53-69.

WILSON, ARTHUR H. "The Great Theme in Charles Dickens." Susquehanna
  University Studies, 6 (Apr.-June 1959), 422-57.

WING, GEORGE. "Edwin Drood and Desperate Remedies: Prototypes of
  Detective Fiction in 1870." SEL, 13 (1973), 677-87.

WINSTEDT, E. O. "Helena Landless." N&Q, 195 (1950), 325.

WINTERS, WARRINGTON. "The Death Hug in Charles Dickens." L&P, 6
  (1966), 109-15.

Christmas Books

Christmas Books

CHARACTERIZATION

Psychological double: Stone, KR, 24 (1962), 666-67.

CRITICAL ASSESSMENT

General: Wilson, Susquehanna University Studies, 6 (Apr.-June 1959), 435-37.

Contemporary reaction: Slater, Di, 65 (1969), 17-18; (Chartist reviewers): Peyrouton, Di, 60 (1964), 78-84, 152.

LANGUAGE and STYLE

Tone: Slater, Di, 65 (1969), 20-21.

PLOT

Fairy tale elements: Stone, KR, 24 (1962), 667-68.

Supernatural elements: Slater, Di, 65 (1969), 21-22.

THEMES

Christmas: C., TLS, 13 Nov. 1943, p. 541; Collins, EA, 23 (1970), 161-67.

Exaltation of home and family: Slater, Di, 65 (1969), 23-24.

Social criticism: Slater, Di, 65 (1969), 22-23.

Bibliography for Christmas Books

C., H. H. "Three Christmases. 1-The Dickens Feast." <u>TLS</u>, 13 Nov. 1943, p. 541.

COLLINS, PHILIP. "'<u>Carol</u> Philosophy, Cheerful Views.'" <u>EA</u>, 23 (1970), 158-67.

PEYROUTON, N. C. "Dickens and the Chartists." <u>Di</u>, 60 (1964), 78-88, 152-61.

SLATER, MICHAEL. "The Christmas Books." <u>Di</u>, 65 (1969), 17-24.

STONE, HARRY. "Fire, Hand, and Gate: Dickens' <u>Great Expectations</u>." <u>KR</u>, 24 (1962), 662-91.

WILSON, ARTHUR H. "The Great Theme in Charles Dickens." <u>Susquehanna University Studies</u>, 6 (Apr.-June 1959), 422-57.

A Christmas Carol

CHARACTERS

Ghost of Christmas Past: Patten, <u>DSA</u>, 2 (1972), 175–76.

Ghost of Christmas Present: Patten, <u>DSA</u>, 2 (1972), 180–81.

Marley: Patten, <u>DSA</u>, 2 (1972), 168–73.

Scrooge, Ebenezer: Cox, <u>PMLA</u>, 90 (1975), 922–23; Gilbert, <u>PMLA</u>, 90 (1975), 22–23, 25–30; 90 (1975), 923–24; Hardy, <u>VS</u>, 5 (1961), 53–55; Johnson, <u>ASch</u>, 21 (1952), 93–98; <u>SatR</u>, 30 Dec. 1967, pp. 13, 42; Morris, <u>SSF</u>, 3 (1965), 46–55; Patten, <u>DSA</u>, 2 (1972), 163–64, 166–96; Steig, <u>VS</u>, 13 (1970), 340–42.

COMPOSITION

Background: Butt, <u>Di</u>, 51 (1954/55), 15–18.

CRITICAL ASSESSMENT

General: Collins, <u>EA</u>, 23 (1970), 158–60; Watt, <u>SatR</u>, 4 Dec. 1943, pp. 16–18.

EXPLANATORY NOTES, HISTORICAL BACKGROUND, and SOURCES

Cooking Christmas dinner: D., <u>N&Q</u>, 178 (1940), 68–69.

Liturgy of Christmas: Patten, <u>DSA</u>, 2 (1972), 188–90.

LANGUAGE and STYLE (<u>See also</u> TECHNIQUES, VARIOUS)

Imagery (anality and excrement): Steig, <u>VS</u>, 13 (1970), 340–43.

A Christmas Carol

SETTING

Time, historical: Patten, <u>DSA</u>, 2 (1972), 169–70.

World of novel: Patten, <u>DSA</u>, 2 (1972), 171–73, 176–96.

TECHNIQUES, VARIOUS

General: Gilbert, <u>PMLA</u>, 90 (1975), 22–30; Morris, <u>SSF</u>, 3 (1965), 47–55.

Dreams, use of: Morris, <u>SSF</u>, 3 (1965), 47–55.

Fires, use of: Greaves, <u>Di</u>, 41 (1944/45), 47.

Food and drink (preparation or consumption): Watt, <u>DSA</u>, 3 (1974), 166–67.

Metaphysical vs. rationalistic narrative: Gilbert, <u>PMLA</u>, 90 (1975), 24–30.

Time, use of: Franklin, <u>DSA</u>, 4 (1975), 15–16; Patten, <u>DSA</u>, 2 (1972), 166–96; (first stave): <u>ibid.</u>, 166–70.

THEMES

General: Butt, <u>Di</u>, 51 (1954/55), 17–18; Morris, <u>SSF</u>, 3 (1965), 46–55; Patten, <u>DSA</u>, 2 (1972), 172–73, 176–96; Slater, <u>Di</u>, 65 (1969), 18–19.

Brotherhood: Wrigg, <u>EJ</u>, 48 (1959), 538–39.

Business rapacity: Johnson, <u>SatR</u>, 30 Dec. 1967, pp. 13, 42.

Christmas, attitude toward: Brown, <u>Di</u>, 60 (1964), 18–19.

Innocence, metaphysical: Gilbert, <u>PMLA</u>, 90 (1975), 24–30.

Social criticism: Johnson, <u>ASch</u>, 21 (1952), 91–98.

Spiritual rebirth: Patten, <u>DSA</u>, 2 (1972), 164–65, 173–96.

Time: Franklin, <u>DSA</u>, 4 (1975), 15–16; Patten, <u>DSA</u>, 2 (1972), 166–96.

Bibliography for
A Christmas Carol

BROWN, F. J. "Those Dickens Christmases." Di, 60 (1964), 17-20.

BUTT, JOHN E. "A Christmas Carol: Its Origin and Design." Di, 51 (1954/55), 15-18.

COLLINS, PHILIP. "'Carol Philosophy, Cheerful Views.'" EA, 23 (1970), 158-67.

COX, DON RICHARD. "Scrooge's Conversion." PMLA, 90 (1975), 922-23.

D., M. H. "At Christmas: Ibsen and Dickens." N&Q, 178 (1940), 68-69.

FRANKLIN, STEPHEN L. "Dickens and Time: The Clock Without Hands." DSA, 4 (1975), 1-35.

GILBERT, ELLIOT L. "The Ceremony of Innocence: Charles Dickens' A Christmas Carol." PMLA, 90 (1975), 22-31.

_____. "Scrooge's Conversion." PMLA, 90 (1975), 923-24.

GREAVES, JOHN. "Fireside Reflections." Di, 41 (1944/45), 43-47.

HARDY, BARBARA. "The Change of Heart in Dickens' Novels." VS, 5 (1961), 49-67.

JOHNSON, EDGAR. "A Christmas Carol." SatR, 30 Dec. 1967, pp. 13, 42.

_____. "The Christmas Carol and the Economic Man." ASch, 21 (1952), 91-98.

MORRIS, WILLIAM E. "The Conversion of Scrooge: A Defense of That Good Man's Motivation." SSF, 3 (1965), 46-55.

PATTEN, ROBERT L. "Dickens Time and Again." DSA, 2 (1972), 163-96.

SLATER, MICHAEL. "The Christmas Books." Di, 65 (1969), 17-24.

STEIG, MICHAEL. "Dickens' Excremental Vision." VS, 13 (1970), 339-54.

WATT, IAN. "Oral Dickens." DSA, 3 (1974), 165-81.

WATT, WILLIAM W. "Christmas 1943--a Dickens Centenary." SatR, 4 Dec. 1943, pp. 16-18.

WRIGG, WILLIAM. "Dickens' Message of Christmas." EJ, 48 (1959), 537-39.

The Chimes

CHARACTERIZATION

General: Slater, DiS, 2 (1966), 110-23, 125-40.

CHARACTERS

Fern, Will (prototype): Smith, VS, 18 (1974), 211-15.
Toby: Tarr, NCF, 27 (1972), 211-15.

COMPOSITION

Ms. and revisions: Slater, DiS, 2 (1966), 109-40.

CRITICAL ASSESSMENT

Contemporary reaction (Bulwer-Lytton): Flower, Di, 69 (1973), 83-84.

EXPLANATORY NOTES, HISTORICAL BACKGROUND, and SOURCES

Dickens's attitude toward the workingman: Smith, VS, 18 (1974), 197-217.

Depiction of the poor: Humpherys, DSA, 4 (1975), 89.

INFLUENCES

(on Dickens) Carlyle: Slater, NCF, 24 (1970), 506-19; Carlyle, Chartism: Smith, VS, 18 (1974), 213-15; Carlyle, Past and Present ("Justice Metaphor"): Tarr, NCF, 27 (1972), 208-15; Jerrold: Slater, NCF, 24 (1970), 520-26.

The Chimes

LANGUAGE and STYLE (<u>See also</u> TECHNIQUES, VARIOUS)

Metaphor (of justice): Tarr, <u>NCF</u>, 27 (1972), 209-15.

Symbolism: Marlow, <u>NCF</u>, 30 (1975), 28-30.

TECHNIQUES, VARIOUS

Realism: Tarr, <u>NCF</u>, 27 (1972), 209-15.

THEMES

General: Slater, <u>DiS</u>, 2 (1966), 108; <u>Di</u>, 65 (1969), 19.

Justice: Tarr, <u>NCF</u>, 27 (1972), 210-15.

Bibliography for *The Chimes*

FLOWER, SIBYLLA JANE. "Charles Dickens and Edward Bulwer-Lytton."
<u>Di</u>, 69 (1973), 79-89.

HUMPHERYS, ANNE. "Dickens and Mayhew on the London Poor." <u>DSA</u>, 4
(1975), 78-90.

MARLOW, JAMES E. "Memory, Romance, and the Expressive Symbol in
Dickens." <u>NCF</u>, 30 (1975), 20-32.

SLATER, MICHAEL. "Carlyle and Jerrold into Dickens: A Study of <u>The
Chimes</u>." <u>NCF</u>, 24 (1970), 506-26.

_____. "The Christmas Books." <u>Di</u>, 65 (1969), 17-24.

_____. "Dickens (and Forster) at Work on <u>The Chimes</u>." <u>DiS</u>, 2
(1966), 106-40.

SMITH, SHEILA M. "John Overs to Charles Dickens: A Working-Man's
Letter and Its Implications." <u>VS</u>, 18 (1974), 195-217.

TARR, RODGER L. "Dickens' Debt to Carlyle's 'Justice Metaphor' in
<u>The Chimes</u>." <u>NCF</u>, 27 (1972), 208-15.

The Cricket on the Hearth

TECHNIQUES, VARIOUS

January-May motif: Manning, <u>Di</u>, 71 (1975), 67-68.

Bibliography for
The Cricket on the Hearth

MANNING, SYLVIA. "Dickens, January, and May." <u>Di</u>, 71 (1975), 67-75.

The Battle of Life

CHARACTERS

Two sisters: Gibson, Di, 58 (1962), 44-45.

COMPOSITION

Background: Gibson, Di, 58 (1962), 43.

CRITICAL ASSESSMENT

Contemporary reaction: Mason, Di, 43 (1946/47), 174.

LANGUAGE AND STYLE

Allusion (religious): Carolan, Di, 69 (1973), 106-10.

LITERARY PARALLELS

Goldsmith, The Vicar of Wakefield: Carolan, Di, 69 (1973), 105-106.

Bibliography for
The Battle of Life

CAROLAN, KATHERINE. "The Battle of Life, a Love Story." Di, 69 (1973), 105-10.

GIBSON, FRANK A. "Nature's Possible: A Reconsideration of The Battle of Life." Di, 58 (1962), 43-46.

MASON, LEO. "Jane Eyre and David Copperfield." Di, 43 (1946/47), 172-79.

The Haunted Man

CHARACTERIZATION

    Psychological double: Stone, <u>KR</u>, 24 (1962), 666–67.

CHARACTERS

    Redlaw: Stone, <u>KR</u>, 24 (1962), 666–67, 668; <u>SAQ</u>, 61 (1962), 496–505; Tick, <u>NCF</u>, 24 (1969), 151–52.

PLOT (<u>See also</u> STRUCTURE/UNITY)

    Fairy tale elements: Stone, <u>SAQ</u>, 61 (1962), 494–99.

SETTING

    World of novel: Stone, <u>SAQ</u>, 61 (1962), 494–99.

STRUCTURE/UNITY (<u>See also</u> PLOT)

    Allegory: Stone, <u>SAQ</u>, 61 (1962), 499–502.

TECHNIQUES, VARIOUS

    General: Stone, <u>SAQ</u>, 61 (1962), 494–505.
    Autobiography, use of: Stone, <u>SAQ</u>, 61 (1962), 503–504.

THEMES

    General: Stone, <u>SAQ</u>, 61 (1962), 500.

Bibliography for
The Haunted Man

STONE, HARRY. "Dickens' Artistry and <u>The Haunted Man</u>." <u>SAQ</u>, 61 (1962), 492-505.

_____. "Fire, Hand, and Gate: Dickens' <u>Great Expectations</u>." <u>KR</u>, 24 (1962), 662-91.

TICK, STANLEY. "The Memorializing of Mr. Dick." <u>NCF</u>, 24 (1969), 142-53.

Appendix I

Selected Books and Reviews, 1940-1975

AMALRIC, JEAN-CLAUDE, ed. Studies in the Later Dickens. Montpellier: Université Paul Valéry, 1973.

    Ford, George H. DSN, 6 (1975), 61-64.
    Rosenberg, Edgar. Di, 70 (1974), 130.

AXTON, WILLIAM F. Circle of Fire: Dickens' Vision and Style and the Popular Theatre. Lexington: Univ. of Kentucky Press, 1966.

    Bailey, J. O. Style, 4 (1970), 81-83.
    Cribb, T. J. RES, N.S. 19 (Aug. 1968), 348.
    Davis, Earle. ELN, 6 (Dec. 1968), 146-48.
    Ford, George H. Cithara, 7 (Nov. 1967), 75-77.
    Lane, Lauriat, Jr. DiS, 3 (1967), 170-75.
    Meisel, Martin. JEGP, 67 (Jan. 1968), 169-70.
    Monod, Sylvère. WHR, 22 (Spring 1968), 173-75.
    Staples, L. C. Di, 63 (1967), 124.
    Worth, Katherine J. VS, 11 (1968), 416-17.

AYLMER, FELIX. Dickens Incognito. London: Hart-Davis, 1959.

    Fielding, K. J. MLR, 55 (1960), 436-37.
    TLS, 27 Nov. 1959, p. 694.
    Wood, Frederick T. ES, 41 (1960), 403.

———. The Drood Case. London: Hart-Davis, 1964.

    Birch, Dennis. Di, 61 (1965), 36-39.
    Fielding, K. J. NCF, 20 (1966), 410-12.
    Peyrouton, N. C. DiS, 1 (1965), 104-106.
    TLS, 5 Nov. 1964, p. 1000.
    Wood, Frederick T. ES, 46 (Dec. 1965), 516.

BAKER, RICHARD M. The Drood Murder Case. Berkeley: Univ. of California Press, 1951.

    Culler, A. Dwight. YR, 41 (1951), 303-308.
    TLS, 19 Oct. 1951, p. 654.

Appendix I

BECKWITH, CHARLES E., ed. Twentieth Century Interpretations of A
    Tale of Two Cities. Englewood Cliffs, N.J.: Prentice-Hall,
    1972.

        Monod, Sylvère. DSN, 4 (1973), 100-102.
        Woodcock, George. Di, 69 (1973), 53-54.

BLOUNT, TREVOR. Charles Dickens: The Early Novels. London: Long-
    mans, Green, 1968.

        TLS, 1 Aug. 1968, p. 834.

BROOK, G. L. The Language of Dickens. London: André Deutsch, 1970.

        Badessa, Richard P. DSN, 2 (1971), 76-78.
        Greenberg, Robert. NCF, 27 (1972), 357-61.
        Holloway, J. Encounter, 34 (June 1970), 63-65.
        Page, Norman. Di, 66 (1970), 250-51.
        Wall, Stephen. EIC, 21 (July 1971), 261-80.

BROWN, ARTHUR WASHBURN. A Sexual Analysis of Dickens' Props. New
    York: Emerson Books, 1971.

        Dodsworth, Martin. Di, 68 (1972), 191-93.
        Horton, Susan. VS, 16 (1972), 251-52.
        Senelick, Laurence. DSN, 4 (1973), 50-52.
        TLS, 8 Oct. 1971, p. 1214.

BROWN, IVOR. Dickens in His Time. London: Nelson, 1963.

        Stone, Harry. NCF, 19 (1964), 308-309.
        TLS, 16 Jan. 1964, p. 48.

BUTT, JOHN E. and KATHLEEN TILLOTSON. Dickens at Work. London:
    Methuen, 1957.

        Carnall, Geoffrey. MLR, 53 (Oct. 1958), 574-75.
        Engel, Monroe. VS, 1 (1958), 288-89.
        Fielding, K. J. Di, 65 (1969), 49-51.
        Howard, Daniel. KR, 21 (1958), 309-20.
        Jump, John D. RES, N.S. 10 (1959), 98-100.
        Lane, Lauriat, Jr. MLN, 74 (1959), 543-46.
        Thomas, Gilbert. English, 12 (1958), 21-22.

CAREY, JOHN. The Violent Effigy: A Study of Dickens' Imagination.
    London: Faber and Faber, 1973; American Title: Here Comes Dick-
    ens: The Imagination of a Novelist. New York: Schocken Books,
    1974.

        Axton, W. F. JEGP, 74 (1975), 251.
        Fielding, K. J. RES, N.S. 26 (May 1975), 235-37.
        Giddings, Robert. DSN, 6 (1975), 115-19.

Goldberg, Michael. NCF, 29 (1974), 354-57.
Hardy, Barbara. Di, 71 (1975), 49-51.
Pickering, Samuel, Jr. MP, 73 (1975), 205.
TLS, 11 Jan. 1974, pp. 21-22.

CLARK, WILLIAM R. Discussions of Charles Dickens. Boston: Heath, 1961.

Fielding, K. J. Di, 58 (1962), 150-51.

COCKSHUT, A. O. J. The Imagination of Charles Dickens. London: Collins, 1961.

Collins, H. P. EIC, 13 (Apr. 1963), 177-80.
Fielding, K. J. Di, 58 (1962), 21-22.
Marcus, Steven. NSN, 62 (1 Sept. 1961), 278-79.
McMaster, R. D. QQ, 69 (Autumn 1962), 482-84.
Stone, Harry. NCF, 17 (1962), 89-91.
TLS, 15 Sept. 1961, p. 615.
Wood, Frederick T. English, 43 (Aug. 1962), 274-75.

COLLINS, PHILIP. Dickens and Crime. London: Macmillan, 1962.

Barnard, Robert. SoRA, 1 (1963), 99-102.
Butt, John E. Di, 59 (1963), 44-45.
Engel, Monroe. VS, 7 (1963), 105-106.
Fielding, K. J. RES, N.S. 14 (1963), 308-309.
Gross, John. NSN, 64 (4 Aug. 1962), 234.
Jump, John D. CritQ, 4 (1962), 371-72.
McMaster, R.D. QQ, 71 (Summer 1964), 278-79.
TLS, 17 Aug. 1962, p. 627.
Wood, Frederick T. ES, 44 (Oct. 1963), 390.

_____. Dickens and Education. London: Macmillan, 1963.

Blount, Trevor. RES, N.S. 17 (1966), 219-21.
Hill, A. G. CritQ, 7 (1965), 374-83.
McMaster, R. D. NCF, 19 (1964), 306-308.
Stone, Harry. VS, 8 (1965), 371-72.
Thomas, Gilbert. English, 15 (Summer 1964), 64.
TLS, 12 Dec. 1963, p. 1034.
VQR, 40 (Spring 1964), 66.

_____. Dickens: The Critical Heritage. London: Routledge and Kegan Paul, 1971.

Hawes, Donald. DSN, 5 (1974), 115-17.
Rantavaara, Irma. Di, 67 (1971), 109-11.
Robson, A. P. VS, 16 (1972), 475-80.
TLS, 5 Mar. 1971, pp. 269-70.
Wall, Stephen. EIC, 21 (July 1971), 261-80.

Appendix I

COOLIDGE, ARCHIBALD C., JR. Charles Dickens as Serial Novelist.
    Ames: Iowa State Univ. Press, 1967.

    Fielding, K. J. Di, 63 (1967), 156-57.
    Ford, George H. Novel, 2 (1969), 184-85.
    Hale, Osborne. North Dakota Quarterly, 35 (Spring 1967),
      55-57.
    Monod, Sylvère. WHR, 22 (1968), 173-75.
    Smith, Grahame. MLR, 64 (Apr. 1969), 409.
    Sutherland, J. A. DiS, 4 (1968), 95-98.
    TLS, 28 Dec. 1967, p. 1265.

COUSTILLAS, PIERRE, ed. Gissing's Writings on Dickens. London:
    Enitharmon Press, 1970.

    Curtis, Anthony. DSN, 4 (1973), 26-28.
    Slater, Michael. Di, 66 (1970), 253.
    TLS, 11 June 1970, p. 630.

CRUIKSHANK, ROBERT J. Charles Dickens. London: Pitman, 1949.

    NCF, 5 (1950), 80-83.

DABNEY, ROSS H. Love and Property in the Novels of Dickens. London:
    Chatto and Windus, 1967.

    Cribb, T. J. RES, N.S. 19 (May 1968), 243.
    Ford, George H. MP, 66 (1969), 381-83.
    Hamilton, Robert. Di, 63 (1967), 110.
    Kettle, Arnold. VS, 11 (1967), 249.
    Lane, Lauriat, Jr. DiS, 3 (1967), 170-75.
    TLS, 4 Jan. 1968, p. 10.

DALESKI, H. M. Dickens and the Art of Analogy. New York: Schocken
    Books, 1970.

    Axton, William F. MLQ, 33 (1972), 203-205.
    Ganz, Margaret. VS, 15 (1971), 234-36.
    Price, Martin. YR, 61 (1972), 271-79.
    Smith, Grahame. Di, 67 (1971), 49-51.
    Sucksmith, Harvey Peter. NCF, 26 (1971), 352-57.
    Thomas, Gilbert. English, 20 (Spring 1971), 25-26.
    Thomson, Patricia. RES, N.S. 22 (1971), 509-12.
    TLS, 25 Dec. 1970, p. 1521.
    Wall, Stephen. EIC, 21 (July 1971), 261-80.
    Wing, George. DSN, 1 (Dec. 1970), 13-15.

DAVIS, EARLE R. The Flint and the Flame: The Artistry of Charles
    Dickens. Columbia: Univ. of Missouri Press, 1963.

    Butt, John E. NCF, 19 (1964), 88-91.
    Coolidge, Archibald C., Jr. MP, 63 (1965), 84-87.
    Lewis, Leslie. ELN, 3 (Dec. 1965), 152-54.
    McMaster, R. D. DR, 45 (Summer 1965), 217-19.
    Miller, J. Hillis. JEGP, 63 (1964), 534-36.
    Peyrouton, N. C. Di, 60 (1964), 40-42.
    Thomas, Gilbert. English, 15 (Summer 1964), 64.
    TLS, 16 Jan. 1964, p. 48; 10 Feb. 1966, p. 104.

Dickens Criticism: Past, Present and Future Directions: A Sym-
    posium. Cambridge, Mass.: Charles Dickens Reference Center,
    1962.

    Fielding, K. J. Di, 59 (1963), 73-77.

DYSON, A. E. Dickens: Modern Judgements. Toronto: Macmillan,
    1968.

    Rosenberg, Edgar. Di, 65 (1969), 187-89.
    TLS, 25 July 1968, p. 783.

_____. The Inimitable Dickens: A Reading of the Novels. London:
    Macmillan, 1970.

    Burton, Anthony. Di, 66 (1970), 244.
    Cribb, T. J. RES, N.S. 22 (Aug. 1971), 388-89.
    Fido, Martin. VS, 15 (1971), 101-102.
    Hornback, Bert G. DSN, 1 (Dec. 1970), 11-13.
    Pritchett, V. S. NSN, 79 (5 June 1970), 807.
    Thomas, Gilbert. English, 20 (Spring 1971), 25-26.
    TLS, 4 June 1970, p. 598.
    Wall, Stephen. EIC, 21 (1971), 261-80.

ELTON, OLIVER. Dickens and Thackeray. New York: Haskell House,
    1970.

    Axton, William F. DSN, 2 (1971), 78-80.

ENGEL, MONROE. The Maturity of Dickens. Cambridge, Mass.: Harvard
    Univ. Press, 1959.

    Butt, John E. RES, N.S. 11 (1960), 440-43.
    Cox, C. B. CritQ, 1 (1959), 360.
    Johnson, Edgar. NCF, 14 (1959), 182-84.
    Kreisel, Henry. UTQ, 31 (Jan. 1962), 246-50.
    L&P, 9 (1959), 23.
    Nisbet, Ada. VS, 3 (1960), 311-13.

Appendix I

Peyrouton, N. C. <u>Di</u>, 55 (1959), 155-56.
Stevenson, Lionel. <u>JEGP</u>, 59 (1960), 308-10.
Thomas, Gilbert. <u>English</u>, 13 (Spring 1960), 24.
Tillotson, Kathleen. <u>MLR</u>, 55 (1960), 597-98.
<u>TLS</u>, 20 Nov. 1959, p. 678.

FANGER, DONALD. <u>Dostoevsky and Romantic Realism: A Study of Dosto-</u>
<u>evsky in Relation to Balzac, Dickens and Gogol</u>. Cambridge,
Mass.: Harvard Univ. Press, 1965.

Becker, George J. <u>MLQ</u>, 26 (Dec. 1965), 606-10.
C., C. <u>ELN</u>, 4 (Sept. 1966), Supp., 56.
Muchnic, H. <u>CL</u>, 19 (Winter 1967), 78-80.
Panichas, George A. <u>MLJ</u>, 51 (1967), 50-51.
<u>TLS</u>, 3 Mar. 1966, p. 165.

FIDO, MARTIN. <u>Charles Dickens</u>. London: Routledge and Kegan Paul,
1968.

Schaefer, William D. <u>NCF</u>, 24 (1969), 249-50.

_____. <u>Charles Dickens: An Authentic Account of His Life and Times</u>.
London: Hamlyn, 1970.

Burton, Anthony. <u>Di</u>, 66 (1970), 246.
<u>TLS</u>, 4 June 1970, p. 618.

FIELDING, K. J. <u>Charles Dickens: A Critical Introduction</u>. London:
Longmans, Green, 1958, 1960.

Jump, John D. <u>RES</u>, N.S. 11 (1960), 223-25.
Nisbet, Ada. <u>VS</u>, 3 (1960), 311-13.
Packenham, Pansy. <u>Di</u>, 55 (1959), 31-32.
<u>TLS</u>, 7 Nov. 1958, p. 642.
Wood, Frederick T. <u>ES</u>, 41 (1960), 115.

_____. <u>Charles Dickens: A Critical Introduction</u>. London: Long-
mans, Green, 1965.

Harvey, W. J. <u>EIC</u>, 15 (July 1965), 353-55.
Kinney, Arthur F. <u>CE</u>, 27 (May 1966), 655-56.
<u>TLS</u>, 4 Aug. 1966, p. 702.

FLEISSNER, ROBERT F. <u>Dickens and Shakespeare: A Study in Histrionic</u>
<u>Contrasts</u>. New York: Haskell House, 1965.

Collins, Philip. <u>NCF</u>, 21 (1967), 401-403.

FORD, GEORGE H. Dickens and His Readers: Aspects of Novel Criticism Since 1836. Princeton, N.J.: Princeton Univ. Press, 1955.

Bevington, Merle. SAQ, 55 (1956), 243-44.
Johnson, Edgar. VQR, 31 (1955), 644-48.
Rolfe, Franklin P. NCF, 10 (1955), 242-45.
Ross, Malcolm. QQ, 62 (Autumn 1955), 469-71.
Stone, Edward. CE, 17 (1955), 124-25.
Tillotson, Geoffrey. SR, 64 (Fall 1956), 671-73.
TLS, 6 Jan. 1956, p. 3.
Wilson, Angus. Encounter, 6 (Apr. 1956), 75-77.

FORD, GEORGE H. and LAURIAT LANE, JR., eds. The Dickens Critics. Ithaca, N.Y.: Cornell Univ. Press, 1961.

Crompton, Louis. CE, 24 (Oct. 1962), 70.
Fielding, K. J. Di, 58 (1962), 150-51.
Garis, Robert E. VS, 7 (1964), 375-86.
Jump, John D. CritQ, 4 (1962), 371-72.
McMaster, R. D. DR, 42 (Autumn 1962), 391-93.
_____. QQ, 69 (Autumn 1962), 483-84.
Pritchard, A. D. UTQ, 32 (July 1963), 413-14.
Stevenson, Lionel. SAQ, 61 (Autumn 1962), 568.
TLS, 15 Feb. 1963, p. 108.

GARIS, ROBERT E. The Dickens Theatre: A Reassessment of the Novels. Oxford: Clarendon Press, 1965.

Bell, Vereen M. SoR, N.S. 6 (1970), 532-35.
Burgan, William. VS, 9 (1966), 208-10.
Cribb, T. J. RES, N.S. 17 (1966), 338-39.
Elliott, George P. HR, 18 (1966), 433-41.
Ford, George H. DiS, 2 (1966), 96-101.
Green, Martin. KR, 27 (1965), 510-16.
Gross, John. PR, 33 (1966), 288-92.
Hartman, Joan. JEGP, 65 (1965), 617-20.
Herring, Paul D. MP, 65 (1968), 259-63.
Hill, A. G. CritQ, 7 (Winter 1965), 374-83.
Johnson, Edgar. NCF, 20 (1966), 395-402.
Price, Martin. YR, 55 (1965), 291-96.
TLS, 10 Feb. 1965, p. 104.
Williamson, C. F. EIC, 16 (1966), 228-37.

GERSON, STANLEY. Sound and Symbol in the Dialogue of the Works of Charles Dickens. Stockholm: Almqvist and Wiksell, 1967.

Levitt, H. RES, N.S. 19 (1968), 448-49.

Appendix I

GOLD, JOSEPH. <u>Charles Dickens: Radical Moralist</u>. London: Oxford
    Univ. Press, 1972.

      Bennett, R. <u>RES</u>, N.S. 25 (Aug. 1974), 371.
      Easson, Angus. <u>Di</u>, 69 (1973), 190–91.
      Fleishman, A. <u>MLQ</u>, 34 (June 1973), 191–99.
      Hornback, Bert G. <u>DSN</u>, 4 (1973), 56–58.
      McMaster, R. D. <u>Humanities Association Review</u>, 24 (1973),
         56–58.
      Myers, William. <u>VS</u>, 17 (1973), 108–10.
      Page, Norman. <u>DR</u>, 52 (1973), 691–95.
      Patten, Robert L. <u>NCF</u>, 28 (1973), 103–107.
      Pickering, Samuel. <u>GaR</u>, 27 (1973), 455–63.
      Steig, Michael. <u>West Coast Review</u>, 7 (Jan. 1973), 76.
      Stevenson, Lionel. <u>SAQ</u>, 72 (1973), 332–33.
      Sucksmith, H. P. <u>YES</u>, 5 (1973), 315.
      Thomas, Gilbert. <u>English</u>, 23 (Spring 1974), 36.
      <u>TLS</u>, 25 Jan. 1974, p. 36.
      Welsh, Alexander. <u>YR</u>, 62 (1973), 285.
      Worth, G. W. <u>CEA Critic</u>, 37 (Nov. 1974), 32–35.

———. <u>The Stature of Dickens: A Centenary Bibliography</u>. Toronto:
    Univ. of Toronto Press for Univ. of Manitoba Press, 1971.

      Altick, Richard D. <u>NCF</u>, 27 (1972), 107–10.
      DeVries, Duane. <u>Di</u>, 68 (1972), 188–91.
      Ellsworth, R. C. <u>QQ</u>, 79 (1972), 108.
      Fielding, K. J. <u>RES</u>, N.S. 24 (Feb. 1973), 100–102.
      Heaney, Howell. <u>DSN</u>, 3 (1972), 7–12.
      Partlow, Robert. <u>DSN</u>, 2 (1971), 103–105.

GOLDBERG, MICHAEL. <u>Carlyle and Dickens</u>. Athens: Univ. of Georgia
    Press, 1972.

      Clubbe, J. <u>SAQ</u>, 73 (Autumn 1974), 569–70.
      D., J. A. <u>ELN</u>, 11 (Sept. 1973), 40–41.
      Dunn, Richard. <u>DSN</u>, 4 (1973), 72–76.
      Fielding, K. J. <u>Di</u>, 69 (1973), 111–18.
      Pickering, S. <u>GaR</u>, 27 (1973), 455.
      Sanders, C. R. <u>NCF</u>, 27 (1973), 490.
      Sharples, E. <u>Criticism</u>, 16 (1974), 180–83.
      Slater, Michael. <u>VS</u>, 17 (1974), 328.
      Steig, Michael. <u>West Coast Review</u>, 8 (3 Jan. 1974), 76.
      Sucksmith, H. P. <u>MLR</u>, 69 (1974), 848.
      <u>TLS</u>, 27 Apr. 1973, p. 478.
      Welsh, Alexander. <u>YR</u>, 62 (Winter 1973), 281.
      Worth, G. W. <u>CEA Critic</u>, 37 (Nov. 1974), 32–35.

GOMME, A. H. Dickens. London: Evans, 1971.

     Brice, Alec W. DSN, 4 (1973), 113-15.
     Fielding, K. J. Di, 68 (1972), 60-61.
     TLS, 29 Oct. 1971, p. 1361.

GRAY, PAUL E. Twentieth Century Interpretations of Hard Times.
    Englewood Cliffs, N.J.: Prentice-Hall, 1969.

     Palmer, William J. DSN, 4 (1973), 81-84.

GREAVES, JOHN. Who's Who in Dickens. London: Elm Tree Books, 1972;
    New York: Taplinger, 1973.

     Cheesewright, Gordon. DSN, 5 (1974), 40-44.
     Overbeck, L. Di, 69 (1973), 57-58.
     TLS, 2 Mar. 1973, p. 235.
     Worth, G. J. CEA Critic, 37 (Nov. 1974), 32-35.

GROSS, JOHN and GABRIEL PEARSON, eds. Dickens and the Twentieth Cen-
    tury. London: Routledge and Kegan Paul, 1962.

     Fielding, K. J. Di, 59 (1963), 45-47.
     Garis, Robert E. EIC, 14 (1964), 197-208.
     _____. VS, 7 (1964), 375-86.
     Johnson, Edgar. ELN, 2 (June 1965), 308-13.
     Lane, Lauriat, Jr. NCF, 18 (1963), 200-202.
     McMaster, R. D. DR, 43 (1963-64), 552-54.
     Thomas, Gilbert. RES, N.S. 15 (1964), 212-14.
     TLS, 15 Feb. 1963, p. 108.
     Wood, Frederick T. ES, 44 (Oct. 1963), 389.

HARBAGE, ALFRED B. A Kind of Power: The Shakespeare-Dickens
    Analogy. Philadelphia: American Philosophical Society, 1974.

     Hulse, Bryan. Di, 71 (1975), 174-75.

HARDWICK, MICHAEL and MOLLIE HARDWICK. The Charles Dickens Compan-
    ion. London: Murray, 1965.

     TLS, 8 July 1965, p. 580.

_____. The Charles Dickens Encyclopedia. Reading: Osprey Publish-
ing, 1973.

     Staples, L. C. Di, 69 (1973), 186-87.

HARDY, BARBARA. Dickens: The Later Novels. London: Longmans,
    Green, 1968.

     Robson, W. W. Di, 65 (1969), 114-16.

Appendix I

_____. The Moral Art of Dickens: Essays. London: Athlone Press, 1970.

    Cribb, T. J. RES, N.S. 23 (Aug. 1972), 372.
    Cushman, Keith. MP, 70 (1972), 166-68.
    Johnson, E. D. H. NCF, 27 (1971), 349-52.
    Lane, Lauriat, Jr. DSN, 2 (1971), 47-49.
    Muir, Kenneth. MLR, 67 (Apr. 1972), 405.
    Price, Martin. YR, 61 (Winter 1972), 271-79.
    Thomas, Gilbert. English, 20 (Spring 1971), 25-26.
    TLS, 25 Dec. 1970, p. 1521.
    Wall, Stephen. EIC, 21 (July 1971), 261-80.
    Wilson, Angus. Di, 67 (1971), 45-47.

HAYWARD, ARTHUR L. The Dickens Encyclopedia: An Alphabetical Dictionary. London: Routledge and Kegan Paul, 1969.

    PBSA, 64 (1970), 258.

HOBSBAUM, PHILIP. A Reader's Guide to Charles Dickens. New York: Farrar, Straus, and Giroux, 1972.

    Cheesewright, Gordon. DSN, 5 (1974), 40-44.
    Kincaid, J. R. Di, 70 (1974), 57-59.
    TLS, 27 Apr. 1973, p. 478.

HORNBACK, BERT G. Noah's Arkitecture: A Study of Dickens' Mythology. Athens: Ohio Univ. Press, 1972.

    Fleishman, A. MLQ, 34 (June 1973), 191-99.
    Gold, Joseph. DSN, 4 (1973), 58-60.
    H., B. Di, 69 (1973), 129-30.
    McMaster, R. D. NCF, 28 (1973), 107-10.
    TLS, 27 Apr. 1973, p. 478.
    Worth, G. J. JEGP, 72 (Apr. 1973), 246-49.

HOUSE, HUMPHRY. The Dickens World. London: Oxford Univ. Press, 1941.

    Butt, John E. RES, 20 (Jan. 1944), 88-90.
    Churchill, R. C. Scrutiny, 10 (1942), 304-307.
    Neff, Emery. MLN, 58 (Apr. 1943), 325-26.
    TLS, 11 Oct. 1941, p. 509.
    Young, George M. Di, 38 (1941/42), 61-62.

HOUSE, MADELINE and GRAHAM STOREY, eds. The Letters of Charles Dickens. Vol. I: 1820-1839. Oxford: Clarendon Press, 1965.

    Best, Geoffrey. Di, 61 (1965), 69-77.
    Butt, John E. RES, N.S. 17 (1966), 99-103.
    Girling, Zoe. QQ, 72 (Winter 1966), 693.

Gross, John. NSN, 69 (19 Mar. 1965), 444, 446.
Haight, Gordon. VS, 9 (1965), 51–53.
Hill, A. G. CritQ, 7 (Winter 1965), 374–83.
Hornback, Bert G. MQR, 7 (1967), 65–67.
Johnson, Edgar. KR, 27 (Summer 1965), 503–10.
McMaster, R. D. UTQ, 35 (1965), 313–14.
Nisbet, Ada. NCF, 20 (1966), 391–95.
Stone, Harry. JEGP, 65 (1966), 342–49.
Tillotson, Geoffrey. SR, 75 (1967), 325–37.
TLS, 11 Feb. 1965, pp. 97–99.

_____. The Letters of Charles Dickens. The Pilgrim Edition.
Vol. II: 1840–1841. London: Oxford Univ. Press, 1970.

Altick, Richard D. DSN, 2 (1971), 34–37.
Cribb, T. J. RES, N.S. 22 (Aug. 1971), 388.
Slater, M. Di, 66 (1970), 242–44.
TLS, 11 Dec. 1970, p. 1420.
Wall, Stephen. EIC, 21 (1971), 261–80.

HOUSE, MADELINE, GRAHAM STOREY, and KATHLEEN TILLOTSON, eds. The
Letters of Charles Dickens. Vol. III: 1842–1843. Oxford:
Clarendon Press, 1974.

Altick, Richard D. DSN, 6 (1975), 17–19.
Ford, George H. Di, 71 (1975), 106–109.
Monod, Sylvère. TLS, 6 Dec. 1974, p. 1359.
Welsh, Alexander. YR, 65 (Oct. 1975), 115.

JOHANNSEN, ALBERT. Phiz: Illustrations from the Novels of Charles
Dickens. Chicago: Univ. of Chicago Press, 1956.

Corrigan, Beatrice. VS, 1 (1957), 99–100.
TLS, 29 Mar. 1957, p. 190.

JOHNSON, E. D. H. Charles Dickens: An Introduction to the Reading
of His Novels. New York: Random House, 1969.

Schaefer, William D. NCF, 24 (1969), 249.

JOHNSON, EDGAR. Charles Dickens: His Tragedy and Triumph. 2 vols.
New York: Simon and Schuster, 1952.

ASch, 22 (1953), 379.
Bevington, Merle. SAQ, 53 (1954), 147–50.
Butt, John E. NCF, 8 (1953), 151–53.
Carlton, W. J. Di, 49 (1952), 53–58.
House, Humphry. Listener, 50 (1952), 693–94.
Ray, Gordon N. VQR, 29 (1953), 297–302.

Appendix I

KINCAID, JAMES R. Dickens and the Rhetoric of Laughter. Oxford:
    Clarendon Press, 1971.

    Fielding, K. J. RES, N.S. 24 (Feb. 1973), 100.
    Ganz, Margaret. DSN, 4 (1973), 89-93.
    Myers, William. VS, 17 (1973), 108-10.
    Quirk, E. F. JEGP, 73 (Apr. 1974), 260-62.
    Schlicke, Paul. Di, 69 (1973), 51-53.
    Sucksmith, H. P. YES, 4 (1973), 323.
    Tennyson, G. B. NCF, 27 (1973), 369-75.
    Thomas, Gilbert. English, 21 (Summer 1972), 71-73.
    Welsh, Alexander. YR, 62 (1973), 286-87.

KORG, JACOB. Twentieth Century Interpretations of Bleak House.
    Englewood Cliffs, N.J.: Prentice-Hall, 1968.

    Blount, Trevor. Di, 66 (1970), 57-58.
    Dick, S. QQ, 76 (Summer 1969), 364-66.

KOTZIN, MICHAEL C. Dickens and the Fairy Tale. Bowling Green, Ohio:
    Bowling Green Univ. Press, 1972.

    Goldfarb, Russell. DSN, 3 (1972), 111-12.
    McMaster, R. D. NCF, 28 (1973), 107-10.
    Myers, William. VS, 17 (1973), 108-10.
    Stone, Harry. Di, 69 (1973), 121-23.

LARY, N. M. Dostoevsky and Dickens: A Study of Literary Influence.
    London: Routledge and Kegan Paul, 1973.

    Frank, Joseph. DSN, 6 (1975), 119-23.
    Greene, M. SEER, 52 (Apr. 1974), 315.
    H., B. Di, 70 (1974), 54-55.
    Peace, R. A. MLR, 69 (Apr. 1974), 478-79.
    Stewart, D. H. WHR, 27 (1973), 418-21.
    Sucksmith, H. P. NCF, 29 (1974), 101-104.
    TLS, 10 Aug. 1973, p. 923.
    Wasiolek, Edward. VS, 17 (1974), 342-43.
    Worth, G. W. CEA Critic, 37 (Nov. 1974), 32-35.

LEAVIS, F. R. and Q. D. LEAVIS. Dickens The Novelist. New York:
    Pantheon, 1970.

    Fielding, K. J. DSN, 2 (1971), 37-39.
    Ford, George H. NCF, 26 (1971), 95-113.
    Hardy, Barbara. NSN, 80 (9 Oct. 1970), 456-57.
    Lane, Lauriat, Jr. SNNTS, 5 (Spring 1973), 125-38.
    Mudrick, Marvin. HR, 24 (1971), 346-54.
    Price, Martin. YR, 61 (Winter 1972), 271-79.
    Robson, W. W. Di, 67 (1971), 99-104.

Shelston, A. CritQ, 13 (Spring 1971), 89-91.
TLS, 25 Dec. 1970, p. 1521.
Wall, Stephen. EIC, 21 (July 1971), 261-80.

LINDSAY, JACK. Charles Dickens: A Biographical and Critical Study.
 New York: Philosophical Library, 1950.

 Bevington, Merle. SAQ, 50 (1951), 441-43.
 Ford, George H. MLQ, 14 (1953), 314-16.
 Grubb, G. G. NCF, 5 (1951), 317-24.
 Stevenson, Lionel. MLN, 66 (1951), 416-17.
 TLS, 14 Apr. 1950, p. 231.

LUCAS, JOHN. The Melancholy Man: A Study of Dickens's Novels. London: Methuen, 1970.

 Ganz, Margaret, VS, 15 (1971), 234-36.
 Meckier, Jerome. DSN, 2 (1971), 100-102.
 Thomas, Gilbert. English, 20 (Spring 1971), 25-26.
 TLS, 25 Dec. 1970, p. 1521.
 Wall, Stephen. EIC, 21 (July 1971), 261-80.

MANNING, JOHN. Dickens on Education. Toronto: Univ. of Toronto
 Press, 1959.

 Bantock, G. H. VS, 4 (1960), 167-70.
 Butt, John E. Di, 56 (1960), 98-99.
 Collins, Philip. RES, N.S. 12 (1961), 312-14.
 Donovan, Robert A. Journal of Modern History, 32 (1960), 173.
 Gordon, Wilhelmina. QQ, 67 (Summer 1960), 316.
 Nisbet, Ada. NCF, 15 (1960), 89-90.
 TLS, 4 Mar. 1960, p. 146.

MANNING, SYLVIA BANK. Dickens as Satirist. New Haven: Yale Univ.
 Press, 1971.

 Allen, Richard J. VS, 15 (1972), 492-94.
 Cribb, T. J. RES, N.S. 24 (1973), 230-33.
 DeVries, D. DSN, 2 (1971), 51-53.
 Helfand, Michael S. Novel, 5 (1972), 186-89.
 Price, Martin. YR, 61 (Winter 1972), 271-79.
 Tennyson, G. B. NCF, 27 (1973), 369-75.
 Trickett, Rachel. Di, 68 (1972), 54-56.

MARCUS, STEVEN. Dickens: From Pickwick to Dombey. London: Chatto
 and Windus, 1965.

 Fielding, K. J. DiS, 1 (1965), 145-48.
 Gross, John. NSN, 69 (19 Mar. 1965), p. 446.
 Hardy, Barbara. VS, 9 (1966), 206-207.
 Hill, A. G. CritQ, 7 (Winter 1965), 374-83.

271

Appendix I

Johnson, Edgar. NCF, 20 (1966), 395-402.
McMaster, R. D. DR, 46 (1966), 106-107.
Moynahan, Julian. Encounter, 24 (May 1965), 84-87.
Steig, Michael. L&P, 15 (1965), 230-37.
_____. Paunch, 23 (1965), 68-78.
Stone, Harry. KR, 27 (1965), 516-23.
Thomas, Gilbert. English, 15 (Summer 1965), 192-93.
Williamson, C. F. EIC, 16 (1966), 228-37.
Wood, Frederick J. ES, 47 (1966), 400-401.

MILLER, J. HILLIS. Charles Dickens: The World of His Novels. Cambridge, Mass.: Harvard Univ. Press, 1958.

Booth, Bradford A. MP, 57 (1959), 69-71.
Hardy, Barbara. MLR, 55 (1960), 433-36.
Howard, D. F. KR, 21 (1959), 309-20.
Johnson, Edgar. SatR, 41 (30 Aug. 1958), 17-18.
McMaster, R. D. DR, 38 (1959), 512-16.
Monod, Sylvère. NCF, 13 (1959), 360-63.
Moynahan, Julian. VS, 2 (1958), 170-72.
Peyrouton, N. C. Di, 55 (1959), 32-33.
Rosenberg, Marvin. JEGP, 58 (1959), 544-45.
Stevenson, Lionel. SAQ, 58 (1959), 478-79.
Tillotson, Kathleen. MLN, 75 (1960), 439-42.
TLS, 16 Jan. 1959, p. 30.
Wood, Frederick T. ES, 41 (1960), 403.

_____ and DAVID BOROWITZ. Charles Dickens and George Cruikshank.
Los Angeles: William Andrews Clark Memorial Library, Univ. of
California, 1971.

Cohen, Jane Rabb. Di, 68 (1972), 58-60.
PBSA, 65 (1971), 435.
Steig, Michael. DSN, 3 (1972), 112-14.
Sucksmith, H. P. YES, 3 (1972), 316.
TLS, 29 Oct. 1971, p. 1361.

MIYAZAKI, KOICHI. A Study of Two of Dickens' Later Novels. Tokyo:
Seijo English Monographs, 1972.

McCullen, Maurice. DSN, 5 (1974), 44-48.

MONOD, SYLVÈRE. Dickens The Novelist. Norman: Univ. of Oklahoma
Press, 1968.

Fielding, K. J. Di, 65 (1969), 49-51.
McMaster, R. D. NCF, 23 (1968), 359-61.
Reed, John R. CLS, 6 (1969), 346-48.
Stoehr, Taylor. Novel, 2 (1968), 81-82.
TLS, 13 Nov. 1969, p. 1319.

NISBET, ADA and BLAKE NEVIUS, eds. <u>Dickens Centennial Essays</u>.
    Berkeley: Univ. of California Press, 1971.

      Bennett, R. <u>RES</u>, N.S. 24 (Nov. 1973), 508-10.
      Gilmour, Robin. <u>DSN</u>, 4 (1973), 76-79.
      Kincaid, James R. <u>Di</u>, 68 (1972), 186-88.
      McMaster, R. D. <u>NCF</u>, 26 (1971), 221-28.
      Pickering, Samuel, Jr. <u>GaR</u>, 27 (1973), 455-63.
      <u>TLS</u>, 27 Apr. 1973, p. 478.

ODDIE, WILLIAM. <u>Dickens and Carlyle: The Question of Influence</u>.
    London: The Centenary Press, 1972.

      D., J. A. <u>ELN</u>, 11 (Sept. 1973), Supp., 41-42.
      Fielding, K. J. <u>Di</u>, 69 (1973), 111-18.
      Sharples, E. <u>Criticism</u>, 16 (Spring 1974), 180-83.
      Slater, Michael. <u>VS</u>, 17 (Mar. 1974), 328-30.
      Tennyson, G. B. <u>DSN</u>, 5 (1974), 24-28.
      ______. <u>NCF</u>, 28 (1973), 115-17.
      <u>TLS</u>, 2 Mar. 1973, p. 235.

PARTLOW, ROBERT B., JR., ed. <u>Dickens the Craftsman: Strategies of
    Presentation</u>. Carbondale and Edwardsville: Southern Illinois
    Univ. Press, 1970.

      Fielding, K. J. <u>RES</u>, N.S. 22 (Aug. 1971), 364-66.
      McMaster, R. D. <u>NCF</u>, 26 (1971), 221-28.
      Meckier, Jerome. <u>DSN</u>, 1 (1970), 9-11.
      Slater, Michael. <u>Di</u>, 67 (1971), 112-14.
      Smith, Grahame. <u>VS</u>, 14 (1971), 459-62.
      <u>TLS</u>, 5 Mar. 1971, pp. 269-70.

_____. <u>Dickens Studies Annual</u>. Vol. I. Carbondale: Southern Illi-
    nois Univ. Press, 1970.

      Cribb, T. J. <u>RES</u>, N.S. 24 (1973), 230-33.
      Daleski, H. M. <u>NCF</u>, 26 (1972), 486-91.
      Davis, Earle. <u>DSN</u>, 1 (Dec. 1970), 7-8.
      Helfand, Michael S. <u>Novel</u>, 5 (1972), 186-89.
      Slater, Michael. <u>Di</u>, 67 (1971), 177.
      Smith, Grahame. <u>VS</u>, 14 (1971), 459-62.
      <u>TLS</u>, 5 Mar. 1971, p. 270.

_____. <u>Dickens Studies Annual</u>. Vol. 2. Carbondale: Southern Illi-
    nois Univ. Press, 1972.

      Davis, Earle. <u>DSN</u>, 4 (1973), 24-26.
      Pickering, Samuel. <u>GaR</u>, 27 (1973), 455-63.
      Tennyson, G. B. <u>NCF</u>, 28 (1973), 115-17.

Appendix I

_____. Dickens Studies Annual. Vol. 3. Carbondale: Southern Illinois Univ. Press, 1974.

    Slater, Michael. Di, 71 (1975), 175.
    Stone, Harry. NCF, 29 (1975), 474-77.
    TLS, 5 July 1974, p. 733.

PEARSON, HESKETH. Dickens: His Character, Comedy, and Career. London: Methuen, 1949.

    Bevington, Merle. SAQ, 49 (1950), 99-100.
    Brown, E. K. VQR, 25 (1949), 611-14.
    Nineteenth Century, 146 (1950), 194.
    Nisbet, Ada. NCF, 4 (1950), 159-63.

POPE-HENNESSY, UNA. Charles Dickens. London: Chatto and Windus, 1945.

    C., G. H. QQ, 54 (1947), 121-23.
    Stuart, Dorothy M. English Magazine of the English Association, 6 (1946), 31-33.

PRICE, MARTIN. Dickens: A Collection of Critical Essays. Englewood Cliffs, N.J.: Prentice Hall, 1967.

    Eriksen, Donald H. Arizona Quarterly, 24 (1968), 181-83.
    McMaster, R. D. DR, 48 (1968), 263-64.
    Rosenberg, Edgar. Di, 65 (1969), 187-89.

QUIRK, RANDOLPH. Charles Dickens and Appropriate Language. Durham, England: Univ. of Durham, 1959.

    Bodelsen, C. A. ES, 41 (1960), 125.

REES, RICHARD. For Love or Money: Studies in Personality and Essence. London: Secker and Warburg, 1960.

    Dobree, Bonamy. Listener, 64 (Aug. 1960), 311.
    Lea, F. A. TC, 168 (1960), 367-68.
    TLS, 26 Aug. 1960, p. 549.
    Wilson, Angus. Observer, 14 Aug. 1960, p. 20.

REID, JOHN C. The Hidden World of Charles Dickens. Auckland: Univ. of Auckland Press, 1962.

    Fielding, K. J. RES, N.S. 15 (1964), 104-106.

SCHILLING, BERNARD, ed. The Comic World of Dickens: The Wellers, Mrs. Gamp, Mr. Chuzzlewit. London: John Murray, 1959.

    Greaves, John. Di, 55 (1959), 156-57.

SLATER, MICHAEL, ed. Dickens 1970: Centenary Essays. New York: Stein and Day, 1970.

Fielding, K. J. RES, N.S. 22 (Aug. 1971), 364-66.
McMaster, R. D. NCF, 26 (1971), 221-28.
Seymour, W. K. Contemporary Review, 217 (1970), 161-62.
Smith, Grahame. VS, 14 (1971), 459-62.
Thomas, Gilbert. English, 20 (Spring 1971), 25-26.
TLS, 4 June 1970, p. 597.
Wall, Stephen. EIC, 21 (July 1971), 261-80.
Welsh, Alexander. Di, 66 (1970), 248-50.

SMITH, GRAHAME. Dickens, Money, and Society. Berkeley: Univ. of California Press, 1968.

Kettle, Arnold. RES, N.S. 21 (1970), 233-35.
Lane, Lauriat, Jr. SNNTS, 2 (1969), 377-78.
Sherwin, Richard E. NCF, 24 (1969), 117-20.
TLS, 13 Nov. 1969, p. 1319.
Williams, Raymond. Di, 65 (1969), 178-80.

SPILKA, MARK. Dickens and Kafka: A Mutual Interpretation. Bloomington: Indiana Univ. Press, 1963.

Baker, Sheridan. MQR, 5 (1966), 68-69.
Hill, A. G. CritQ, 7 (1965), 374-83.
Houk, M. Ann. L&P, 14 (1964), 37-39.
Mateer, Ruth. EIC, 15 (1965), 224-29.
McMaster, R. D. QQ, 70 (Winter 1964), 621-22.
Miller, J. Hillis. NCF, 18 (1965), 404-407.
Peyrouton, N. C. Di, 60 (1964), 115-16.
TLS, 16 Jan. 1964, p. 48.
West, Paul. VS, 7 (1963), 214-15.

STEVENSON, LIONEL, ed. Victorian Fiction: A Guide to Research. Cambridge, Mass.: Harvard Univ. Press, 1964.

Cockshut, A. O. J. RES, N.S. 17 (Aug. 1966), 341-42.
Poston, Lawrence. CE, 26 (Dec. 1964), 244.
Smith, Sheila. MLR, 62 (Jan. 1967), 120-21.
Tillotson, Geoffrey and Kathleen Tillotson. NCF, 19 (1965), 405-10.
TLS, 15 Apr. 1965, p. 289.

STEWART, GARRETT. Dickens and the Trials of Imagination. Cambridge, Mass.: Harvard Univ. Press, 1974.

Collins, Philip. TLS, 19 Sept. 1975, p. 1066.

Appendix I

STOEHR, TAYLOR. Dickens: The Dreamer's Stance. Ithaca, N.Y.:
     Cornell Univ. Press, 1965.

     Angus-Smith, Joanne. DR, 46 (1966), 393-94.
     Bell, Vereen M. SoR, N.S. 6 (1970), 529-38.
     Bodelsen, C. A. ES, 47 (1966), 77-79.
     Cribb, T. J. RES, N.S. 17 (1966), 338-39.
     Fielding, K. J. Di, 62 (1966), 22-24.
     Hardy, Barbara. MLQ, 27 (1966), 230-33.
     Herring, Paul D. MP, 65 (1968), 259-63.
     Muir, Kenneth. MLR, 63 (Jan. 1968), 219-20.
     Price, Martin. YR, 55 (1966), 293-95.
     Senelick, Lawrence. DiS, 2 (1966), 152-55.
     Steig, Michael. L&P, 15 (1965), 230-37.
     Stone, Harry. NCF, 20 (1966), 402-406.
     Thomas, Gilbert. English, 16 (1966), 66-67.
     Welsh, Alexander. VS, 9 (1966), 207-208.

SUCKSMITH, HARVEY PETER. The Narrative Art of Charles Dickens: The
     Rhetoric of Sympathy and Irony in His Novels. Oxford: Claren-
     don Press, 1970.

     DeVries, Duane. JEGP, 71 (Jan. 1972), 152.
     Fielding, K. J. VS, 14 (1971), 211-12.
     Lane, Lauriat, Jr. SNNTS, 5 (Spring 1973), 125-38.
     Partlow, Robert B., Jr. NCF, 26 (1972), 494-97.
     Smith, Grahame. Di, 67 (1971), 49-51.
     Spence, G. W. AUMLA, 35 (1971), 106-107.
     Stange, Richard. DSN, 1 (1970), 5-7.
     Steig, Michael. Criticism, 13 (1971), 319-21.
     Thomas, Gilbert. English, 20 (Spring 1971), 25-26.
     Thomson, P. RES, N.S. 22 (1971), 509-12.
     TLS, 25 Dec. 1970, p. 1521
     Wall, Stephen. EIC, 21 (1971), 261-80.

TOMLIN, E. W. F., ed. Charles Dickens. London: Weidenfield and
     Nicolson, 1969.

     Blount, Trevor. DSN, 2 (1971), 49-51.
     Fleissner, Robert. SNNTS, 2 (1970), 384-86.
     Gerson, Stanley. AUMLA, 34 (1970), 131.
     McMaster, R. D. NCF, 26 (1971), 221-28.
     Smith, Grahame. VS, 14 (1971), 459-62.
     Staples, L. C. Di, 66 (1970), 54-57.

WAGENKNECHT, EDWARD. Dickens and the Scandalmongers. Norman: Univ.
     of Oklahoma Press, 1965.

     Bell, Vereen M. SoR, N.S. 6 (1970), 529-38.
     Ford, George H. NCF, 20 (1966), 406-10.

McMaster, R. D. DR, 46 (1966), 107–108.
Peyrouton, N. C. DiS, 2 (1966), 45–46.
Stone, Harry. KR, 28 (1966), 142–43.
TLS, 27 Jan. 1966, p. 64.

WALL, STEPHEN, ed. Charles Dickens: A Critical Anthology. Harmondsworth: Penguin, 1970.

Dunn, R. J. DSN, 3 (1972), 46–50.
Rantavaara, Irma. Di, 67 (1971), 109–11.
TLS, 25 Dec. 1970, p. 1521.

WELSH, ALEXANDER. The City of Dickens. Oxford: Clarendon Press,
1971.

Burgan, William. VS, 16 (1972), 122–23.
Cribb, T. J. RES, N.S. 24 (1973), 230–33.
Kincaid, James R. DSN, 3 (1972), 81–84.
Lane, Lauriat, Jr. SNNTS, 5 (1973), 125–38.
Price, Martin. YR, 61 (Winter 1972), 271.
Shrock, Ruth. ELN, 10 (Sept. 1972), 57–60.
Slater, Michael. NCF, 26 (1972), 492–94.
Sucksmith, H. P. YES, 2 (1972), 310–12.
TLS, 29 Oct. 1971, p. 1361.
Williams, Raymond. Di, 68 (1972), 53–54.

WILLIAMS, MARY. The Dickens Concordance. New York: Haskell House,
1970.

Gold, Joseph. DSN, 3 (1972), 14–16.

WILSON, ANGUS. The World of Charles Dickens. London: Secker and
Warburg, 1970.

Donoghue, Denis. NCF, 27 (1972), 216–18.
Fido, Martin. VS, 15 (1971), 101–102.
Fielding, K. J. Di, 66 (1970), 248.
Holloway, John. Encounter, 34 (June 1970), 63–68.
Lane, Lauriat, Jr. SNNTS, 5 (Spring 1973), 125–38.
Monod, Sylvère. DSN, 2 (1971), 39–42.
Price, Martin. YR, 61 (Winter 1972), 271–79.
TLS, 4 June 1970, pp. 597–98.
Wall, Stephen. EIC, 21 (July 1971), 261–80.

WILSON, EDMUND. The Wound and the Bow. Boston: Houghton Mifflin,
1941.

DeVane, W. YR, 31 (1941), 384–87.
Leavis, F. R. Scrutiny, 11 (1942), 72–73.

Appendix I

WING, GEORGE D. <u>Dickens</u>. Edinburgh: Oliver and Boyd, 1969.

    B., A. <u>Di</u>, 66 (1970), 244.
    <u>Contemporary Review</u>, 216 (1970), 56.
    Kissane, James. <u>DSN</u>, 3 (1972), 12-14.
    <u>TLS</u>, 23 Apr. 1970, p. 450.

Appendix II

Editions and Reviews, 1940-1975

PICKWICK PAPERS

PATTEN, ROBERT L., ed. The Posthumous Papers of the Pickwick Club.
Harmondsworth: Penguin English Library, 1972.

Shillingsburg, Peter L. DSN, 4 (1972), 119-23.
TLS, 11 Aug. 1972, p. 946.
Trickett, Rachel. Di, 69 (1973), 119.

Additional Paperback Editions:

Rev.: Peter L. Shillingsburg, DSN, 3 (1972), 119-23.

Washington Square Press (New York, 1960, reissued as a Col-
lateral Classic, 1967), with an Introduction by Joseph
Mersand.
Dell, Laurel Edition (New York, 1964), with an Introduction by
Edgar Johnson.
New American Library, Signet Classic (New York, 1964), with an
Afterword by Steven Marcus.
Airmont Books (New York, 1969), with an Introduction by Beryl
Rowland.

OLIVER TWIST

FAIRCLOUGH, PETER, ed. Oliver Twist. Harmondsworth: Penguin English Library, 1966.

Patten, Robert L. DSN, 3 (1972), 84-92.
TLS, 29 Sept. 1966, p. 901; 6 Apr. 1967, p. 285.

TILLOTSON, KATHLEEN, ed. Oliver Twist. Oxford: Clarendon Press,
1966.

Altick, Richard D. VS, 11 (1968), 415-16.
Bodelsen, C. A. ES, 48 (1967), 466-67.
Bowers, Fredson. NCF, 23 (1968), 226-39.
Cribb, T. J. RES, N.S. 19 (1968), 87-91.
Fielding, K. J. Di, 63 (1967), 14-16.

Appendix II

> McMaster, R. D. <u>DR</u>, 47 (1967), 100-101.
> Muir, Kenneth. <u>MLR</u>, 63 (1968), 687-88.
> Patten, Robert L. <u>DiS</u>, 3 (1967), 160-68.
> Tillotson, Geoffrey. <u>SR</u>, 75 (1967), 325-37.
> <u>TLS</u>, 6 Apr. 1967, p. 285.

<u>Additional Paperback Editions</u>:

> Rev.: Robert L. Patten, <u>DSN</u>, 3 (1972), 84-92.

> Washington Square Press (New York, 1948; 16th printing 1970), with an Introduction (1957) by Edgar Johnson.
> New American Library, Signet Classic (New York, Afterword copyright 1961; 8th printing), with an Afterword by Edward Le Compte.
> Holt, Rinehart and Winston, Rinehart Edition (New York, 1962), with an Introduction by J. Hillis Miller.
> Airmont Books (New York, 1963).
> Washington Square Press, Reader's Enrichment Series (New York, 1965; 2nd printing 1966); supplemental materials by Harry Shefter, Walter James Miller, and James Manning.
> Lancer Books, Magnum Easy Eye Books (New York, 1968).
> AMSCO School Publications, AMSCO Literature Series (New York, n.d.).

NICHOLAS NICKLEBY

THORNDIKE, DAME SYBIL, ed. <u>Nicholas Nickleby</u>. New Oxford Illustrated Dickens. London: Oxford Univ. Press, 1950.

> <u>NCF</u>, 5 (1950), 251.

<u>The Life and Adventures of Nicholas Nickleby</u>. Reprinted in Parts in Facsimile. Menston, Yorkshire: The Scolar Press, 1973.

> Brennan, E. <u>Di</u>, 69 (1973), 187-89.
> Meckier, Jerome. <u>DSN</u>, 6 (1975), 96-98.
> <u>TLS</u>, 22 June 1973, p. 723.

THE OLD CURIOSITY SHOP

EASSON, ANGUS, ed. <u>The Old Curiosity Shop</u>. Harmondsworth: Penguin English Library, 1972.

> Patten, Robert L. <u>Di</u>, 69 (1973), 54-56.
> <u>TLS</u>, 11 Aug. 1972, p. 946; 15 Sept. 1972, p. 1060.

BARNABY RUDGE

SPENCE, GORDON, ed. Barnaby Rudge. Harmondsworth: Penguin English
Library, 1973.

> Contemporary Review, 224 (1974), 56.
> TLS, 11 Jan. 1974, p. 22; 1 Feb. 1974, p. 109.
> Westburg, Barry. Di, 70 (1974), 133-34.

MARTIN CHUZZLEWIT

FURBANK, P. N., ed. The Life and Adventures of Martin Chuzzlewit.
Harmondsworth: Penguin English Library, 1968.

> Easson, Angus. Di, 65 (1969), 51-52.

DOMBEY AND SON

FAIRCLOUGH, PETER, ed. Dombey and Son. Introduction by Raymond Williams. Harmondsworth: Penguin English Library, 1970.

> Collins, Philip. Di, 67 (1971), 47-49.
> Levine, Richard A. DSN, 3 (1972), 53-57.

HORSMAN, ALAN, ed. Dombey and Son. Oxford: Clarendon Press, 1974.

> Barfoot, C. C. ES, 56 (1975), 443.
> Dunn, Richard J. Di, 71 (1975), 47-49.
> Fielding, K. J. DUL, 67 (1975), 249-51.
> Page, Norman. DSN, 6 (1975), 19-23.
> Slater, Michael. TLS, 20 Sept. 1974, p. 1020.

Additional Paperback Editions:

> Rev.: Richard A. Levine, DSN, 3 (1972), 53-57.

> > Dell, Laurel Edition (New York, 1963), edited with an Intro-
> > duction by Edgar Johnson.
> > New American Library, Signet Classic (New York, 1964), with an
> > Afterword by Alan Pryce-Jones.

DAVID COPPERFIELD

BLOUNT, TREVOR, ed. The Personal History of David Copperfield.
Baltimore: Penguin English Library, 1966.

> Burgess, Anthony. Spectator, 218 (10 Feb. 1967), 171.
> TLS, 17 Mar. 1966, p. 224; 6 Apr. 1967, p. 285.

Appendix II

BLEAK HOUSE

ZABEL, MORTON D., ed. Bleak House. Boston: Houghton Mifflin, 1956.

    Burns, Wayne. CE, 19 (1958), 189.

GUERARD, A. J., ed. Bleak House. New York: Holt, Rinehart and
Winston, 1970.

    Blount, Trevor. Di, 67 (1971), 168-72.
    Lane, Lauriat, Jr. Humanities Association Bulletin, 21 (Sum-
       mer 1970), 66-68.

DeVRIES, DUANE, ed. Bleak House. New York: Crowell, 1971.

    Blount, Trevor. Di, 67 (1971), 168-72.

PAGE, NORMAN, ed. Bleak House. Introduction by J. Hillis Miller.
Harmondsworth: Penguin English Library, 1971.

    Blount, Trevor. Di, 67 (1971), 168-72.

HARD TIMES

FORD, GEORGE H. and SYLVÈRE MONOD, eds. Hard Times: An Authorita-
tative Text; Backgrounds, Sources, and Contemporary Reactions;
Criticism. New York: Norton, 1966.

    Fielding, K. J. Di, 63 (1967), 149-52.
    Smith, Anne. DSN, 4 (1973), 115-22.

CRAIG, DAVID, ed. Hard Times for These Times. Harmondsworth: Penguin English Library, 1969.

    Fielding, K. J. Di, 65 (1969), 189.
    Smith, Anne. DSN, 4 (1973), 115-22.

Additional Paperback Editions:

    Rev.: Anne Smith, DSN, 4 (1973), 115-22.

       Dutton, Everyman's Library (New York, 1907; last reprinted
         1970), with an Introduction by G. K. Chesterton and an
         Afterword on "Dickens and Hard Times" by Joanna Richardson.
       New American Library, Signet Classic (New York and Toronto,
         Afterword copyright 1961; 9th printing), with an Afterword
         by Charles Shapiro.
       Harper and Row. Harper Classic (New York, Introduction copy-
         right 1965), with a biography of Dickens and Introduction by
         Walter Allen.

Fawcett Publications Inc., Fawcett Premier (Greenwich, Conn.,
Introduction copyright 1966), with an Introduction by Raymond Williams.
Holt, Rinehart and Winston, Rinehart Edition (New York, 1967;
12th printing), with an Introduction by W. W. Watt.

LITTLE DORRIT

HOLLOWAY, JOHN, ed. Little Dorrit. Baltimore: Penguin English Library, 1967.

Burgan, William. DSN, 3 (1972), 22-24.

McMASTER, R. D., ed. Little Dorrit. New York: Odyssey Press, 1969.

Burgan, William. DSN, 3 (1972), 22-24.

A TALE OF TWO CITIES

ESTES, HELEN J. and LEE WYNDHAM, eds. A Tale of Two Cities. Englewood Cliffs, N.J.: Prentice-Hall, 1962.

Weisbach, Arthur. EJ, 51 (Sept. 1962), 447.

Additional Paperback Editions:

Rev.: R. D. McMaster, DSN, 3 (1972), 16-21.

Dutton, Everyman's Library (New York, 1906, last reprinted
1962), with an Introduction by G. K. Chesterton.
Washington Square Press (New York, 1939, last reprinted 1967),
with an Introduction (1957) by Edgar Johnson.
Houghton Mifflin, Riverside Edition (New York, 1962), with an
Introduction by Paul Pickrel and suggestions for reading and
discussion by Robert Hillegrass.
Airmont Books (New York, 1963), with an Introduction by
David C. Pitt.
Dell, Laurel Edition (New York, 1963).
New American Library, Signet Classic (New York and Toronto,
1963), with an Afterword by Edgar Johnson.
Allyn and Bacon, Academy Classics (Boston, 1966), with a life
of Dickens, notes and other aids by A. B. DeMille.
Macmillan, Collier Books (New York, 1967), with an Introduc-
tion by Steven Marcus.
Random House, Modern Library College Edition (New York, 1967),
with an Introduction by Edward Wagenknecht.
Lancer Books, Magnum Easy Eye Books (New York, 1968).
Penguin Books, Penguin English Library (Harmondsworth, 1970),
edited with an Introduction by George Woodcock.

Appendix II

AMSCO School Publications, AMSCO Literature Series (New York, n.d.).
Harper and Row, Harper Classic (New York, n.d.), with an Introduction by Walter Allen.

GREAT EXPECTATIONS

SHAW, BERNARD, ed. Great Expectations. London: Hamish Hamilton, 1947.

  TLS, 9 Aug. 1974, p. 404.

WAGENKNECHT, EDWARD, ed. Great Expectations. New York: Pocket Books, 1956.

  Shannon, Edgar F., Jr. CE, 19 (1958), 234.

CROMPTON, LOUIS, ed. Great Expectations. Indianapolis: Bobbs-Merrill, 1964.

  Boyle, Ted E. CE, 27 (1966), 650-51.
  DeVries, Duane. DSN, 5 (1974), 56-61.

CALDER, ANGUS, ed. Great Expectations. Harmondsworth: Penguin English Library, 1965.

  DeVries, Duane. DSN, 5 (1974), 56-61.
  Senelick, Laurence. DiS, 2 (1966), 157-58.
  TLS, 6 Apr. 1967, p. 285.

McMASTER, R. D., ed. Great Expectations. Toronto: Macmillan, 1965.

  DeVries, Duane. DSN, 5 (1974), 56-61.
  Orrell, John. Humanities Association Bulletin, 17 (Spring 1966), 66.

Additional Paperback Editions:

  Rev.: Duane DeVries, DSN, 5 (1974), 56-61.

  Collier Books (New York, 1962), with an Introduction by Frank Chapman.
  Houghton Mifflin Co., Riverside Edition (Boston, 1962), with an Introduction by Monroe Engel and suggestions for reading and discussion by Louis G. Dickins.
  New American Library, Signet Classic (New York, 1963), with an Afterword by Angus Wilson.
  Airmont Publishing Company, Inc., Classics Series (New York, 1965), with an Introduction by Mary M. Threapleton.
  Harper and Row, Harper Classics (New York, 1965), with an Introduction by Walter Allen.

Lancer Books, Magnum Easy Eye Books (New York, 1968).
AMSCO School Publications, Inc., AMSCO Literature Series (New York, 1970).
Holt, Rinehart and Winston, Rinehart Editions, Second Edition (New York, 1972), with an Introduction by Earle Davis.
Pocket Books, Washington Square Press Enriched Classics Edition (New York, 1973), with an Introduction by Warrington Winters and a Reader's Supplement.

OUR MUTUAL FRIEND

GILL, STEPHEN, ed. Our Mutual Friend. Harmondsworth: Penguin English Library, 1971.

Fisher, Benjamin Franklin, IV. DSN, 5 (1974), 87-90.
Gilmour, Robin. Di, 67 (1971), 173-74.
Wall, Stephen. EIC, 21 (1971), 261-80.

Additional Paperback Editions:

Rev.: Benjamin Franklin Fisher, IV, DSN, 5 (1974), 87-90.

Random House, Inc., The Modern Library (New York, 1960), with a "Note to Our Mutual Friend" by Monroe Engel.
New American Library, Signet Classic (New York, 1964), with an Afterword by J. Hillis Miller.

THE MYSTERY OF EDWIN DROOD

CARDWELL, MARGARET, ed. The Mystery of Edwin Drood. Oxford: Clarendon Press, 1972.

Barfoot, C. C. ES, 54 (1973), 366.
Cox, Arthur J. Mystery and Detection Annual 1973, pp. 307-12.
Fisher, Benjamin Franklin, IV. NCF, 28 (1973), 229-32.
Rosenberg, Edgar. DSN, 5 (1974), 70-84.
TLS, 11 Aug. 1974, p. 946; 18 Aug., p. 970; 25 Aug., pp. 996-97.
Wilson, Angus, Di, 69 (1973), 48-51.

COX, ARTHUR J., ed. The Mystery of Edwin Drood. Introduction by Angus Wilson. Harmondsworth: Penguin English Library, 1974.

Stewart, J. I. M. Di, 70 (1974), 211-12.

Appendix II

CHRISTMAS BOOKS

SLATER, MICHAEL, ed. <u>The Christmas Books</u>. Harmondsworth: Penguin
English Library, 2 Vols., 1971.

Easson, Angus. <u>DSN</u>, 4 (1973), 68.
Monod, Sylvère. <u>Di</u>, 68 (1972), 122-24.

A CHRISTMAS CAROL

ADAMS, FREDERICK B., JR., ed. <u>A Christmas Carol</u>. Introduction by
Monica Dickens. A Facsimile of the Manuscript in the Pierpont
Morgan Library. New York: The Folio Press, 1967.

<u>Di</u>, 67 (1971), 118.

DICKENS, CEDRIC CHARLES, ed. <u>A Christmas Carol</u>. London: Routledge
and Kegan Paul, 1972.

Easson, Angus. <u>DSN</u>, 4 (1973), 68-71.
<u>TLS</u>, 3 Mar. 1972, p. 256.

Author Index

The AUTHOR INDEX notes each page on which a critic is cited in the SUBJECT INDEX and in the two APPENDIXES. In addition, the first appearance of each article in one of the BIBLIOGRAPHY sections is indicated by a page number followed by an asterisk; to identify all articles by an individual commentator in the SUBJECT INDEX, refer to those pages with asterisks in the AUTHOR INDEX.

N.B.: In many instances, a critic is cited more than once on a page.

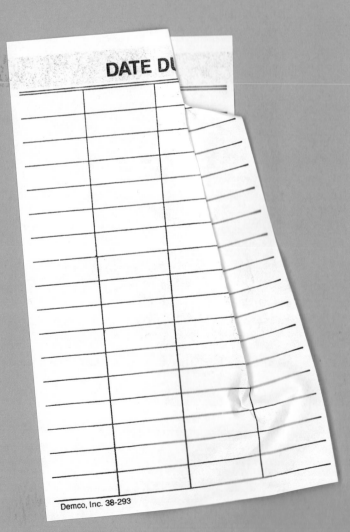

DATE DU

Demco, Inc. 38-293